D1225025

DATE			

Disequilibrium Macroeconomics in Open Economies

Disequilibrium Macroeconomics in Open Economies

John T. Cuddington
Per-Olov Johansson
Karl-Gustaf Löfgren

Basil Blackwell

First published 1984
Basil Blackwell Publisher Limited
108 Cowley Road, Oxford OX4 1JF, England

British Library Cataloguing in Publication Data

Cuddington, John T.
Disequilibrium macroeconomics in open economies.
1. Equilibrium (Economics)
I. Title II. Johansson, Per-Olov
III. Löfgren, Karl-Gustaf
330.028   HB145

ISBN 0-631-13532-4

Typeset by Unicus Graphics Ltd, Horsham, West Sussex
Printed in Great Britain by The Camelot Press Ltd, Southampton

To our Parents

Contents

Acknowledgments

A number of people have taken valuable time to provide constructive criticisms and suggestions on various chapters of the book: Avinash Dixit, Jean Drèze, Seppo Honkapohja, Thor Gylfason, Oliver Landmann, Torsten Persson, Steven Van der Tak, and José Viñals. To them we extend our greatest thanks. They, of course, share no blame for any deficiencies in the final product. In addition, John Cuddington and Per-Olov Johansson wish to thank the Institute for International Economic Studies in Stockholm and its research staff for their hospitality and support during their extended stays there. Financial support from the Swedish Council for Research in Humanities and Social Sciences and permission from the *Review of Economic Studies* to reprint portions of Cuddington (1981) in chapter 6 are gratefully acknowledged.

Finally, thanks are due to Elizabeth Cannon, Eva Cederblad, Monica Göransson, Marie Loise Harder, Helen Lindström, Marie Näsström, Ing Marie Nilsson, and Debbie Olson for their typing and editorial assistance, without which this book would not have come to fruition!

1

Introduction

1   Intellectual Origins of the Study

In retrospect the 1970s will undoubtedly be viewed as a revolutionary period in macroeconomics. Policymakers were confronted with many novel situations, often international in scope: persistent worldwide inflation, the breakdown of the Bretton Woods fixed exchange rate commitment, the emergence of the OPEC cartel and the 1973 oil embargo, the raw materials price shocks of 1973–74, soaring international debt, and the record high interest rates of 1981–82.

Against this background and in some cases in response to it, macroeconomic theory itself began a period of soul-searching and critical reevaluation. Two areas of research have been particularly influential. One, spearheaded by neoclassical rational-expectations school associated with Thomas Sargent and Robert Lucas among others, has already made tremendous advances elucidating an alternative paradigm to Keynesian macroeconomic orthodoxy. As basic working hypotheses, this school assumes that (1) expectations about the future values of key economic variables are formed rationally in the sense that they embody all currently available information about the structure and past behavior of the economy in a (statistically) optimal way and (2) all prices are perfectly flexible, adjusting continuously to equate supply and demand in their respective markets. It is the objective of such models to provide "equilibrium" theories of the business cycle and to define bounds for the efficacy of aggregate demand management as well as "supply-side" policies within this context.

A second body of research, rather than abandoning existing macroeconomic paradigms, has attempted to refurbish and generalize the standard Keynesian framework. Unlike the neoclassical macroeconomics, this literature assumes that many prices and wages are sticky in the short run. In fact, in his important book *On Keynesian Economics and the Economics of Keynes*, Axel Leijonhufvud (1968) maintains that the central message of Keynes' (1936) *General Theory* is that quantity adjustments take place much more rapidly than price adjustments, and that markets in "disequilibrium" are the normal state of the economy. Consistent trading is created through quantity adjustments and the effects that perceived quantity constraints in one market (such as the labor market) have on the demands or supplies in other markets (such as the markets for commodities). Hence the initial impacts of changes in market conditions are to be found in changes in order books, delivery dates, inventories, unemployment lines, hours of work, and so on. Changes in relative prices come about only gradually over time.

As recent microtheoretic work on *temporary equilibrium* models with quantity constraints or "rationing" makes clear, neo-Keynesian models are most appropriately viewed not as models of "disequilibrium" and dynamic adjustment toward equilibrium, but as particular models of non-Walrasian equilibrium.[1] They are *fix-price* models in the sense of Hicks (1965). That is, even if prices vary, the causes are to be found outside the model. An alternative justification of the rigid price assumption is that the speed at which price adjustment occurs is very slow relative to the speed at which actual and perceived quantity constraints change. Hence, the former can be ignored in the time frame relevant for *short-run* analyses.

The intellectual origins of the fix-price, quantity-constraint models – which are still often referred to as "disequilibrium" models for simplicity – are relatively old and scattered. The first explicit treatment of how firms act in "disequilibrium," i.e., when they cannot buy or sell unlimited quantities at ruling prices, can be found in Don Patinkin's (1956) seminal work, *Money, Interest and Prices*. The corresponding decision problem facing households was analyzed in a pioneering article by Robert Clower (1965), following earlier microtheoretic work by James Tobin and Hendrik Houthakker (1950–51). Clower considered a situation where the (exogenous) price vector facing households is such that they perceive a binding constraint on employment. That is, they are unable to find demanders for all of the labor they wish to supply given the prevailing wage and commodity prices. Their *effective* demand for goods, therefore, will differ from *notional* demand in that it reflects the perceived constraint on employment as well as the usual budget constraint.

[1] See Grandmont (1977a) for a survey of temporary equilibrium models.

The nontrivial problem of combining the behavior of quantity-constrained firms and households in a general disequilibrium model was solved in an article by R. Barro and H. Grossman (1971). The basic framework has since provided the basis for a stream of important contributions to what is variously known as macroeconomic "disequilibrium" theory or fix-price equilibrium theory with quantity rationing.[2] The model set forth by Barro and Grossman and elaborated upon by others considered a closed economy. In recent years there have been several attempts to generalize the model to the open-economy context.[3]

2 Scope of the Study

It is the objective of this volume to provide a reasonably complete synthesis of research on fix-price equilibrium in open economies. Because research in this area is very recent, any claim of a definitive treatment would be premature. In fact, in several important instances, we have attempted to fill in major gaps in the literature so as to provide a more systematic treatment of economic policy in the open-economy fix-price equilibrium context.

Extending closed-economy work to the open-economy context is essential; virtually all countries have important foreign sectors. The inclusion of a foreign sector thus makes the models more realistic. Another, and perhaps more important, reason in the present context is that we believe that it is important to develop "disequilibrium" models of open economies as a complement to existing Walrasian equilibrium models typically employed in international trade theory. The generalization of "disequilibrium" models in this direction gives new insights into the working of economic policy and hopefully will pave the way for an integration of pure trade, commercial policy, and international macroeconomics within a single theoretical framework.

3 Plan of the Book

Chapter 2 gives a comprehensive review of the origins of fix-price theory. The seminal contributions of various researchers are summarized. The theoretical issue of *why* prices are fixed or adjust only

[2] These contributions include books by Barro and Grossman (1976) and Malinvaud (1977, 1980). See Drazen (1980) and chapter 2 of the present book for surveys of the literature.
[3] See Dixit (1978), Cuddington (1980, 1981), Neary (1980), Johansson and Löfgren (1980, 1981), and Steigum (1980).

sluggishly is discussed, but admittedly remains unresolved in the literature.

The fix-price models of chapter 2 are models of closed economies. In chapter 3 we introduce a single-sector fix-price model of the open economy. The model is similar to that in Dixit (1978), but emphasizes the intertemporal aspects of the households' choice problem, as Muellbauer and Portes (1978) did in the closed-economy context. The model is used to some extent to analyze the effects of economic policy. For example, factors affecting the effectiveness of exchange rate devaluation are considered. The primary purpose of the chapter, however, is to introduce the reader to open-economy fix-price models in their simplest, most transparent form so that the more complex models to follow can be more easily comprehended. In the latter models our primary objective is to emphasize the usefulness of macroeconomic disequilibrium analysis for the study of economic policy in open economies. There lies the major contribution of this book.

Chapter 4 lays out a *two-sector* fix-price framework for analyzing stabilization policies in open economies. The particular model, which distinguishes between tradeable and nontradeable goods, is used to analyze the effects of fiscal policy and real wage adjustments (via wage-price policies or devaluations) under different disequilibrium regimes. The assumption of fixed exchange rates is maintained throughout the chapter.

One of the problems of introducing flexible exchange rates properly into a fix-price setting is to integrate multiple asset holdings into a microtheoretic framework in a way that accurately captures both the intertemporal decision-making process giving rise to asset demands and the role of money in facilitating transactions. Previous attempts to deal with the flexible exchange rate case have been inadequate. They assume that money is the only asset and impose the condition that the exchange rate adjusts to continually clear the foreign exchange market. In the absence of nonmonetary assets, this amounts to assuming that the *trade balance*, which is identically equal to domestic income minus expenditure, is zero in each and every period. This period-by-period constraint is much stronger than the intertemporal budget constraint implicit in the fixed exchange rate case. Hence earlier comparisons of fixed versus flexible exchange rate regimes have been contaminated by the asymmetric treatment of the intertemporal budget constraint.

Chapter 5 solves this problem in the context of a financial market setup where there is perfect capital mobility. In so doing it develops a model which, under the Keynesian unemployment regime, is closely related to the well-known Mundell–Fleming (M–F) model. It goes beyond the M–F model, however, by explicitly specifying the effects of quantity rationing in a two-sector economy. Various stabilization policies – such as fiscal, monetary, and wage policies – under flexible versus fixed exchange rates are studied in this context. Perhaps the most striking finding is that bond-financed increases in government spending are shown to be *contractionary* in the presence of classical unemployment under flexible exchange rates. This is a consequence of the adverse effect of the resulting exchange rate appreciation on the tradeable good sector.

Chapter 6 returns tô a fixed exchange rate setting. The model of chapter 4 is modified by distinguishing between exportables and importables rather than tradeables and nontradeables, and by allowing for the possibility that firms and households may perceive quantity constraints in the markets for internationally traded commodities. Rationing occurred in the nontraded goods market, but not the tradeable goods market, in chapter 4. Using the exportables–importables framework, chapter 6 analyzes different commercial policies such as quantitative import restrictions and policy changes in disequilibrium prices and wages.

Chapter 7 continues the discussion of commercial policy by examining the effects on sectoral employment, output, and the trade balance of import tariffs under fixed exchange rates. The last half of the chapter considers the effects of tariffs under flexible exchange rates using the perfect capital mobility model from chapter 5.

The efficacy of economic policy is most often discussed in terms of its influence on variables like employment, output, the price level, and external balance. From these effects, we hope to infer something about national welfare, which is difficult to define and estimate in the conventional macroeconomic models. The present fix-price framework, however, is built on solid microfoundations for macrotheory. This facilitates a more rigorous welfare analysis based on microeconomic principles. As an illustration of this, chapter 8 derives cost–benefit rules to be used in the presence of rationing in the labor and product markets. We show that disequilibrium shadow pricing rules are regime-sensitive and that the rules derived from partial equilibrium analysis, which are found in most cost–benefit manuals, can be very misleading in disequilibrium conditions. Because this chapter extends the literature on cost–benefit analysis to an open economy in disequilibrium, it should be of interest to students of public finance as well as international economics.

The main text concludes with a chapter suggesting avenues for future research. The book also contains two technical appendices: one on the microeconomics of rationing, and a second on short-run quantity adjustment and long-run price adjustments.

4 Comparison of the Present Work with that of Dornbusch

At this point it is perhaps informative to briefly contrast the coverage of the present book with standard open-economy macroeconomics texts. To do this, obviously at the potential cost of being too narrow, we focus on Rudiger Dornbusch's (1980) monograph, *Open Economy Macroeconomics*.

Our book spends much more time analyzing the production side of the economy than is typical in open-economy macroeconomics. We deal at length with a two-sector setup where prices and wages do not necessarily adjust immediately to market-clearing levels. The various types of disequilibrium situations that arise – including the usual Keynesian unemployment regime as one case – are discussed using a sound microtheoretic framework. The book analyzes the effects of monetary and fiscal policies on employment, aggregate and sectoral output, and the trade balance in considerably more detail than is possible in the standard open-economy models, e.g., Dornbusch (1980). These models ignore important differences between notional and effective demands in their typically *ad hoc* specification of non-Walrasian equilibrium situations.

In contrast to our approach, Dornbusch's models (which often assume full employment) are more detailed in their treatment of financial and monetary considerations, adjustment dynamics, and exchange rate expectations. To date, these issues have received only scant treatment in the fix-price literature.

The present book provides an extensive analysis of commercial policies, including both tariffs and quotas, in a *macrotheoretic* framework. It allows for trade imbalances and unemployment, however, thereby avoiding major inadequacies in the way that pure trade models treat commercial policy issues. Our framework permits a thoroughgoing macroeconomic analysis of import substitution policies, which is nonetheless consistent with microeconomics under sticky prices and rationing constraints.

Finally we go beyond the usual scope in macroeconomics by specifying how benefit–cost analyses and hence other welfare issues can be tackled within a general disequilibrium model. Although these issues are treated to some extent in graduate-level pure trade theory,[4] a Walrasian market-clearing setup is typically employed. In cases where wage stickiness is considered, only the case of classical unemployment has been treated. Our framework permits an extension of this work to the Keynesian unemployment case, thereby making explicit the linkages between conventional macroeconomic models and the microtheoretic models used for modern welfare analysis and pure trade theory.

---

[4] See, e.g., chapters 21, 22, and 23 in the recent book by Bhagwati and Srinivasan (1983).

PART I

Analytical Preliminaries and Earlier Work

2

Macroeconomics with Quantity Rationing in Closed Economies

1   Introduction

Classical economists since the time of Walras as well as the modern neoclassical macrotheorists[1] have typically assumed that prices adjust rapidly to restore equilibrium in the face of excess supplies or demands. While this may be the case for many markets, such as those for agricultural products, raw materials, financial assets, and foreign exchange, it is not always an accurate characterization. In the markets for many manufactured goods, services, and particularly in the labor market, transactions take place at prices that differ from Walrasian equilibrium levels. That is, various agents' desired supplies and demands at prevailing prices need not equal the actual size of their transactions for considerable periods of time.

Recognizing the importance of imperfect price flexibility and the phenomenon of persistent non-market-clearing, John Hicks (1965) distinguished between "flex-price" and "fix-price" goods. To analyze the implications of price stickiness, Hicks employed the "fix-price" method, which in its pure form assumes that all prices are completely fixed during the period under consideration.

The main purpose of this chapter is to introduce the reader to what Grandmont (1977b) calls "the logic of the fix-price method."[2] This method is introduced here in a simple closed-economy setting. A variation of the method will be used in the open-economy analysis in later chapters, the main deviation from the pure fixed-price method being that sometimes certain prices will be assumed to be flexible even in the short run.

[1] The real classical revival is no longer to be found within the old Chicago school with Friedman, Metzler, Brunner, and others, but rather within the rational-expectations paradigm, which has been developed during the 1970s. For a review compare Kantor (1979).
[2] For a comprehensive survey see Drazen (1980).

11

2   Flex-price and Fix-price Tâtonnement

Within the neoclassical general equilibrium framework described by Walras at the end of the nineteenth century, trades take place in frictionless markets. All agents are assumed to have perfect knowledge about the characteristics and prices of all commodities in the economy. To coordinate trading Walras introduces the fiction of the auctioneer. All agents – firms and consumers – are in contact with the auctioneer who starts the trading process by announcing an arbitrary price vector, which includes all prices. Agents specify what they are willing to buy and sell at the announced prices. If the buying and selling decisions are inconsistent the auctioneer adjusts the price vector according to the following rule: If, in a particular market, the aggregate quantity demanded exceeds the aggregate quantity supplied – i.e., a positive excess demand – the auctioneer raises the price; if there is an excess supply he lowers the price. The agents are allowed to renew their bids, and the sketched process – the tâtonnement process – continues until the simultaneous consistency of the buying and selling decisions in all markets is achieved. Then actual trading takes place.

There is of course no auctioneer in reality, but in economic theory it is typically assumed that all markets work as if one existed. If one accepts this view of how markets work, stabilization policy and unemployment become nonissues. Every unemployment situation must be of a very temporary nature. Unemployment or excess supply in the labor market as well as disequilibrium in the goods markets will quickly disappear without government intervention.

Although the neoclassical paradigm introduced by Walras was esthetically appealing, its implications often proved to be a poor description of reality, as the case of the great depression in the 1930s made clear.

In a widely read, but perhaps not sufficiently clearly written, book, *The General Theory*, Keynes (1936) introduced a theoretical alternative to Walras' self-regulating "market-clearing machine." Keynes claimed that unemployment in certain market situations is not automatically eliminated – not even in a long run. Keynes' exact explanation for this is still debated by his many interpreters, but if one believes there is something fundamentally new in Keynes, his explanation of involuntary unemployment cannot revolve solely around institutionally determined price rigidities.

Price rigidities can explain unemployment even within the neoclassical paradigm. What Keynes presumably claimed to have shown is that unemployment can, under certain conditions, persist even if one allows for complete price and wage flexibility. Translated into the consequences for stabilization policy, Keynes claimed that an active stabilization policy might be necessary to create full employment.

Keynes' ideas received a high degree of acceptance. By the late 1960s Milton Friedman (1968) claimed "we are all Keynesians now." However, much macroeconomic debate centered around what Keynes really meant. Out of these concerns grew the neo-Keynesian paradigm to which the present study belongs.

2.1 Don Patinkin's Contribution

One aspect of the macroeconomic debate following the publication of *The General Theory* concerned what came to be called the *Dunlop–Tarshis*[3] *problem*: Empirical observations of the movement of real wages over the business cycle indicated that real wages moved pro-cyclically, not countercyclically as would be expected from the profit-maximizing behavior of firms. A profit-maximizing firm is in equilibrium if the marginal productivity of labor equals the real wage rate, and this equality determines the level of employment. If one disregards productivity changes the only way to increase employment in this setting is by lowering the real wage rate; but the empirical works of both Dunlop and Tarshis seemed to tell a different story.[4]

There are, of course, many possible answers to this puzzle.[5] An interesting one was given by Don Patinkin (1956) in his *Money, Interest and Prices*. He considers a situation where firms are competitive, in the sense that they perceive that they cannot influence the prevailing price, but yet cannot sell their profit-maximizing output. If price adjustments are sluggish, the best they can do in the short run is to adjust output to a level that equals anticipated sales.[6] This behavior implies, as we will show below, that there is no longer a one-to-one relationship between the real wage rate and the level of employment. Hence the logical necessity of a countercyclical movement in real wages disappears.

---

[3] Dunlop (1938) and Tarshis (1939).
[4] Later studies, e.g., by Bodkin (1969), tend to confirm the Dunlop–Tarshis findings.
[5] Keynes participated in the debate, and suggested that the procyclical behavior of real wages could be explained if the assumption of perfect competition was abandoned. Under monopolistic conditions, output increases are compatible with real wage increases as long as demand elasticities increase with increases in aggregate demand. See Keynes (1939).
[6] We disregard here the fact that the commodity may be storable.

To see this, consider a typical firm that produces one output, Y_i, using one variable input labor, L_i. The twice continuously differentiable and strictly concave production function is given by:[7]

$$Y_i = F(L_i).$$

Under competitive conditions the firm maximizes profit π subject to the production function and the given prices in the markets for labor and its output:

$$\underset{L_i}{\text{Max}} \; \pi = pF(L_i) - wL_i \tag{2.1}$$

where w is the nominal wage and p is product price. The first-order condition for an interior maximum:

$$\frac{d\pi}{dL_i} = pF_L(L_i) - w = 0, \tag{2.2}$$

where $F_L(L_i)$ is the marginal product of labor, implicitly contains the usual labor demand function for the firm as a function of the real product wage:

$$L_i = F_L^{-1}\left(\frac{w}{p}\right) = L_i\left(\frac{\bar{w}}{p}\right). \tag{2.3}$$

Provided the marginal product of labor is a decreasing function of the level of employment and output, the demand for labor will be a decreasing function of the real wage rate. This is denoted by the minus sign above the argument in equation (2.3). Diagrammatically, the profit-maximizing level of employment is shown in figure 2.1 at the point where the marginal product of labor equals the real wage.

The firm's supply of the commodity is obtained by substituting the demand function into the production function:

$$Y_i = F\left(L_i\left(\frac{\bar{w}}{p}\right)\right) = Y_i\left(\frac{\bar{w}}{p}\right). \tag{2.4}$$

Hence, the supply of the commodity is also a decreasing function of the real wage rate and a positive function of the product's price. The market supply curve is obtained by aggregating the supply curves of the individual firms:

$$Y = Y\left(\frac{w}{p}\right) = \sum_{i=1}^{N} Y_i\left(\frac{w}{p}\right). \tag{2.5}$$

---

[7] The fix-price model introduced below coincides with the seminal version of the Barro and Grossman model developed in Barro and Grossman (1971).

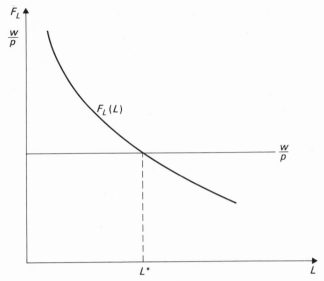

FIGURE 2.1   The neoclassical determination of the demand of labor

The aggregate supply given by equation (2.5) can be sold if and only if aggregate demand D exceeds or equals aggregate supply:

$$Y \leq D.$$

If $D < Y$ at prevailing prices, on the other hand, all firms will not be able to sell their profit-maximizing levels of output. At least some firms will face a quantity constraint on their sales. That is, agents on the long side of the market face quantity rationing, by which we mean an inability or perceived inability to complete their desired level of market transactions at prevailing prices. The profit-maximization problem of these rationed firms takes the form:

$$\operatorname*{Max}_{L_i} \pi = pF(L_i) - wL_i \tag{2.6}$$

subject to $F(L_i) \leq \bar{Y}_i$ where $\bar{Y}_i$ is the perceived sales constraint facing firm i. The Lagrangian of the maximization problem can be written:

$$H(L_i, \lambda) = pF(L_i) - wL_i + \lambda[\bar{Y}_i - F(L_i)] \tag{2.7}$$

and the Kuhn–Tucker necessary conditions for a maximum are:

$$(p - \lambda)\, F_L(L_i) - w \leq 0, \qquad L_i[(p - \lambda)\, F_L(L_i) - w] = 0, \quad \text{(2.8a)}$$

$$\bar{Y}_i - F(L_i) \geq 0, \qquad \lambda[\bar{Y}_i - F(L_i)] = 0, \tag{2.8b}$$

$$\lambda \geq 0, \qquad L_i \geq 0, \tag{2.8c}$$

where the Lagrange multiplier λ is the value of one unit relaxation in the perceived sales constraint. If the constraint is binding, we have $\lambda > 0$. Condition (2.8b) then implies:

$$\bar{Y}_i = F(L_i), \tag{2.9}$$

i.e., the firm will choose to produce exactly the amount that it believes it can sell. The good is assumed to be perishable so that the firm never produces for inventory. The amount of labor necessary for this level of production is found by inverting the production function and evaluating it at the constraint level $\bar{Y}_i$:

$$\tilde{L}_i = F^{-1}(\bar{Y}_i) = \tilde{L}_i(\bar{Y}_i). \tag{2.10}$$

The firm's labor demand when subject to the sales constraint (2.9) is referred to as *effective* labor demand to distinguish from the *notional* demand (2.3) when the firm faces no quantity constraints.

In (2.10) employment will be an increasing function of the perceived sales constraint. Given the binding sales constraint, (2.8b) implies that $\lambda \geqslant 0$. It then follows from (2.8a) that the marginal product of labor will be larger than the ruling real wage rate:

$$F_L(\tilde{L}_i) = \frac{w}{(p-\lambda)} \geqslant \frac{w}{p}. \tag{2.11}$$

Therefore, if the real wage was set equal to $w/(p-\lambda)$, the firm would perceive no restriction on its sales. Neary and Roberts (1980) call shadow prices (or wages) with this property "virtual prices." In appendix A it is shown that these virtual prices are handy when comparing the derivatives of behavioral functions under rationing to the corresponding derivatives of behavioral functions in an environment without perceived quantity constraints.

It should be emphasized that in the above circumstance where the firm faces a sales constraint, its *effective* labor demand is independent of the real wage.[8] The firm's effective demand for labor is depicted in figure 2.2. It is an increasing function of the demand for the firm's product, as increased demand relaxes the sales constraint that the representative firm faces. The real wage rate no longer determines the level of employment, and the marginal product of labor may exceed the real wage rate. Hence we have opened up the possibility, at least

---

[8] The main reason for this is that the commodity is assumed to be perishable. In an intertemporal planning problem with storable goods, the firm's demand for labor and its supply of goods will, in general, depend on the real wage rate in the current period and the expectations of future sales possibilities. Compare Peisa (1977), Muellbauer and Portes (1978), and Neary and Stiglitz (1983).

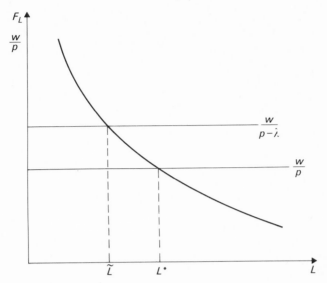

FIGURE 2.2   Equilibrium demand for labor under rationing compared to the neoclassical equilibrium demand for labor

in a partial equilibrium setting, that output and real wages can move in the same direction. We will show below that this possibility is preserved in a general equilibrium fix-price model.

2.2   Robert W. Clower's Contribution

One somewhat embarrassing property of some of the aggregate behavioral equations that emerged from the interpretations of Keynes' *General Theory* was that they depended not just on (output and factor) prices as the Walrasian general equilibrium model dictates, but also on *quantities*. The aggregate consumption function, for example, depended on the level of real output. This brought the microfoundations of the Keynesian theory into question.

In a now well-known paper, Robert W. Clower (1965) pointed to an elegant solution to the search for microfoundations of Keynesian macroeconomics. He assumed that households under non-market-clearing prices would recognize that there are restrictions on their trading possibilities, and take these explicitly into account in their utility-maximizing process. Given such perceived quantity constraints, it is straightforward to show that demand functions will depend on quantities as well as relative prices. Consider a household with a twice continuously differentiable and strictly quasi-concave utility function:[9]

$$U = U\left(D_i, L_i^s, \frac{M_i}{p} + m_i^d\right) \tag{2.12}$$

where D_i = the demand for goods by household i,

L_i^s = the supply of labor by household i,

M_i/p = household i's initial holdings of real balances,

$m_i^d = M^d/p - M_i/p$ = household i's flow demand for real balances.

Under "neoclassical conditions" this utility function is maximized (with respect to D_i, L_i^s, and m_i^d) subject to the budget constraint:

$$pD_i + pm_i^d = wL_i^s + \pi_i, \tag{2.13}$$

where π_i is nominal profit income in the current period. The first-order conditions for an interior maximum can be written:

$$\begin{aligned}
U_1 - \mu p &= 0, \\
U_2 + \mu w &= 0, \\
U_3 - \mu p &= 0, \\
\pi_i + wL_i^s - pD_i - pm_i^d &= 0,
\end{aligned} \tag{2.14}$$

where the subscripts on U indicate the partial derivatives and μ is the Lagrange multiplier associated with the budget constraint (2.13). From the first-order conditions, the household's commodity demand, labor supply, and the excess money (or saving) function can be obtained. They take the form:

$$\begin{aligned}
D_i &= D_i\left(p, w, \pi_i, \frac{M_i}{p}\right), \\
L_i^s &= L_i^s\left(p, w, \pi_i, \frac{M_i}{p}\right), \\
m_i^d &= m_i^d\left(p, w, \pi_i, \frac{M_i}{p}\right).
\end{aligned} \tag{2.15}$$

It is easy to show that the neoclassical demand functions are homogeneous of degree zero in prices, wages, profit income, and nominal money. Therefore, dividing all variables in the behavioral

---

[9] In chapter 3 below it will be further discussed how money balances (nominal or real) should enter the utility function.

functions in (2.15) by $1/p$, the demand for goods, the supply of labor, and savings can be written as functions of the real wage rate, real profit income, and real balances:[10]

$$D_i = D_i\left(\frac{w}{p}, \frac{\pi_i}{p}, \frac{M_i}{p}\right),$$

$$L_i^s = L_i^s\left(\frac{w}{p}, \frac{\pi_i}{p}, \frac{M_i}{p}\right), \qquad (2.16)$$

$$m_i^d = m_i^d\left(\frac{w}{p}, \frac{\pi_i}{p}, \frac{M_i}{p}\right).$$

The desired level of transactions implied by these functions can be carried out provided that aggregate demand does not exceed aggregate supply, and that aggregate labor supply does not exceed labor demand, i.e., $\Sigma_{i=1}^n D_i \leqslant Y$ and $\Sigma_{i=1}^n L_i^s \leqslant L$. However, if relative prices are such that the inequalities are reversed, some households will perceive binding constraints on their trading possibilities.

Clower calls demand functions derived from the maximization of utility subject only to a budget constraint "notional demand functions." The agent assumes that the desired level of transactions can be effected without facing quantity constraints in either goods or labor markets.

Suppose, on the other hand, that there is excess supply in the labor market and that households, being the long side of the market, expect to face quantity constraints on their labor supply. Clower then argues that it is reasonable to assume that household i takes account of the restrictions perceived in the labor market, when it expresses its demand in the market for goods.

The Clower effective demand concept was defined more precisely by Benassy (1973) as follows:

Effective Demand (Clower–Benassy): Effective demand in market i equals the demand in market i that results from the maximization of utility (profit) subject to the budget constraint (production function), and subject to the restrictions perceived in all other markets $j \neq i$.

Thus, if an agent perceives constraints only on his trading possibilities in the labor market, his effective labor supply (i.e., effective demand for leisure) will coincide with his notional supply of labor.

---

[10] As real profits is a function of the real wage rate, it would also be correct to say that demand is a function of the real wages and the real balances provided households perceive the relationship between wages and profits in the short run.

According to Clower, therefore, the household's effective demand for goods when it perceives a quantity constraint in the labor market would be found by maximizing:

$$U = U\left(D_i, L_i^s, \frac{M_i}{p} + m_i^d\right)$$ (2.17)

subject to the budget constraint:

$$pD_i + pm_i^d = wL_i^s + \pi_i,$$ (2.17a)

as well as the perceived restriction in the labor market:

$$L_i^s \leqslant \bar{L}_i.$$ (2.17b)

Any perceived constraint on the goods market itself is ignored when determining the effective demand function.[11] Necessary conditions for an interior optimum, assuming a binding constraint in the labor market, are:

$$U_1 - \mu p = 0,$$

$$U_2 + \mu w - \gamma = U_2 + \mu(w - \gamma/\mu) = 0,$$ (2.18)

$$U_3 - \mu p = 0,$$

where μ and γ are the Lagrange multipliers corresponding to the budget constraint and employment constraint respectively.

In appendix A it will be shown that $w - \gamma/\mu$ in (2.18) can be interpreted as the "virtual" price of leisure time. That is, it is the price that would induce the household to supply an amount of labor equal to $\bar{L}_i$, when utility is maximized subject to no other restriction than the budget constraint.[12] The virtual price $w - \gamma/\mu$ can be used to compare the derivatives of the constrained (effective) and the notional behavior functions.

---

[11] The Clower (Benassy) definition of effective demand should be distinguished from an alternative definition proposed by Drèze (1975). In the latter, the demand for each good is obtained by maximizing utility subject to the budget constraint and *all* perceived constraints including the market in question. Thus, the *Drèze* effective supply of labor equals the perceived constraint level L_i, not the notional supply function. The distinction between Clower and Drèze effective demands becomes paramount if long-run price adjustments are to be modeled as functions of effective excess demands. This will be discussed further in appendix B when we return to price adjustment.

[12] Note that μ in (2.18) will in general differ from μ in (2.14). The same symbol is used solely for notational convenience.

It is fairly easy to show that the effective demand functions implicit in (2.18) can be written in the form:

$$\hat{D}_i = \hat{D}_i\left(\frac{\pi_i}{p}, \frac{w}{p}, \frac{M_i}{p}, \bar{L}_i\right) = \hat{D}_i\left(\frac{\pi_i}{p} + \frac{w}{p}\bar{L}_i, \frac{M_i}{p}, \bar{L}_i\right),$$

$$\hat{m}_i^d = \hat{m}_i^d\left(\frac{\pi_i}{p}, \frac{w}{p}, \frac{M_i}{p}, \bar{L}_i\right) = \hat{m}_i^d\left(\frac{\pi_i}{p} + \frac{w}{p}\bar{L}_i, \frac{M_i}{p}, \bar{L}_i\right).$$

(2.19)

These effective demands depend on quantities as well as prices, as the marginal utilities in (2.18) are evaluated with (2.17b) holding as a strict equality.

A special, but illuminating, case is obtained if we assume a one-household economy.[13] For the economy as a whole, real income (Y) equals real value added:

$$Y = \frac{\pi}{p} + \frac{w}{p}\bar{L}_i.$$

Substituting this expression into the effective demand functions of the single household yields:

$$\hat{D} = \hat{D}\left(Y, \frac{M}{p}, \bar{L}\right),$$

$$\hat{m}^d = \hat{m}^d\left(Y, \frac{M}{p}, \bar{L}\right).$$

(2.20)

The resulting effective demand for goods (the consumption function) and the effective demand for additional money balances (which equals saving in the present single-asset context) look very Keynesian indeed. In particular, these functions depend on real output, employment, and real balances. It is straightforward to show[14] that the marginal propensities to consume and to save sum to unity:

$$\frac{\partial \hat{D}}{\partial Y} + \frac{\partial \hat{m}^d}{\partial Y} = 1.$$

(2.21)

---

[13] Alternatively, it could be assumed that the *distribution* of profits and wages does not affect demand. The first person to suggest that the Keynesian consumption function can be derived from neoclassical microtheory augmented with an employment constraint was A. Lindbeck. See Lindbeck (1963, pp. 33 and 44).

[14] Differentiate the budget constraint with respect to real profit income after setting L to the constrained level $\bar{L}$.

We will return below to the properties of the effective demand functions under different kinds of possible market imbalances. Here we note only that the marginal rate of substitution between goods and labor will be smaller than the real wage rate when the ration "bites" in the labor market ($\gamma > 0$). From the first-order conditions (2.18) we obtain:

$$\frac{-U_2}{U_1} = \frac{w - \gamma/\mu}{p} \leqslant \frac{w}{p}, \tag{2.22}$$

where

$$\frac{-U_2}{U_1} = \left(\frac{\partial D}{\partial L^s}\right)_{u=k}$$

is the marginal rate of substitution along the indifference curve. The inequality (2.22) indicates that the household is forced to consume too much leisure when it faces a labor supply constraint. Assuming that $\hat{m}^d$ is optimally chosen, given the constraint (2.17b), a cross-section picture of the utility function and the budget constraint in (L^s, D) space looks like the one in figure 2.3.

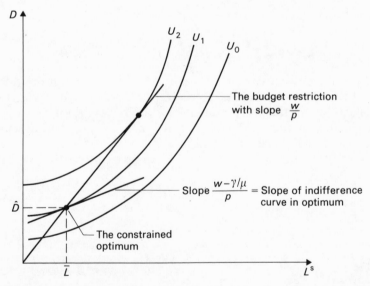

FIGURE 2.3 The household's optimum when it is constrained in the labor market

The consequences of employing alternative excess demand concepts when specifying long-run price adjustments are not clear from Clower's paper. A fairly natural approach, however, would be to use *effective* demand and supply functions as the measure of the market imbalances, and as the force that governs price adjustments. This idea will be discussed at some length in appendix B.

Moreover, it is not clear from Clower's analysis (except perhaps from the partial point of view of the consumer) if and how trade takes place outside the Walrasian equilibrium. This problem is dealt with to some extent in an important book written by Axel Leijonhufvud (1968).

2.3   Axel Leijonhufvud's Contribution

Axel Leijonhufvud's interpretation of Keynes is fairly close to Clower's views on the same matters. According to Leijonhufvud, Keynes does not question the neoclassical decision theory based on complete rationality. This means, among other things, that the price system "works" in the sense that changing the price vector leads to a change in behavior, and Keynes does not deny the existence of a price vector which would, once established, guarantee a full-employment Walrasian equilibrium. What Keynes eliminates from neoclassical theory is the Walrasian auctioneer, who, by making repeated price adjustments and allowing recontracting, generates the necessary conditions for consistent trading.

Leijonhufvud argues that Keynes regards quantity adjustments as being considerably faster than price adjustments.[15] The normal state of a market is hence one of disequilibrium in the Walrasian sense. Leijonhufvud is not very explicit on how to model the trade process at disequilibrium prices. One useful approach, however, would be to regard prices as fixed in the short run, and allow the auctioneer to use quantity adjustments to create consistent trading. This is, in fact, the *Hicksian fix-price method* in its pure form.

A "Keynesian" version of the *tâtonnement process* in a simple economy with a single household and a single firm could schematically be described in the following manner. On market day the auctioneer starts the process by announcing an arbitrary chosen price vector, which is fixed in the short run. The firm then announces its notional supply of goods and notional demand for labor. Similarly,

[15] This is, in fact, the revolutionary element in Keynes' *General Theory*, according to Leijonhufvud.

the household informs the auctioneer about its notional demand for goods and notional supply of labor.

Let us assume that these first-round demands and supplies result in excess supply in both the goods and labor markets. In this situation no trades occur. The tâtonnement process continues. In the next step the auctioneer informs the firm about the *quantities* of goods the household is willing to buy, and the household is informed about the amount of labor the firm wants to buy.[16] The resulting quantity constraints from the short side of each market are then used, together with the first-round prices, as restrictions on the decision problems of the firm and the household in the second round of the process. This round generates effective demands for goods and labor and the corresponding perceived transactions of labor and goods.[17] The latter are equal to the first-round demand for labor and the first-round demand for goods. The second-round effective demands are likely to be smaller than the corresponding first-round entities, as both the household and the firm now have additional constraints on their decision problems. Hence, in the next step of this recontracting process (where no trades actually occur until the process is complete) the household and the firm are informed about the new restrictions on their decision problems, which was reflected in their second-round effective demands for goods and labor. The sketched process continues until the perceived transactions of labor and goods converge toward the effective demands generated when perceived constraints are used together with the invariable prices as restrictions on the decision problems of the household and the firm. Note that the effective supplies of goods and labor are constant during the whole process, as neither the firm nor the household perceive any restrictions on the demand for labor and goods, respectively. The fix-price equilibrium is, hence, the fixed point[18] of the tâtonnement or "perceived quantity-constraint adjustment" process, which maps effective demands into effective demands.

Consistent trading can now take place at the fix-price equilibrium. We can then allow prices to change in the direction indicated by the sign (positive or negative) of effective excess demands. The short-run equilibrium tâtonnement process on perceived quantity constraints

---

[16] The information set should also contain information about profit income, but we disregard this for the moment.

[17] The perceived transactions of labor and goods equal the quantity constraints perceived by the household and the firm.

[18] Consider a function $y = F(x)$. A fixed point is a point x^* which is mapped onto itself, i.e., $x^* = F(x^*)$.

then starts all over again at the new vector of fixed prices. In other words, two time frames are being distinguished: quantity adjustments create a short-run equilibrium at fixed prices within each period, but between periods prices can adjust. A long-run equilibrium is present when the fix-price equilibrium attained within the period is such that there is no tendency for prices to adjust over time (i.e., between periods) so that the within-period equilibrium is sustained indefinitely.

If price adjustments are governed by effective excess demands the Walrasian equilibrium is a long-run equilibrium. When prices are at their general equilibrium levels, nobody will perceive any quantity restrictions on trades once the tâtonnement process on quantities is complete. Effective excess demands at that time will coincide with notional excess demands, which are zero (by definition) at the Walrasian equilibrium. From this special case where price adjustments are governed by effective excess demand it should be fairly obvious that the nature of the long-run equilibrium will, in general, depend on the specification of the price adjustment process.

2.4   Robert Barro's and Herschel I. Grossman's Contribution

The tâtonnement process in quantities described above is perhaps not explicit in Barro and Grossman's (1971) paper, but it is at least implicit. Barro and Grossman are the first to show how the ideas of Patinkin and Clower can be combined into a general disequilibrium model, where consistent trading can take place at fixed non-market-clearing prices.

Their seminal paper analyzes the simple three-market, one-household, one-firm economy discussed above. Two fundamentally different disequilibrium situations are analyzed. The first one is a general excess supply, i.e., at the initial price vector there are excess supplies of both labor and goods. In a different terminology one could say that there is unemployment (underemployment), and a deficiency of aggregate demand for output. This situation is appropriately labelled *Keynesian unemployment.*

The second disequilibrium situation is characterized by general excess demand, i.e., excess demand in both the labor market and the market for goods. Hence the firm perceives a constraint on its demand for labor, and the household perceives a constraint on its demand for goods. As prices and wages are fixed and cannot rise to alleviate these excess demands in the short run, this situation has been called *repressed inflation*.[19]

One disequilibrium combination not analyzed by Barro and Grossman (1971) is the case of excess demand for goods and excess supply of labor.[20] This situation has been called *classical unemployment* due to the fact that the neoclassical remedy for unemployment, lower wages, is potent.[21]

One could think of another possible disequilibrium configuration with an excess supply of goods and an excess demand for labor. If the good is nonstorable and labor is the only variable input in the short run, however, this situation never arises. This is so because the production function is a one-to-one relation between input of labor and output of goods, implying that the firm cannot simultaneously perceive constraints in both the labor and goods markets.[22]

In an intertemporal framework with nonperishable goods, however, the *underconsumption* case, characterized by an excess supply of goods and an excess demand for labor, can arise. It was initially discussed by Malinvaud (1977) and, in a more explicit intertemporal framework, by Muellbauer and Portes (1978).

The properties of fix-price equilibria within all four of the above-mentioned regimes will not be discussed here. This will be done in appendix B where price adjustment and matters of stability are considered. We will, however, analyze the properties of the fix-price equilibrium under Keynesian unemployment to show, among other things, that the previously discussed partial equilibrium result that employment and real wages can move in the same direction is preserved in a general equilibrium setting.

We start with figure 2.4a showing how the different regimes depend on the real wage and real balances.

The broken curves show $(w/p, M/p)$ combinations where *notional* demands and supplies are equalized in the labor and goods markets respectively. The full curves are the loci denoting equality between *effective* demands and supplies in the corresponding markets.

Point W in figure 2.4a shows the real wage rate/real balances combination (ω^*, m^*) that generates the unique Walrasian equilibrium.

---

[19] It has also been called the Hansen-region (H-region), due to the fact that Bent Hansen (1951) was the first to analyze this disequilibrium situation in his study on inflation, although he did not explicitly consider *repressed inflation* with spillover effects. See also Löfgren (1979) and Raymon (1981).

[20] This situation is treated in Barro and Grossman (1976).

[21] Malinvaud (1977) is responsible for this terminology. Löfgren (1979) calls this situation the Ω-region.

[22] For a formal proof see, e.g., Barro and Grossman (1976).

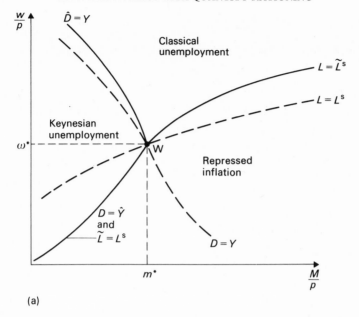

(a)

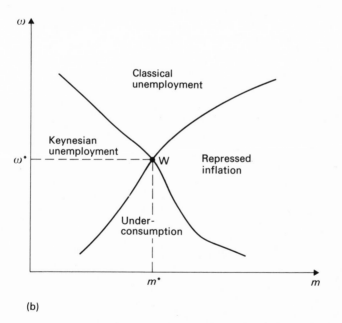

(b)

FIGURE 2.4   (a) Disequilibrium regimes. (b) Disequilibrium regimes including
                an underconsumption regime

If the real wage rate is kept constant while real balances are decreased, the economy moves into the region of Keynesian unemployment. Given the constant real wage, firms want to buy the same amount of labor and supply the same amount of goods as before, regardless of the level of the real balances – see equations (2.3) and (2.4) above. On the other hand, as real wealth of the household is decreased, a lower demand for goods and a larger supply of labor emerges. (Leisure is assumed to be a normal good.) Hence, an excess supply is generated in both markets. The opposite holds if real balances are increased while the real wage rate is kept constant: an excess supply of goods and an excess demand for labor, i.e., repressed inflation, emerges.

Suppose real balances are kept constant at the Walrasian equilibrium level while the real wage rate is increased. Firms will demand less labor and supply less output. The household will demand more goods and supply more labor as the increase of the real wage makes leisure more expensive relative to goods.[23] The net effects are an excess demand for goods and an excess supply of labor as we move north from (ω^*, m^*) in figure 2.4a. This is the classical unemployment region.

The border between the regions of Keynesian and classical unemployment is the locus of points where effective demand for goods just equals notional supply: $\hat{D} = Y$. The border between the region of Keynesian unemployment and the region of repressed inflation is the locus of points where the effective supply of goods (when the firm perceives a binding constraint on its demand for labor) just equals notional demand: $D = \hat{Y}$. It is also the locus of points where the effective demand for labor, when the firm perceives a binding constraint on its supply of goods, just equals notional labor supply: $\tilde{L} = L^s$.

There is no region of excess supply of goods and excess demand of labor in this figure for reasons mentioned above.[24] In the intertemporal approach used in chapter 3, however, an underconsumption regime is a distinct possibility. The diagram describing the different disequilibrium regimes under such circumstances would look like figure 2.4b, with the underconsumption regime situated between the Keynesian unemployment and repressed inflation regions.

[23] As the economy is assumed to have only one household and one firm, all income effects from an increased real wage rate net out. The household gets less profit income at the same level of employment and more labor income.

[24] From a technical point of view, there is a problem of discontinuity of the effective excess demand functions on this border when the long-run price adjustment process is governed by the effective excess demand functions. We return to this problem in appendix B.

Returning for the moment to figure 2.4a, note that the regions of classical unemployment and underconsumption shrink when they are delineated by effective rather than notional behavior functions. The reason is this: when there is excess supply in the labor market this lowers effective demand in the goods market in relation to notional demand. An analogous argument can be applied for the labor market when there is excess supply in the goods market. Consequently, the region of general excess supply under the notional behavior functions will be included in the region of general effective excess supply, i.e., the region of Keynesian unemployment. Similar spillover effects are at work so that the region of general effective excess demand is magnified in relation to the region of general notional excess demand.

In the chapters to follow we will consider different assumptions regarding price inflexibility. One particularly interesting case is when the price of goods adjusts quickly to clear the goods market, while the wage rate is fixed thereby generating unemployment. In figure 2.4a, this situation is characterized by real wage/real balance combinations which lie on the border between the classical unemployment and Keynesian unemployment regions. This regime is called *orthodox Keynesian unemployment* due to its similarities with the standard textbook macroeconomic models.[25]

Assume now that the (ω, m) vector is such that the economy is in the region of Keynesian unemployment. What will determine the nature of the fix-price equilibrium? First of all, the restriction on sales that the firm perceives must coincide with the household's effective demand for goods (equation (2.20) if there is a single household or if income distribution effects are assumed away):

$$\bar{Y} = \hat{D}\left(\bar{Y}, \frac{M}{p}, \bar{L}\right). \tag{2.23}$$

Moreover, the restriction on the supply of labor perceived by the household, $\bar{L}$, must equal the labor input demanded by the firm in light of the sales constraint it perceives:

$$\bar{L} = \tilde{L}(\bar{Y}). \tag{2.24}$$

That is, the household's perceived employment constraint must coincide with the firm's effective demand for labor. Given the prevailing level of real wages and money balances, equations (2.23) and (2.24) jointly determine the levels of employment and domestic

---

[25] For a recent use of the properties of this regime in cost–benefit analysis, see Roberts (1982).

output, $\bar{L}$ and $\bar{Y}$. It is therefore possible, in principle, to solve for the fix-price equilibrium (provided one exists; see section 2.5 below).

Regarding our earlier discussion of the Dunlop–Tarshis problem in section 2.1 above, it can easily be shown that the marginal productivity of labor exceeds[26] the real wage rate and that inequality (2.22) is valid in general disequilibria with unemployment. Hence, the fix-price equilibrium in the Keynesian unemployment region is characterized by:

$$\frac{-U_2}{U_1} \leqslant \frac{w}{p} \leqslant F_L \qquad \text{(Keynesian unemployment)},$$

where at least one of the inequalities will hold with strict inequality. For a fix-price equilibrium of the classical unemployment variety, it must be the case that:

$$\frac{-U_2}{U_1} \leqslant \frac{w}{p} = F_L \qquad \text{(classical unemployement)}.$$

In the region of repressed inflation, it can be shown that

$$F_L \geqslant \frac{w}{p}, \qquad \frac{-U_2}{U_1} \geqslant \frac{w}{p} \qquad \text{(repressed inflation)}.$$

At least one of the inequalities must be a strict inequality. The latter inequality indicates that the household is forced to buy too little leisure.[27] In other words the household is overemployed.

2.5   Jean P. Benassy's Contribution

In two papers, Jean P. Benassy (1975, 1976b) generalized the Barro–Grossman model to an economy consisting of H households, F firms, and N commodities, and presented conditions under which a fix-price equilibrium exists.[28] Although we will not go into all the details in Benassy's papers, some complications that emerge when an increased number of goods and agents are introduced should be briefly mentioned. The first complication is that the volumes on the short sides of the markets have to be allocated to the various agents on the long sides of the markets. This problem was solved by Benassy by

---

[26] Equality is of course possible. This is true at the border between the classical and Keynesian regions, i.e., in the region of orthodox Keynesian unemployment.
[27] Malinvaud (1977) provides hints for proving these propositions.
[28] This was also done in Drèze (1975). Benassy's contributions are now collected in a monograph – see Benassy (1982).

introducing for each market n the actual transaction possibilities for every household and firm as function of the effective demands of all agents $(\ldots H + F)$, i.e.

$$\bar{x}_{hn} = F_{hn}(\tilde{x}_{1n}, \ldots, \tilde{x}_{H+Fn}) \qquad h = 1, \ldots, H+F, \qquad (2.25)$$

where $\bar{x}_{hn}$ is the net trade of the agent h in the nth market and $\bar{x}_{hn} > 0$ (<0) implies that the agent is a net demander (supplier) in the nth market.

These *rationing rules* can in practice take many forms. In the goods market there may exist a queueing system or a coupon system; in the labor market one can think of different types of priority systems which determine the employment possibilities. The "theoretical" reason for these functions is to inform the agents during the tâtonnement process about their actual trading possibilities. It is neither necessary nor desirable that any trading takes place during the process. The purpose of the quantity adjustments is to create a situation that makes consistent trading possible.[29] At the same time the quantities traded must be consistent with optimizing behavior at the individual level, when the perceived trading possibilities (i.e., rationing constraints) are explicitly considered.

Rationing functions are usually assumed to have the following properties:

$$|\bar{x}_{hn}| \leqslant |\tilde{x}_{hn}| \qquad \text{and} \qquad \bar{x}_{hn}\tilde{x}_{hn} \geqslant 0 \qquad \text{for all } h \text{ and } n, \qquad (2.26a)$$

$$\tilde{x}_n\tilde{x}_{hn} \leqslant 0 \quad \Rightarrow \quad \bar{x}_{hn} = \tilde{x}_{hn} \qquad \text{for all } h \text{ and } n. \qquad (2.26b)$$

Property (2.26a) means that trade is voluntary, i.e., the agent is not forced by the rationing function to trade more than his effective demand (supply). Property (2.26b) means that the short side of the market can always realize its effective demand. When these properties prevail, we say we have a "frictionless market."

The rationing functions may be thought of as a substitute for the Walrasian auctioneer, which signals in every step of the tâtonnement process. As a requirement of consistency it is reasonable to assume that all goods are distributed. Formally:

$$\bar{x}_n = \Sigma \bar{x}_{hn} = 0 \qquad \text{for all } n. \qquad (2.27)$$

Finally, one needs rules to translate the effective demands into *perceived* restrictions on trades. Benassy (1975) assumes that the

---

[29] Note that even if the firm and the household are given the labor and the goods they demand in the first round of the tâtonnement process, too much will be produced.

perceived restrictions on trade are continuous functions of the effective demands:

$$\bar{\bar{x}}_{hn} = f(\tilde{x}_{1n}, \dots, \tilde{x}_{H+Fn}) \qquad \text{for all } n \text{ and } h, \qquad (2.28)$$

where $\bar{\bar{x}}_{hn}$ is the restriction on trade in the nth market perceived by the hth agent. These functions are assumed to have the following properties:

$$|\bar{x}_{hn}| < |\tilde{x}_{hn}| \quad \Rightarrow \quad \bar{\bar{x}}_{hn} = \bar{x}_{hn} \qquad h = 1, \dots, H+F \quad (2.29a)$$

$$\bar{x}_{hn} = \tilde{x}_{hn} \quad \Rightarrow \quad (\bar{\bar{x}}_{hn} - \bar{x}_{hn}) \, \tilde{x}_{hn} \geqslant 0, \qquad (2.29b)$$

$$\tilde{x}_{hn} \tilde{x}_n < 0 \quad \Rightarrow \quad (\bar{\bar{x}}_{hn} - \bar{x}_{hn}) \, \tilde{x}_{hn} > 0. \qquad (2.29c)$$

Property (2.29a) means that if the agent is constrained in the nth market (i.e., his effective net demand exceeds the quantity which is allocated to him through the rationing function), then the perceived restriction on trade coincides with the actual trade. If the agent is allowed to trade his effective net demand it is reasonable to assume that he may perceive some further transaction possibilities in the same direction. This is expressed by property (2.29b). In particular, this should be the case if he is on the short side of the market; this is formalized in property (2.29c).

Rationing functions (F) and the functions expressing the perceived restrictions on trades (f) in combination with the optimization by individual agents (which generate the effective net demand vectors $\tilde{x}$), map effective net demand vectors into net effective demand vectors. This is illuminated in figure 2.5 borrowed from Malinvaud (1977).

The fix-price equilibrium is the fixed point of this circular scheme. Under suitable concavity assumptions on the maximization problems

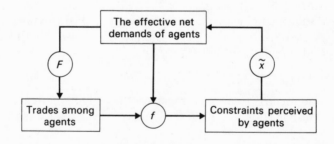

FIGURE 2.5   The tâtonnement process under fixed prices

and assuming the function f and F are continuous, it can be shown that a fix-price equilibrium exists. It can also be shown that a fix-price equilibrium maximizes the utility of every agent given all the restrictions he perceives. In other words, the fix-price equilibrium is the best possible for the agent under the circumstances of completely inflexible prices. They are in addition Nash equilibria. (See Benassy (1982), chapters 7 and 10.)

More formally, a *fix-price equilibrium* is defined as the effective demands, perceived restrictions, and actual transactions fulfilling the following three conditions:

(i) $\bar{\bar{x}}_{hn} = f(\tilde{x}_{1n}, \ldots, \tilde{x}_{H+Fn})$ for all h and n,

(ii) $\tilde{x}_{hn}$ is obtained as the hth agent's effective demand, when his choice set is constrained by initial endowments, the fixed prices, and perceived restrictions $\bar{\bar{x}}_{hn}$,

(iii) $\bar{x}_{hn} = F(\tilde{x}_{1n}, \ldots, \tilde{x}_{H+Fn})$ for all h and n.

Conditions (i) and (ii) take care of the fixed-point property of the equilibrium mentioned above. Note that the effective demands that generate the perceived restrictions in (i) are in turn generated by a maximization problem where the perceived restrictions are among the constraints. The purpose of (iii) is to generate the actual transactions.

The definition of fix-price equilibrium emphasizes an important point: the vector of equilibrium excess demands and equilibrium trades depends on the particular rationing scheme that is assumed to prevail in the economy.[30] Changing the rationing rule will, in general, change resource allocation and ultimate consumption vectors in the fix-price equilibrium.

Stability conditions on the quantity adjustment process will be discussed to some extent in appendix B. Here it suffices to note that agents' perceptions of how the actual trades are generated is important. Hence, if the rationing functions are such that "overbidding pays" (i.e., if overstating true demand reduces the severity of the rationing an individual experiences), general "overbidding" with unbounded sequence of effective demands is likely to result. (Different types of nonmanipulative and manipulative rationing schemes are discussed by Benassy (1977).)

---

[30] It might also be mentioned that a Benassy-equilibrium (K-equilibrium) defined above differs from a Drèze-equilibrium based on the alternative effective demand concept proposed by Drèze (see footnote 11). In a Benassy-equilibrium effective demands may differ from actual trades, while these concepts coincide in a Drèze equilibrium. Silvestre (1982) and Benassy (1982) discuss conditions under which the two equilibrium concepts are equivalent.

2.6   Extensions of the Closed-economy Fix-price Model

It is well known that the vector of Clower effective demands may violate the budget constraint and therefore be infeasible. Another related problem with the Clower effective demand concept is that it implies that an agent believes that it is worthwhile to express an effective demand in excess of what he perceives it possible to trade.[31] In this sense every rationing scheme within fix-price models using the Clower effective demand concept must be manipulative.

One way out of these dilemma is to use some kind of stochastic rationing scheme. Even in stochastic environments, of course, there can be manipulative rationing schemes. Gale (1979) has proved the existence of equilibrium in a model allowing for a very general, stochastic, manipulative rationing scheme. Svensson (1980) considers the properties of a stochastic fix-price model with a nonmanipulative rationing scheme.[32]

Perhaps the most unsatisfactory feature of the Barro–Grossman model discussed above is that intertemporal considerations enter only implicitly, via the real balance effect in the utility function. This method obscures the important role of expectations by implicitly assuming that the next period's price level will be the same as this period's, and that the disequilibrium regime that prevails today does not affect expectations about the regime that will prevail tomorrow.

Muellbauer and Portes (1978) attempt to eliminate these difficulties by considering a stochastic model where both households and firms plan for two periods. Instead of assuming that households and firms hold point expectations about *future* prices and quantity constraints, they take an explicitly probabilistic, von Neumann–Morgenstern view. Muellbauer and Portes show that the conditional utility function to be maximized subject to the first-period budget constraint:

$$pD + M = wL^s + \pi + M_0$$

can be written:

$$U = V(D, L^s, M; \theta), \tag{2.30}$$

---

[31] The most natural way out of this dilemma is to work with a simultaneous determination of both prices and quantities. Compare the discussion of the theory of conjectural equilibria below.

[32] A similar approach is followed in Futia (1977). The difference is that Futia studies a sequence of markets while Svensson allows for the consumers to express their demands simultaneously for all goods.

where θ absorbs the parameters concerning the subjective probabilistic expectations of future-period values of profit income, prices, wages, and quantity constraints on trade. The reader should note that *nominal* (not real) money balances is the argument in the conditional utility function. The effects of future prices are embodied in the expectations parameter θ and hence affect the functional form of the utility function in D, L^s, and M.

The alternative way to introduce intertemporal considerations into fix-price models is to introduce *point* expectations about future prices and future constraints in a two-period setting. This is done by Neary and Stiglitz (1983)[33] who analyze the efficiency of economic policy under rational constraint expectations, i.e., perfect foresight about future quantity constraints. They show that rational expectations may enhance rather than reduce the effectiveness of government policy in the fix-price context with expectations regarding future quantity constraints. This conclusion stands in contrast to the literature on neoclassical macromodels where rational expectations greatly reduces and sometimes eliminates entirely the efficacy of government policy.

3   Why are Prices Fixed in Fix-price Equilibria?

So far, we have not explicitly addressed the important question of why price adjustments are slower than quantity adjustments. The view taken in sections 1 and 2 above is that the fix-price equilibria brought about by quantity adjustments are best looked at as short-run equilibria, and that the long-run equilibrium may well be a full-employment flexible-price equilibrium. We feel that it is fair to say that there are no commonly agreed-upon explanations of rigid prices. There are, however, a few promising attempts to account for slow price adjustments and non-Walrasian equilibria. Some of these attempts will be discussed below. The reader is also referred to Solow's (1979, 1980) interesting discussion of the relevance of, and possible explanations for, wage–price stickiness.

[33] The paper by Neary and Stiglitz has been circulating since 1979 and has inspired related efforts, including a paper by Persson and Svensson (1983) asking the question: "Is optimism a good thing in a Keynesian economy?"

3.1 *Partial Equilibrium and/or Incomplete Explanations of Rigid Prices*

This section will review some of the recent attempts to explain slow price adjustments or short-run price rigidities. The explanations are incomplete in the sense that there is no strictly formal reason to believe that the equilibria discussed are "long-run" equilibria in the same sense as the Walrasian equilibria under competitive conjectures about the trading possibilities (i.e., when agents perceive that they can trade any amounts at the ruling market prices).

One can easily point out institutional reasons for relative prices to be rigid outside the Walrasian full-employment equilibrium. Trade unions activity, the indexation of wage agreements, central bank intervention, and government-administered prices provide some motivation for the study of short-run fix-price equilibria. There may, however, exist an even more fundamental, doctrinal reason for the study of such equilibria. Keynes regarded unemployment due to union policy as "voluntary" but retained the first postulate of classical economics: the equality of marginal productivity of labor and the real wage rate, in his *General Theory*.[34] Hence, Keynes assumed perfect competition and also price flexibility in the goods market in his theory of involuntary unemployment. He does not have perfect wage flexibility but explains why lower wages will not help once there is unemployment.

It is obvious that involuntary unemployment cannot coexist in classical economics with both perfect competition and price flexibility, but Keynes' purpose was to construct a theoretical framework which made this (involuntary unemployment and price flexibility) possible.

Armen Alchian (1970) – and to some extent one of Keynes' most well-known interpreters, Axel Leijonhufvud (1968) – base their explanation of sluggish price adjustments on the high information costs associated with adjusting prices quickly and continuously. Alchian, in particular, has argued that stable prices reduce the need for search. A restaurant, for example, does not continuously vary its prices to fill all empty chairs. If price were adjusted continuously to achieve market clearing, consumers might be faced with extreme price uncertainty. Hence diners would have to plan routinely on a period of search before dinner instead of a quick meal at a pre-chosen restaurant. The alternative is an implicit commitment by

---

[34] See Keynes (1936, pp. 5–6).

firms to maintain constant prices for a period of time so that consumers can reduce the resources allocated to search activity.

Leijonhufvud regards the equilibrium state in Keynes' *General Theory* as a short-run equilibrium. There is an ongoing tendency for prices to fall in markets characterized by excess supply, just as the short-run solution with very fast price adjustment in Marshall's model. Leijonhufvud's point is that Keynes implicitly or explicitly turned Marshall's ranking of the relative speeds of price and quantity adjustments upside down.[35]

In later writings Leijonhufvud (1973) has stressed the concept of the corridor. The corridor is defined as a neighborhood around the Walrasian equilibrium where price adjustments are fast. For small deviations from the Walrasian equilibrium the system will swiftly return to the full-employment equilibrium, while for large deviations from the Walrasian equilibrium it is conjectured that the system might end up in a Keynesian short-run equilibrium characterized by extremely slow price adjustments. The theoretical or institutional justification for the corridor is unclear in Leijonhufvud's writings and later investigations have also cast some doubt on its relevance for neo-Keynesian economics.[36]

Another proposed reason for price rigidities is that employers and employees in an uncertain world may find it optimal to agree on a fixed real wage rate. The writings in this area are often lumped together under the heading of *contract theory*.[37] The structure and main content of contract theory can be summarized as follows: firms are assumed to be risk-neutral while consumers are risk-averse. The theory can hence be interpreted as a special case of a more general theory of risk-bearing developed by Borch (1962), Arrow (1971), and others. The markets for output are assumed to clear by auction, with output prices fluctuating with changes in effective demand. In the simplest version of the theory, there are only two states of nature with different levels of prices: state 1 occurs with probability θ and state 2 occurs with probability $1-\theta$. The state-dependent prices relevant for a particular firm are p_1 and p_2. The general price levels under the two possible states are P_1 and P_2. The indirect utility function of households i is assumed to be a function of the real wage rate:

$$v = v\left(\frac{w}{P}\right), \tag{2.31}$$

[35] See Leijonhufvud (1968, p. 53).
[36] See Grossman (1974), Löfgren (1979), and Raymon (1981).
[37] The reader is referred to Baily (1974), Gordon (1974), and Azariadis (1975, 1976).

where v is assumed to be strictly concave in $\omega = w/P$, which is equivalent to an assumption of risk aversion.[38] Moreover, the utility function is an increasing function of the real wage rate.

The expected utility of household i in a Walrasian auction setting is:

$$v_F = \theta v \left(\frac{w_1^a}{P_1}\right) + (1-\theta) v \left(\frac{w_2^a}{P_2}\right), \tag{2.32}$$

when $w_j^a =$ the nominal wage rate resulting from a market-clearing auction in state $j = 1, 2$.

The firm offers a contract $[(w_1, L_1)(w_2, L_2)]$ promising to employ L_1 individuals at wage w_1 in state 1. This contract is constrained by the fact that the representative household will not accept it unless it promises an expected utility larger than or equal to that attainable by selling labor in the spot market each period (defined by v_F in (2.32)). The problem of the firm is therefore to determine a contract offer that will maximize its expected profits:

$$\underset{w_i, L_i}{\text{Max}} \; E(\pi) = \frac{\theta}{P_1} [p_1 F(L_1) - w_1] + \frac{1-\theta}{P_2} [p_2 F(L_2) - w_2 L_2],$$

subject to the constraint that it must leave workers no worse off than they would be by foregoing a contract and engaging in spot-market transactions:

$$\theta \frac{L_1}{L} v \left(\frac{w_1}{P_1}\right) + \theta \frac{(L-L_1)}{L} \bar{v} + (1-\theta) \frac{L_2}{L} v \left(\frac{w_2}{P_2}\right)$$

$$+ (1-\theta) \frac{L-L_2}{L} \bar{v} \geqslant v_F,$$

$$L_i \leqslant L, \qquad i = 1, 2,$$

where L is the supply of labor and $\bar{v}$ is the utility of being unemployed. Assuming the determination of *who* is employed and unemployed in each state i is made randomly, the probability of being unemployed is $(L-L_i)/L$. The above restriction implies that the expected utility of the employee must be at least as large as the expected utility of a full-employment contract (at the spot-market wage rates).

---

[38] The fact that real balances are not included as an argument in the indirect utility function might be justified if the household perceives that it can preserve the real value of its assets across states of nature. If real balances are included in the utility function, the equilibrium contract will no longer specify a real wage rate that is independent of the state of the economy.

It can be shown that the optimal contract must fulfill the conditions:

$$\mu = \frac{L}{v_1(\omega_1)} = \frac{L}{v_1(\omega_2)} \tag{2.33a}$$

and

$$\theta \frac{L_1}{L} v(\omega_1) + \theta \frac{L - L_1}{L} \bar{v} + (1 - \theta) \frac{L_2}{L} v(\omega_2)$$

$$+ (1 - \theta) \frac{L - L_2}{L} \bar{v} = v_F, \tag{2.33b}$$

where μ is the Lagrange multiplier. It can be interpreted as the increase in the firm's expected profit resulting from a decrease of the household's expected utility of the full-employment contract by one unit. Condition (2.33a) implies the important result that the real wage will be state-independent ($\omega = \omega_1 = \omega_2$), thereby providing a theoretical justification of wage stickiness. Condition (2.33b) tells us that the firm offers a contract with expected utility exactly equal to the expected utility of the full-employment contract.

It then remains to be shown that one could expect the optimal contract, which produces wage rigidities, to involve some degree of unemployment. Negishi (1979) emphasizes that this is considerably more difficult than initially suggested by the seminal works in contract theory mentioned above.[39] In sum, the problem with a contract theoretical explanation of rigid wages/prices seems to be that although contract theory can explain rigid wages in certain circumstances, it cannot simultaneously explain involuntary unemployment.[40] In general, optimal contracts will specify not only wage (or price) profiles but also employment (or quantity) determination rules. The latter may be quite different from those implied by the rationing rules used in fix-price models.

Recently Solow (1979) has emphasized the possible role of unemployment compensation benefits (from some source other than the firm) in generating cyclical employment variations within the implicit contracts framework. He also provides further references to this line of thought, which may eventually provide a good theoretical expla-

---

[39] See in particular Negishi (1979, chapter 18).

[40] The reader should note that even if the optimal contract involves unemployment, it is not very precise to call this unemployment "involuntary" in the sense of Keynes. The unemployed can be compared with a buyer of a lottery ticket who does not win the lottery prize.

nation of real wage stickiness and involuntary unemployment. To date, however, contract theory is only a partial equilibrium approach. It may or may not be useful when extended to a general equilibrium setting.

Before we leave this section, the works of Arthur Okun (1975, 1981) should be referenced. They contain interesting attempts to model price-setting behavior. He distinguishes "auction" and "customers" markets. The latter markets are characterized by price stickiness attributable to Alchian-like considerations of intertemporal comparison shopping.

A recent paper[41] by Alan Blinder (1982) also discusses the phenomenon of "sticky prices." He analyzes a micromodel where the firm sells a storable good under monopolistic market conditions, and shows the conditions under which demand fluctuations will cause small output and large price responses rather than the converse.

For an excellent survey of output fluctuations and gradual price adjustment, the reader is referred to Gordon (1981).

3.2 Non-Walrasian Long-run Equilibria: Conjectural Equilibria

The fix-price equilibrium discussed in section 2 above was regarded as a short-run equilibrium. The long-run equilibrium is typically defined, at least implicitly, as a short-run equilibrium where there is no tendency for either prices or quantities to change. If price movements are governed by effective excess demand and the economy is competitive (i.e., both households and firms are price takers, and perceive that they can trade any amount they desire at the ruling prices), then the Walrasian equilibrium is a long-run equilibrium. As shown in two papers by Varian (1975, 1977), there may under certain conditions exist long-run equilibria that are non-Walrasian, but the assumptions necessary to create this possibility have no ready economic interpretation.

If the assumption of *competitive conjectures* with respect to prices (i.e., agents who believe that their actions have no effect on market prices and that they can achieve their desired transactions at those prices) is abandoned, however, then the set of long-run equilibria may include, but need not coincide with, the set of Walrasian equilibria. Consider a situation where certain agents change the prices at

---

[41] His paper is closely related to some unpublished works by Patricia Reagan and a paper by Edward Zabel (1972).

which they are willing to transact whenever they consider this to be in their interest. The stationary point or equilibrium will have to be a set of signals such that agents see no further opportunities for "profit" by changing prices and/or trades. Hence, it is apparent that the set of stationary points cannot be independent of how prices and quantity signals are formed.

That such equilibria may exist is easy to establish. The Walrasian equilibrium is a "conjectural equilibrium" – to use the terminology introduced by Frank Hahn[42] – provided that the agents have *competitive* conjectures about their trading possibilities. The fix-price equilibria considered in section 2 are "conjectural" *long-run* equilibria only under a (probably very uninteresting) set of conjectures, which specifies that all agents perceive it to be unprofitable to change the ruling prices.[43]

The point to be made in the present context by a theory of conjectural equilibria is that in some sense "rational"[44] and/or "reasonable" conjectures could generate equilibria that are non-Walrasian and are characterized by involuntary unemployment. The degree of rationality of conjectures turns out to be crucial for the existence of a non-Walrasian equilibrium. What Hahn has proved is loosely speaking the following: there exist *non-Walrasian conjectural equilibria* where the market signals are such that each agent, given his conjectures, is in equilibrium and where, for each agent, price behavior actually does lead to a *local profit maximum*.[45]

To give the reader an idea of how conjectural equilibria can be modeled more explicitly, we end this chapter by briefly sketching Negishi's (1979) derivation of a *Keynesian long-run conjectural equilibrium* involving unemployment.

The economy is assumed to be competitive in the sense that there are many agents, but the agents have noncompetitive conjectures. Prices and wages are perfectly flexible. In a Walrasian economy with perfect information such assumptions imply that no exchanges take place until general equilibrium is established. At that point, prices

---

[42] See Hahn (1977a, 1977b, 1978).

[43] A more advanced form of fix-price equilibria with price-setting behavior is discussed by Benassy (1976b). Equilibrium is here reached by a two-time system of fast quantity adjustment and price adjustment that begins only once the quantity adjustments have reached a fix-price equilibrium.

[44] Loosely defined, agents do the right thing for the right reason.

[45] For a more thorough discussion the reader is referred to Hahn (1977a, 1977b, 1978) and Drazen (1980). The latter paper, by the way, provides an excellent review of disequilibrium macrotheory.

are no longer changed and all agents behave as if "unlimited" quantities can be bought and sold at ruling prices. Even in a non-Walrasian economy, where information is imperfect, a firm (or a household) may perceive an infinitely elastic demand curve if it can sell all it wishes at the ruling price, i.e., if the firm's conjecture is not falsified by its actual trade. If demand falls short of supply, however, the firm cannot perceive the demand curve to be infinitely elastic. Negishi argues that the perceived, imperfectly elastic demand curve has a kink at the currently realized point (the only point where it coincides with the actual demand curve). According to Negishi, the kinked demand curve is due to asymmetric behavior of customers in a world of imperfect information rather than to asymmetric reactions of rivals. Competitive firms cannot, he argues, exceed the current price ruling in the market since a higher price would induce customers to search for lower-price suppliers. A lower-price, on the other hand, may not be fully advertised to customers who are currently buying from firms that are not lowering their prices.

Thus, the representative firm perceives a demand function:

$$p_i = p_i(y_i, \bar{p}_i, \bar{y}_i), \qquad (2.34)$$

where $\bar{y}_i$ is the current sales of the firm and the current market price $\bar{p}_i$ equals:

$$\bar{p}_i = p_i(\bar{y}_i, \bar{p}_i, \bar{y}_i),$$

with

$$p_i = \bar{p}_i \qquad \text{for } y_i \leqslant \bar{y}_i,$$

$$\left(\frac{\partial p_i}{\partial y_i}\right) < 0 \qquad \text{for } y_i > \bar{y}_i.$$

Given the wage, w, the production function, $F_i(L_i)$, and the perceived demand function (2.34), the firm calculates the p_i and y_i which are expected to maximize profit. Generally, however, this combination of price and sales cannot be realized in the market. Subjective estimation of the perceived demand function and profit maximization is repeated until the maximization conditions, $p_i \geqslant w/F_i'(L_i)$ and $p_i + p_i'F_i(L_i) \leqslant w/F_i'(L_i)$, are satisfied at the "starting point," i.e., the kink of the final perceived demand function. When these conditions are satisfied (i.e., when $P = MR \geqslant MC$ for a decrease in production, and $MR \leqslant MC$ for an increase in production), the firm is in a conjectural equilibrium in the Hahn (1977a) sense that its short-term expectations are realized. Figure 2.6 shows the conjectural equilibrium of the firm.

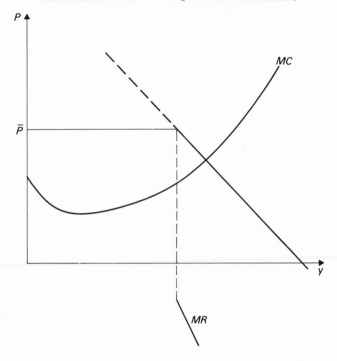

FIGURE 2.6   The conjectural equilibrium of the firm

If effective demand changes, variations in the level of sales can be completely absorbed by changes in output if the maximization conditions are satisfied in the inequality form. In other words, the market is in Walrasian excess supply: firms would want to supply more at the ruling price if it were perceived possible. However, the firms will not perceive any incentive to make changes, unless effective demand changes are large enough to make the maximization conditions hold with strict equality.

In the presence of unemployment, households face a similar decision problem. They realize that an increase in employment from the current level is impossible unless the wage is lowered. However, if a worker lowers his wage offer, so will other workers, so that the probability of obtaining a job will not rise to unity. On the other hand, if a worker increases his "reservation wage," other workers will not follow suit and the individual's probability of employment will be zero. Thus, the perceived "demand curve" for labor is assumed to be infinitely elastic with respect to the left of this point. Given this perception, maximization of a simple indirect utility function:

$$\underset{\theta}{\text{Max}} \; U = \theta U \left(\frac{w}{p}\right) + (1-\theta) \, \bar{U},$$

subject to:

$$\frac{w}{p} = g \left(\theta, \frac{\bar{w}}{\bar{p}}, \bar{\theta}\right),$$

where $\bar{U}$ represents the utility of being unemployed, and θ is the probability of being employed, in a sense "locks in" the household. It does not perceive any incentive to increase its wage bid and is also reluctant to accept a wage below the prevailing level, even though it realizes that a wage cut would increase the probability of employment. Once again, a Keynesian equilibrium results since workers are willing to supply more labor at the ruling wage than is demanded at this real wage rate.

Negishi formally proves that a Keynesian equilibrium exists and that the real wage rate might be lower at such an equilibrium than at the full-employment equilibrium. Furthermore, it is shown that a new Keynesian equilibrium can be established following changes in effective demand without changing prices and wages. Hence, although prices and wages are assumed to be flexible, they will in fact remain constant as the economy moves between Keynesian equilibria. Given the conjectures, price-setting agents do not perceive any incentive to change prices.

3.3 To Sum Up

Sections 3.1 and 3.2 above discuss different reasons for imperfect price flexibility. The "Leijonhufvud–Alchian" view is that prices adjust slowly, much slower than quantities, but they adjust as long as markets are not cleared in the Walrasian sense. The contract theoretic explanation of price rigidities is longer run in character. Unfortunately, to generate a contact involving rigid prices over the business cycle, one has to introduce some quite strong assumptions. Furthermore, in its present form the theory cannot properly explain *involuntary* unemployment. The theory of conjectural equilibria, on the other hand, can generate non-Walrasian long-run equilibria. Here, the issue is whether the conjectures used are in some sense rational or at least reasonable.[46]

In the open-economy models introduced in the following chapters we *assume* imperfect price flexibility without introducing any explicit explanation of why prices should remain fixed in the equilibrium states generated by our models. Therefore, we prefer to regard these equilibrium states as short-run equilibria in the sense of Leijonhufvud.[47] Although the theoretical research justifying long-run equilibria involving unemployment is still in a state of flux, there are numerous, more or less institutionally determined, reasons for a short-run price rigidities.

[46] For a formal definition of what could be meant by rational and reasonable conjectures, see Hahn (1977a). Loosely speaking, a reasonable conjecture is a conjecture where an agent may be right in his belief that he cannot locally improve his utility (profit) for the "wrong" reason. If he is right for the "right" reason, his conjecture is called rational.

[47] Appendix B discusses long-run price behavior to some extent, but the text focuses almost exclusively on short-run considerations. See, however, the brief discussion of the *international adjustment process* in chapter 3.

3

Disequilibrium Analysis in Open Economies: A One-sector Framework

1 Introduction

Chapter 2 surveyed the extensive literature on closed-economy macromodels with quantity rationing. Much of this literature assumes a single production sector. The present chapter lays the groundwork for the two-sector open-economy models used in the rest of the book by considering a single-sector model of the open economy. Using this framework, a number of key aspects of fix-price models can be discussed. Furthermore, the uninitiated reader should find the model more easily digestible than the two-sector models to follow. Several simple policy analyses will be used to illustrate the usefulness of even the simple one-sector model.

The model is similar to that in Dixit (1978) but emphasizes the intertemporal aspects of the household's choice problem, as Muellbauer and Portes (1978) did in the closed-economy context. It is the intertemporal view of the household's decision problem that we want to emphasize here as providing the underlying justification for the analysis in the remainder of the text. Hence it is elaborated upon in section 5 below by turning to an explicit two-period setup. In so doing, we hope to convince the reader that a utility function containing only current consumption, labor supply, and end-of-first-period wealth (or money balances if money is the only asset) can be used if interpreted appropriately. Doing so has the advantage of enabling us to make use of most previous works on fix-price trade models which, although they use such a utility function, are uniformly sketchy regarding intertemporal considerations.

2 The Dixit Model

The simplest open-economy, temporary-equilibrium model with quantity rationing is that of Dixit (1978). In his setup, there is a single good which the "small country" under consideration can buy or sell without limit at the fixed foreign-currency price p^*. Given a fixed exchange rate e and assuming the law of one price holds, the domestic-currency price is also fixed: $p = ep^*$. The good is assumed to be perishable (implying no inventory holding) and there is no capital investment.

It is important to determine *why* prices are fixed before presuming that the fix-price framework *with quantity rationing* is appropriate. By the "small country" assumption we mean that the foreign net supply curve is perfectly elastic at price p^*. Hence quantity rationing never occurs in the goods market even though it is in some sense a "fix-price" market from the small country's point of view. This specification of the goods market serves to make the one-sector open-economy model described in Dixit considerably simpler than its closed-economy counterparts. In particular, Keynesian unemployment – caused by a deficiency of demand for domestic output – can never arise.

In addition to the goods market, Dixit's model contains a labor market and a money market. Only in the former is rationing a possibility. The central bank buys or sells domestic money so as to continually equate money supply and money demand at the official or target exchange rate (without exchange controls or other quantitative restrictions). Money is the only private store of wealth; the private sector of the domestic economy holds no foreign money balances.

Within this environment firms maximize profits given the fixed wage w and the price of the tradeable good, which equals the exchange rate e after normalizing so that $p^* = 1$. The first-order conditions for profit maximization give rise to the usual *unconstrained* or *notional* labor demand function:

$$L = L(w, e), \qquad \frac{\partial L}{\partial w} < 0, \qquad \frac{\partial L}{\partial e} > 0. \tag{3.1}$$

Inserting (3.1) into the production function, where labor is the sole variable factor, yields notional output supply:

$$Y = Y(w, e), \qquad \frac{\partial Y}{\partial w} < 0, \qquad \frac{\partial Y}{\partial e} > 0. \tag{3.2}$$

If labor supply L^s falls short of the firms' demand for labor at (w, e), however, firms will face a quantity constraint $\bar{L} = L^s < L^d(w, e)$ on the labor market. Output then falls short of the profit-maximizing level. The firm's *effective* output supply $\hat{Y}$, which recognizes the constraint on labor availability, equals:

$$\hat{Y} = \hat{Y}(\bar{L}) < Y(w, e), \qquad \frac{\partial \hat{Y}}{\partial \bar{L}} > 0, \tag{3.3}$$

This is found by inverting the production function. Throughout the book, bars over variables indicate quantity constraints. A hat ($\hat{}$) over a variable indicates a *constrained* or *effective* supply/demand in the goods market given the constraint the agent faces on the labor market.

Households are assumed to maximize utility:

$$U(D, L^s, M') \qquad \text{s.t.} \quad eD + M' = wL^s + \pi_0 + M - T, \tag{3.4}$$

where D, L^s, and M' are consumption of goods, labor supply ($\partial U / \partial L^s < 0$), and desired money holdings. M is initial money balances; π_0 is distribution of last-period profits and hence is predetermined in the current decision period. T equals the lump-sum tax levied on households.

Several aspects of Dixit's specification are worth pointing out because they are typical in the literature. First, there is the (admittedly rather arbitrary) assumption that all labor income is received by households in the current period but profit income is not distributed until the beginning of the subsequent period.[1] This, of course, implies that the marginal propensity to save out of current-period profits is unity. Consequently any policy change that affects income distribution alters national saving. In the open-economy context this assumption may have (unintended) implications for the current account of the balance of payments, which according to the well-known accounting identity is just equal to the difference between national saving and domestic investment. As we shall emphasize below, explicit treatment of the intertemporal nature of household's saving-consumption decision is important for a clear understanding of the current account.

---

[1] Below, we consider the alternative assumption that current-period profits are distributed in the current period rather than in the subsequent period. The careful reader will notice that it is not the point in time when profits are distributed that is important. Rather the issue is whether *expected* profit income has any effect on current expenditure decisions, even though the income may be received at the beginning or the end of the period. See also section 6 of chapter 8 for some further consequences of the profit distribution assumption.

Second, money is the only asset in virtually all fix-price quantity rationing models. There are two possible justifications for including money balances in the utility function. The first is that money yields utility directly by providing some monetary services that eliminate the inefficiencies of barter. Presumably it is *real* money balances that are important here, where "real" is defined in terms of *current* prices of consumption goods. The utility function need involve no intertemporal considerations.

A preferable interpretation for our purposes is that the utility function including money balances is a mixed direct–indirect utility function. Underlying it is a multiperiod optimization problem, but future consumption and leisure choice variables have been eliminated by the recursive substitution technique familiar from dynamic programming. In this case money balances are a store of wealth that reflects a desire for *future* consumption. Whether the store of wealth is "money" or some nonmonetary asset is immaterial.

Future consumption, of course, depends on future prices, which are buried in the dynamic programming procedure. To emphasize the dependence of utility on expectations about future prices (as well as future quantity constraints) Muellbauer and Portes (1978) include the parameter θ in the utility function. Other authors deflate money balances by the current price of goods in the utility function, as was done in chapter 2. This amounts to implicitly assuming that future prices are always equal to current prices. All price changes would then have to be interpreted as permanent rather than temporary changes. The intertemporal framework will be explored more systematically in sections 5 and 6 below.

The usual first-order conditions for the utility maximization problem in (3.4) – where there are no quantity constraints – yield the *notional* commodity demand, labor supply, and "money" demand functions:

$$D = D(\bar{e}, \overset{+}{w}, \overset{+}{M} + \pi_0 - T), \tag{3.5}$$

$$L^s = L^s(\bar{e}, \overset{+}{w}, \bar{M} + \pi_0 - T), \tag{3.6}$$

$$M = M(e, w, M + \pi_0 - T). \tag{3.7}$$

The standard assumptions regarding the partial derivatives in (3.5) and (3.6) have been noted. The signs of the partials in the end-of-period money demand function are often left unspecified, and with good reason. From the budget constraint, we see that nominal money demand must equal:

$$M'(e, w, M + \pi_0 - T) = wL^s(e, w, M + \pi_0 - T) + M + \pi_0$$
$$- T - eD(e, w, M + \pi_0 - T). \tag{3.8}$$

Given the assumed signs of the partial derivatives in (3.5) and (3.6), it can be seen from (3.8) that the partials in (3.7) are uncertain *a priori*.

It should be emphasized that the commodity demand and labor supply functions (3.5) and (3.6) need not be homogeneous of degree zero in the nominal variables. This depends on the interpretation of money in the utility function. If the utility function contains real money balances in terms of current output and if current and future prices are always equal, then (3.5) and (3.6) are indeed homogeneous of degree zero and can be written:

$$D = D\left(\frac{w}{e}, \frac{M + \pi_0 - T}{e}\right), \tag{3.9}$$

$$L^s = L^s\left(\frac{w}{e}, \frac{M + \pi_0 - T}{e}\right). \tag{3.10}$$

Comparing (3.6) and (3.10) it is clear that the negative real wage effect of a change in the price of goods on labor supply must overpower the positive effect of the fall in real balances in order to be compatible with the gross substitution assumption that $\partial L^s/\partial e < 0$ in (3.6).

If the utility function is parameterized, at least implicitly, on unchanged *future* prices, however, the behavioural functions in (3.5) and (3.6) are homogeneous of degree zero in $(e, w, M + \pi_0)$ *and* future prices. In this case the specification in (3.9) and (3.10) is potentially misleading because it ignores the relative price of future consumption in terms of current consumption.

By writing the behavioral functions in extensive form as in (3.5)–(3.7) we leave open either of the above interpretations about price and wage changes. In the absence of an explicit intertemporal framework, it is often unclear whether existing fix-price analyses have in mind permanent or temporary effects in their comparative static exercises. We return to this problem in section 6 below after laying out a two-period consumer choice framework in section 5.

When there is unemployment so that households face a quantity constraint on the labor market, they maximize utility in (3.4) subject to the budget constraint plus the employment constraint: $\bar{L} \geq L^s$. The resulting *effective* demands for goods and money take the form:

$$\hat{D} = \hat{D}(\bar{e}, \overset{+}{w}, \overset{+}{M} + \pi_0 - T, \overset{+}{\bar{L}}), \tag{3.11}$$

$$\hat{M}' = \hat{M}'(e, w, M + \pi_0 - T, \bar{L}). \tag{3.12}$$

The sign of the partial derivative $\partial \hat{D}/\partial \bar{L}$ depends on two factors. The first is the positive income effect of the rise in employment (at the prevailing wage). The second factor depends on the complementarity or substitutability between labor/leisure and consumption. If leisure and consumption are substitutes, for example, an increase in the employment constraint $\bar{L}$, which reduces leisure, raises the utility of goods. This shifts the demand for goods upward at prevailing prices and wages. Hence both influences contribute to $\partial \hat{D}/\partial \bar{L}$ being positive when leisure and consumption are substitutes. In the event that they are complements, the sign of $\partial \hat{D}/\partial \bar{L}$ would be ambiguous. However, it is generally assumed in the literature that $\partial \hat{D}/\partial \bar{L}$ is positive, implying that the income effect must dominate in the complements case.[2]

The partial derivatives of the effective money demand function in (3.12), like those for the notional demand function in (3.7), are uncertain *a priori*.

3 Short-run Fix-price Equilibria

A small open economy by definition faces a perfectly elastic world demand for its output and neither domestic firms nor households face rationing in the goods market. Short-run wage rigidity can nevertheless lead to labor market disequilibrium. Two disequilibrium regimes are possible: classical unemployment and repressed inflation.

Classical unemployment
In the first disequilibrium regime, the wage rate is sticky at a level which, given the fixed exchange rate and the level of the domestic money supply, results in an excess supply of labor:

$$\bar{L} = L^{\mathrm{d}}(w, e) < L^{\mathrm{s}}(e, w, M + \pi_0 - T). \tag{3.13}$$

This situation, in which households face an employment constraint $\bar{L}$, is known as *classical unemployment*. It is caused by excessive real wages rather than the deficiency of aggregate demand for output that characterizes *Keynesian unemployment*. Of course, the latter type of unemployment cannot arise in the Dixit model due to its "small open-economy" assumption.

Given labor demand in (3.13), national output is given by (3.2). Domestic demand for goods, of course, is affected by the presence of

---

[2] The effects of quantity constraints on consumer and firm behavior are discussed in detail in appendix A.

unemployment. Households' consumption demand, given their labor market constraint $\bar{L}$, is the *effective* demand shown in (3.11).

The difference between domestic output and domestic demand (by both the private and public sectors) is the country's (real) balance of trade:

$$BT = Y(w,e) - \hat{D}(e,w,M+\pi_0-T,\bar{L}) - G, \qquad (3.14)$$

where $\bar{L}$ is defined by (3.13) and G is government expenditure on current output.

Repressed inflation

The second disequilibrium regime that can arise in the simple Dixit model is similar to Malinvaud's *repressed inflation* case. There is an excess demand for labor, as the real wage is fixed below the Walrasian equilibrium level. Firms, therefore, face a constraint $\bar{L}$ on their labor demand:

$$\bar{L} = L^s(e,w,M+\pi_0-T) < L^d(e,w). \qquad (3.15)$$

Unlike Malinvaud's closed-economy version, where there is also excess demand for goods, the goods market clears in the small open-economy context. It might, therefore, be more accurate to call this case *repressed wage inflation*, but we retain Malinvaud's label to emphasize the similarity of policy analyses in the closed- and open-economy versions of the repressed inflation regime.

Given the employment level in (3.15), national output equals the labor-supply-constrained level in (3.3). Household demand for goods equals the *notional* demand in (3.5), because they are unconstrained in the labor market. Consequently, the balance of trade equals:

$$BT = \hat{Y}(\bar{L}) - D(e,w,M+\pi_0-T) - G, \qquad (3.16)$$

where $\bar{L}$ is defined by (3.15).

3.1   Aggregate Demand Management in Small Open Economies

It should be clear with a little reflection that "expansionary" government spending financed by money creation has no stimulative short-run effect on the level of employment or output in the present small open-economy context. When world demand for domestic output is perfectly elastic at the prevailing world price, domestic output is determined by the short-run level of employment rather than by the level of aggregate demand. Employment, in turn, depends on the prevailing level of wages relative to world prices and also, in the repressed inflation case, on the level of money balances and taxes through their effect on labor *supply*. Policies aimed at affecting domestic output, therefore, must focus on the domestic labor market.

Classical unemployment

In the classical unemployment case, the level of employment (3.13) is determined by the profit-maximizing decisions of firms. Hence employment can only be increased by policies that, one way or another, reduce the real product wage. Reducing wages or raising the domestic-currency price of output (by devaluing the domestic currency, for example) are two possible methods. These policies are considered in the following section. Other "supply-side" policies designed to shift the short-run production function through increased capital investment or technological innovation might also be effective in combating classical unemployment in the intermediate, if not the short, run.

Repressed inflation

Under repressed inflation, employment (3.15) is limited by labor *supply* rather than demand. Changes in income taxation might be designed to increase labor supply, thereby increasing national output. Again the efficacy of these policies depends on their labor market or "supply-side" effects, not on their aggregate demand management aspects.

The foregoing discussion brings out an important point. In small open economies, policymakers should not underestimate the potential of supply-side policies aimed directly at increasing employment as an alternative to textbook prescriptions, which focus on monetary and fiscal policies designed to stimulate aggregate demand.[3] As we will see in chapter 4, the latter policies do become more potent in open economies with significant sheltered or nontraded goods sectors.[4] But in that context, the policies' sectoral resource allocation effects must also be taken into consideration. We defer further discussion of aggregate demand management policies until the tradeables–nontradeables model is introduced in chapter 4.

---

[3] Casual empiricism suggests that policymakers in the small open economies of Western Europe are not unaware of the efficacy of the types of employment policies alluded to here.
[4] Similar conclusions are also obtained in the exportables–importables model in chapter 6 where there is a less than perfectly elastic export demand curve.

3.2   *Wage Policy*

In situations of labor market disequilibrium due to wage stickiness, it is sometimes possible to institute policies (e.g., employment taxes or subsidies on firms or households' labor income, depending on the disequilibrium regime) that can alter wages – particularly in an upward direction – more quickly than they would adjust without policy inducement. Analyzing the effect of policy-induced wage increases on domestic output and employment is straightforward using the analytical framework developed above. In the presence of classical unemployment (CU), wage increases reduce firms' profit-maximizing level of output, thereby worsening unemployment. Under repressed inflation (RI), in contrast, allowing wages to rise will increase labor supply (given our gross substitutability assumption). This reduces the labor shortage being experienced by producers thereby leading to an *increase* in domestic output. Thus it is critical for policymakers to know the state of the labor market if wage policy is to have the desired effects on output and employment.

The differing output effects of wage increases in the CU and RI cases suggest that trade balance effects may also depend critically on the type of disequilibrium being experienced in the labor market. Under classical unemployment, the trade balance effect of a wage increase is found by differentiating (3.14):

$$\frac{\mathrm{d}BT}{\mathrm{d}w} = \frac{\partial Y}{\partial w} - \frac{\partial \hat{D}}{\partial w} - \frac{\partial \hat{D}}{\partial \bar{L}} \frac{\mathrm{d}\bar{L}}{\mathrm{d}w} \gtrless 0, \qquad (3.17)$$

$$\quad\;\;(-)\quad\;(+)\quad\;(+)\;(-)$$

where $\mathrm{d}\bar{L}/\mathrm{d}w < 0$ from (3.13). The wage increase reduces output and has several effects on consumption demand. The first effect of the wage increase is to cause households to substitute away from leisure toward consumption. This, of course, is not possible if households' demand for less leisure (implying greater labor supply) cannot be effected. Consequently, $\partial \hat{D}/\partial w$ in (3.17) involves no substitution component, only a positive income effect, in the case where households are rationed in the labor market. The second effect of a wage increase on consumption demand is the labor income effect due to the increased severity of labor market rationing on households as employment falls, reflecting an upward movement along the firm's labor demand curve. Whether total labor income rises or falls, therefore, depends on the wage elasticity of producers' labor demand. The net effect of an increase in w on consumption demand, therefore, depends on whether total labor income goes up or down.

Hence the short-run effect on the trade balance is indeterminate under classical unemployment.[5]

Under repressed inflation, the trade balance effect of a rise in domestic wages is found using (3.16):

$$\frac{\mathrm{d}BT}{\mathrm{d}w} = \underset{(+)}{\frac{\partial \hat{Y}}{\partial \bar{L}}} \underset{(+)}{\frac{\mathrm{d}\bar{L}}{\mathrm{d}w}} - \underset{(+)}{\frac{\partial D}{\partial w}} \gtrless 0, \tag{3.18}$$

where $\partial \bar{L}/\partial w > 0$ from (3.15). Again the trade balance effect is indeterminate. Although domestic *demand* unambiguously rises in this case (in contrast to classical unemployment), output also rises as the labor shortage facing firms is reduced. Whether the supply or demand change dominates is unclear *a priori*.

3.3   Exchange Rate Policy

Countries often elect to devalue their currencies in order to alter domestic employment or the balance of trade. Unfortunately, the payments equilibrium (or "external balance") is not always simultaneously attainable using exchange rate policy alone. Furthermore, the policy's effects depend on the initial state of the economy.

Classical unemployment

If the economy is suffering from classical unemployment, exchange rate depreciation reduces the real wage (assuming no change or at least a less-than-proportional change in nominal wages due to indexation, say). Hence total employment and national output rise (see (3.1) and (3.2)). Domestic demand for output, on the other hand, may rise or fall with the rise in e due to the opposing influences of the negative substitution effect and the positive employment effect. Therefore the real trade balance may improve or deteriorate following a devaluation:

$$\frac{\mathrm{d}BT}{\mathrm{d}e} = \underset{(+)}{\frac{\partial Y}{\partial e}} - \underset{(-)}{\frac{\partial \hat{D}}{\partial e}} - \underset{(+)}{\frac{\partial \hat{D}}{\partial \bar{L}}} \underset{(+)}{\frac{\mathrm{d}\bar{L}}{\mathrm{d}e}} \gtrless 0. \tag{3.19}$$

[5] This result depends critically on the usual assumption in the literature that profit income is not distributed to households in the current period. If both wage and profit income were distributed to households in the current period, the wage increase would cause domestic demand to fall, but by a smaller proportion than the reduction in national income. Hence the trade balance would unambiguously deteriorate.

Repressed inflation

Under repressed inflation, devaluation reduces employment in (3.15). Consequently, domestic output *falls*, in contrast to the classical unemployment case:

$$\frac{d\hat{Y}}{de} = \frac{d\hat{Y}}{d\bar{L}} \frac{d\bar{L}}{de} < 0. \tag{3.20}$$

$$\quad\;\; (+)\;\; (-)$$

This fall in output and the negative effect of the devaluation on demand work in opposite directions. Therefore, the effect of devaluation under repressed inflation is uncertain, although not because of an uncertain effect on domestic demand (as was the case under classical unemployment):

$$\frac{dBT}{de} = \frac{d\hat{Y}}{de} - \frac{\partial D}{\partial e} \gtrless 0. \tag{3.21}$$

$$\quad\;\; (-)\quad\; (-)$$

It is clear from the foregoing analysis that policymakers must determine the nature of labor market disequilibrium (i.e., classical unemployment or repressed wage inflation) before the direction of output changes following devaluation can be predicted. Under either disequilibrium regime, the balance-of-trade effect is uncertain. Hence policymakers require detailed estimates of various supply and demand elasticities before the impact of devaluation on the trade balance can be ascertained.

This completes our policy analysis based on the single-sector disequilibrium model described up to this point. Although the model has limitations (e.g., it precludes the possibility of Keynesian unemployment), it nevertheless provides some useful insights about the efficacy of fiscal, wage, and exchange rate policies in open economies. These insights carry over to the more complex, two-sector disequilibrium analysis in part II of this book. The present model, however, has the advantage of being more manageable while bringing out important analytical issues in open-economy disequilibrium theory. The remainder of this chapter is devoted to some of these issues, most notably the fundamentally intertemporal nature of household behavior and current account imbalances. First, however, the international adjustment process is briefly discussed.

4   Short-run Walrasian Equilibrium and the International Adjustment Process

Short-run Walrasian equilibrium in the open economy occurs when the nominal wage rate w is allowed to adjust (relative to the fixed domestic-currency price of output e and predetermined $M + \pi_0 - T$) so as to achieve full employment. That is, w must equate notional labor demand in (3.1) to notional labor supply (3.6):

$$L(\bar{w}, \overset{+}{e}) = L^s(\bar{e}, \overset{+}{w}, \bar{M} + \pi_0 - T). \tag{3.22}$$

The locus of wage rate–money supply combinations consistent with full employment at the fixed exchange rate is shown as the FE locus in figure 3.1. Full-employment output then follows immediately from (3.22) by plugging equilibrium labor demand into the production function in (3.2).

The balance of trade is determined by taking the difference between domestic output and total domestic demand for goods at the equilibrium wage (determined by (3.22)):

$$BT = Y(\bar{w}, \overset{+}{e}) - D(\bar{e}, \overset{+}{w}, \overset{+}{M} + \pi_0 - T) - G, \tag{3.23}$$

where G equals government demand for goods.[6] Here BT has been defined in units of real output or, what amounts to the same thing as long as the foreign-currency price p^* and the exchange rate e are fixed, units of foreign exchange.

Equation (3.23) shows that the excess domestic supply of output, which can be sold at the prevailing world price (given the small country assumption), is mirrored in the trade balance.

In the short run, nothing insures that the trade balance is zero even if the wage adjusts immediately to the Walrasian equilibrium level. In other words, while wage flexibility achieves "internal balance," to use James Meade's terminology, "external balance" need not be attained in the short run.

Over time, however, external balance is ultimately restored. Trade surpluses imply an inflow of foreign exchange over time, which the private sector converts into domestic money at the fixed exchange rate offered by the central bank. (Conversely, trade deficits imply foreign reserve outflows and concomitant contractions in the domestic money supply.) Thus a gradual adjustment of the domestic

---

[6] This government expenditure can be assumed to be tax-financed, in which case $eG = T$. Money finance would, of course, affect the adjustment path of the economy over time.

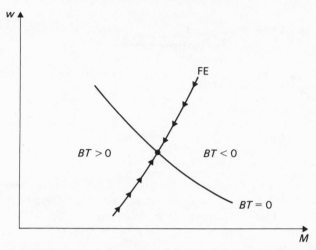

FIGURE 3.1 The international adjustment process

money supply occurs whenever there is a trade imbalance. As the money supply expands (contracts), domestic expenditure rises (falls) until it eventually equals domestic income so that external balance is achieved. The decrease in the labor supply (as M rises) reduces output, which also contributes to the adjustment. This *international adjustment process* whereby a steady state with external equilibrium is ultimately attained is well known from Hume's discussions of the so-called *price-specie-flow mechanism*. More recently the international adjustment process has been emphasized in writings on the *monetary approach to the balance of payments*.

In order to properly describe adjustment toward the steady state, it is necessary to recognize that, although profits (or expected profits) might be considered predetermined at a given moment in time, they adjust endogenously over time.[7] Current-period profits equal:

$$\pi(\bar{w}, \overset{+}{e}) = eY(w, e) - wL(w, e). \tag{3.24}$$

For the study of adjustment dynamics it simplifies matters somewhat to assume that profits are distributed to households in the current

[7] As mentioned above, in subsequent chapters we adopt the specification that current-period profits are distributed immediately, not next period. Of course this distinction disappears if the dynamic analysis is conducted in continuous rather than discrete time.

period. Thus the short-run labor market equilibrium in (3.22) should be reinterpreted with π endogenously determined via (3.24). Similarly the profit function is substituted into the expression for the trade balance in (3.23).

In the present model, the steady state achieved by endogenous adjustment in the domestic money supply M is defined by a trade balance equal to zero:

$$BT = Y(w, e) - D(e, w, M + \pi - T) - G = 0, \tag{3.25}$$

where profits are defined by (3.24). Equation (3.25) indicates the locus of (w, M) combinations consistent with long-run equilibrium in the economy. It is easy to see that wage increases must be accompanied by decreases in money holdings if the trade balance is to be kept in equilibrium. In other words the $BT = 0$ locus is downward sloping in figure 3.1. To confirm this, totally differentiate (3.25) to find the slope:

$$\frac{dw}{dM} = \frac{-\partial D}{\partial \pi} \left[\frac{\partial D}{\partial w} - \left(\frac{\partial Y}{\partial w} - \frac{\partial D}{\partial \pi} \frac{\partial \pi}{\partial w} \right) \right]^{-1} < 0, \tag{3.26}$$

and note that $\partial Y / \partial w$ is larger in absolute value than $\partial \pi / \partial w$ (from (3.24)).

Given an arbitrary initial money stock M, the economy's short-run equilibrium wage rate is determined from the full employment (FE) locus in figure 3.1. If this point (w, M) on the FE locus is to the left of the long-run equilibrium locus where $BT = 0$, the country has a trade surplus. Consequently its money supply will grow gradually as the international adjustment process moves the economy along the FE locus toward its steady state. Wages necessarily rise to maintain labor market equilibrium as the money supply increases due to the trade surplus. Similarly, if the short-run equilibrium involves a trade deficit, the economy is at a point on the FE locus to the right of $BT = 0$. Hence wages must fall over time, thereby improving international competitiveness, as the money supply gradually shrinks to bring about external balance.

Using the full-employment model just described, it would be possible to examine the effects of various government policies aimed at either raising the full-employment level of output or altering the speed with which external payments imbalances are eliminated. For the most part, however, real-world policy decisions must recognize the existence (or potential, at least) for short-run wage stickiness as in section 3 above, rather than assuming that wages adjust freely and continuously to clear the labor market. It would be desirable, therefore, to carry out an analysis of the international adjustment process in the presence of wage stickiness. Although there are a number of published papers on fix-price disequilibrium dynamics in the closed-economy context (see appendix B), the important task of extending this work to open economies has not yet (to our knowledge) been undertaken. Yet it is obviously important for a thorough understanding of the international adjustment process.

The existing closed-economy literature on adjustment dynamics in fix-price (dis)equilibrium models as well as the Walrasian model of the adjustment process in the present section are all based on an extremely *myopic* behavioral specification. It treats successive temporary equilibria as completely unrelated. In particular, the behavioral functions – (3.5) to (3.7) in the present model – depend only on *current* prices and wages even though these variables may be adjusting over time toward their steady-state levels as shown in figure 3.1. Even if agents lack perfect foresight, they presumably have some idea of the direction of change for wages (say, in the present context) or, more generally, wages and prices. The demand for goods as well as the supply of labor should depend not only on current wages and prices but also on their expected future values. It would seem most satisfactory to do this in an explicitly intertemporal framework that recognizes the interdependence between successive temporary equilibria and the importance of expectations generating processes. Although we do not attempt such a dynamic analysis here, the intertemporal model developed below should bring out the temporal interdependence that is inherent, although greatly underemphasized, in existing treatments of *macroeconomic* disequilibrium theory. Microeconomic discussions of disequilibrium theory, however, place greater emphasis on the sequential nature of temporary equilibria (see, e.g., Grandmont, 1977a).

5 An Intertemporal View of Household Behavior

It is becoming clear as a result of recent research in macroeconomics that much can be learned by explicitly formulating the intertemporal aspects of households' consumption decisions, as well as the capital investment decisions of firms. Such a framework is necessary for an understanding of the permanent income hypothesis and for the comparison of temporary as opposed to permanent economic shocks or policy changes, just to give two examples. Much of the recent microtheoretic work on the current account of the balance of payments is also exploiting the intertemporal decisions that underlie the current account (see, e.g., Svensson and Razin, 1983). Recall that, according to a well-known accounting identity, the current account just equals the difference between domestic saving and investment. Both saving and investment decisions are inherently intertemporal in nature.

A thorough understanding of open-economy models with quantity rationing and macroeconomic disequilibrium is greatly facilitated by an intertemporal interpretation of the household choice problem. Although we have not undertaken the ambitious task of using an explicit intertemporal framework throughout the book, much of it can be reinterpreted using such a framework. To help the reader to appreciate the usefulness of the intertemporal approach, we will briefly explore its implications for household decision making.

Consider a household that consumes a single good and supplies labor in each of two periods. It can save income earned in period 1 for future consumption by purchasing bonds that yield a market-determined interest rate r and have a single-period maturity date. We assume this asset provides no monetary services *per se* and hence does not enter the direct utility function. Hence it will not be referred to as "money," thereby avoiding the existing confusion between money and nonmonetary assets in the fix-price literature. In chapter 5, the analysis will be extended by forcing households to hold money for transactions purposes, while bonds continue to function as a store of value for future consumption. This enables previous work on macroeconomic quantity-rationing models to be extended to include the asset choice problem.[8]

In the absence of quantity constraints in the current period as well as expected constraints in the future,[9] households maximize the utility function:

$$U(D, L, D', L')\qquad(3.27)$$

subject to the intertemporal constraints:

$$eD + \left(\frac{e'}{1+r}\right)D' = wL + \pi + W - T + \frac{1}{1+r}(w'L' + \pi' - T'),$$

$$(3.28)$$

---

[8] Recent work by Persson (1982a, 1982b) pursues a similar approach.
[9] For an analysis of the effects of expected future constraints, see Muellbauer and Portes (1978), Neary and Stiglitz (1983), and Persson and Svensson (1983).

where primes ($'$) on variables indicate second-period values. Here π and π' are first- and second-period profits. W is beginning-of-first-period wealth. T and T' are lump-sum taxes. Both borrowing and lending are allowed at the prevailing interest rate r.

Once the possibility of borrowing or lending at the prevailing interest rate is introduced, the issue of whether profits are distributed in the period in which they are generated or in the subsequent period becomes less important. It only affects the prices that are appropriate in defining profits. In what follows it will be assumed that *all* current income (labor and profit) is distributed within the *current* period. This specification avoids the unintended income distribution effects alluded to in section 2 above.

Maximizing (3.27) subject to the intertemporal budget constraint (3.28) yields notional commodity demand and labor supply functions for the first period of the following form:

$$D = D\left(e, w, \frac{e'}{1+r}, \frac{w'}{1+r}, I\right), \tag{3.29}$$

$$L = L\left(e, w, \frac{e'}{1+r}, \frac{w'}{1+r}, I\right), \tag{3.30}$$

where I is the present value of nonlabor income less taxes, plus initial financial wealth. Equations (3.29) and (3.30) differ from those commonly used in the fix-price literature in that: (1) the intertemporal nature of the household choice problem is made explicit by including *future* prices (e', w') and the interest rate r in addition to current prices (e, w), and (2) the functions include the present value of current and future-period profit income in addition to initial financial asset holdings.[10]

The following assumptions are made regarding the partial derivatives of the notional commodity demand and labor supply functions in (3.29) and (3.30):

$$\frac{\partial D}{\partial e} < 0, \qquad \frac{\partial D}{\partial w} > 0, \qquad \frac{\partial D}{\partial e'} > 0, \qquad \frac{\partial D}{\partial w'} > 0, \qquad \frac{\partial D}{\partial I} > 0, \tag{3.31}$$

$$\frac{\partial L}{\partial e} < 0, \qquad \frac{\partial L}{\partial w} > 0, \qquad \frac{\partial L}{\partial e'} < 0, \qquad \frac{\partial L}{\partial w'} < 0, \qquad \frac{\partial L}{\partial I} < 0. \tag{3.32}$$

[10] Furthermore it should be noted that the behavioral relations in (3.29) and (3.30) *are* homogeneous of degree zero in prices and the initial level of nominal wealth. Recall our discussion regarding the (non)homogeneity of (3.5) and (3.6) above.

These assumptions are obtained by assuming that present and future consumption and leisure are all gross substitutes.[11]

Next consider the situation where the household faces a current-period employment constraint ($\bar{L} \geqslant L^s$) but expects to be unrationed in all subsequent periods. As the discussion in section 2 above would suggest, the *effective* commodity demand function takes the form:

$$\hat{D} = \hat{D}\left(\bar{e}, \overset{+}{w}, \frac{\overset{+\prime}{e}}{1+r}, \frac{\overset{+\prime}{w}}{1+r}, \overset{+}{I}, \overset{+}{\bar{L}}\right), \tag{3.33}$$

where $\partial\hat{D}/\partial\bar{L} > 0$. As in the unconstrained case, gross substitutability among current and future consumption and leisure is assumed in order to sign the other partial derivatives. All of them have the same sign as they did in the notional commodity demand function (3.29).

For completeness let us finally consider situations where the representative household is rationed on the goods market. Even though this situation never arises in the simple model employed in this chapter (because of the small-country assumption), it does arise in closed-economy models and multisector open-economy models.

If the household perceives a current-period quantity constraint $\bar{D}$ on its demand for current consumption, its labor supply and wealth accumulation decisions will certainly be affected. Maximizing (3.27) subject to (3.28) and the quantity constraint $D \leqslant \bar{D}$ yields the effective labor supply function:

$$\tilde{L} = \tilde{L}\left(\overset{+}{e}, \overset{+}{w}, \frac{e'}{1+r}, \frac{\overset{-}{w'}}{1+r}, \overset{-}{I}, \overset{+}{\bar{D}}\right), \tag{3.34}$$

where presumably $\partial\tilde{L}/\partial\bar{D} > 0$. That is, a reduction in the severity of rationing in the goods market should be expected to increase current-period labor supply. Note that the sign of $\partial\tilde{L}/\partial e$ is positive in this case: as long as the quantity constraint $\bar{D}$ is binding and leisure is a normal good, an increase in the price of goods induces an increase in labor supply to (at least partially) offset the increased expenditure on rationed goods. The effect of an increase in the nominal wage $\partial\tilde{L}/\partial w$ is still assumed to be positive, although it is (according to Le Chatelier's principle) presumably smaller in magnitude than it would be if consumers were unrationed in the goods market (in which case they could spend their additional labor income on increased current consumption).

---

[11] The *gross substitutability* assumption is widely employed in the literature. In some cases the weaker assumption of *net substitutes* has proved sufficient for obtaining definite results. See Johansson and Löfgren (1981).

6   Transitory versus Permanent Price and Wage Changes

Once the intertemporal aspects of the household's decision problem are made explicit, the question arises as to whether comparative static analyses in the existing literature are, in fact, examining *temporary* or *permanent* changes in prices, wages, and various policy control variables. In the case of temporary changes, prices revert to their initial level in the subsequent periods. With permanent changes, they remain at their new level. The demand and supply functions in the literature are typically specified as functions of current-period prices only; the role of future prices is not explicit. Yet for many policy-induced changes in wages or prices it might be presumed that the changes are permanent in the sense that current and future prices change by the same amount.

In any event, it seems necessary to consider what is expected to happen to future prices (e' or w') when current prices (e or w) change. It so happens that the assumption of gross substitutes among current and future consumption and leisure enables straightforward and useful results to be obtained. Rewriting (3.29) and (3.30) in elasticities form:

$$\dot{D} = \epsilon_1 \dot{e} + \epsilon_2 \dot{w} + \epsilon_3 \left(\frac{\dot{e}'}{1+r} \right) + \epsilon_4 \left(\frac{\dot{w}'}{1+r} \right) + \epsilon_5 \dot{I}, \qquad (3.35)$$

$$\dot{L} = \mu_1 \dot{e} + \mu_2 \dot{w} + \mu_3 \left(\frac{\dot{e}'}{1+r} \right) + \mu_4 \left(\frac{\dot{w}'}{1+r} \right) + \mu_5 \dot{I}, \qquad (3.36)$$

where ϵ_i and μ_i are notional commodity demand and labor supply elasticities respectively and dots over variables denote *percentage* changes, gross substitutability implies that the own-price elasticities (i.e., $\epsilon_1 < 0$ and $\mu_2 > 0$) are larger in absolute value than any of the cross-price elasticities.[12] Now consider a change in the current price of goods $\dot{e}$ which (potentially) causes a change in the household's point expectation regarding the future price denoted $\dot{e}'$. From (3.35) the change in goods demand equals:

$$\dot{D} = [\epsilon_1 + \epsilon_3 (\dot{e}'/\dot{e})]\dot{e}. \qquad (3.37)$$

Gross substitution implies $|\epsilon_1| > \epsilon_3$. Thus as long as households have regressive expectations so that $\dot{e}'/\dot{e} \leq 1$, current-period demand for goods will decline as e rises. More specifically, equation (3.37) is unambiguously negative for *either* temporary ($\dot{e}'/\dot{e} = 0$) or permanent

---

[12] The elasticities always satisfy the adding-up condition, i.e., they sum (over i) to zero.

($\dot{e}'/\dot{e} = 1$) price changes. The absolute value of the total derivative in (3.37) is, of course, smaller for permanent price changes than for temporary changes because there is no intertemporal substitution effect in the former.

Analogously, it follows from gross substitution and the assumption that the elasticity of future price expectations with respect to current prices does not exceed unity (i.e., regressive expectations) that:

$$\dot{L} = [\mu_2 + \mu_4(\dot{w}'/\dot{w})] \dot{w} > 0 \qquad (3.38)$$

from the notional labor supply function in (3.36).

Equations (3.35) and (3.36) and (3.37) and (3.38) pertain to the household's unconstrained or *notional* commodity demand and labor supply functions. In the case where the household faces a current-period constraint on the labor market ($\bar{L} \geqslant L^s$), the assumptions of gross substitutes and less-than-unity expectations of future prices with respect to current prices are again sufficient to insure that:

$$\dot{D} = [\epsilon_1 + \epsilon_3(\dot{e}'/\dot{e})] \dot{e} < 0, \qquad (3.39)$$

$$\dot{D} = [\epsilon_2 + \epsilon_4(\dot{w}'/\dot{w})] \dot{w} > 0. \qquad (3.40)$$

The hats ($\hat{}$) which should be included over both D and the elasticities have been omitted to avoid notational clutter, but these variables now pertain to the *effective* demand function (3.33).

Finally, in the case where the household is rationed in the goods market, the effective labor supply function (3.34) has total price and wage effects of the following form:

$$\dot{L} = [\mu_1 + \mu_3(\dot{e}'/\dot{e})] \dot{e} \gtrless 0, \qquad (3.41)$$

$$\dot{L} = [\mu_2 + \mu_4(\dot{w}'/\dot{w})] \dot{w} > 0. \qquad (3.42)$$

Again hats ($\hat{}$) on L and the elasticities have been omitted for notational simplicity, but we are referring to (3.34) not (3.30). Gross substitution implies that $\mu_2 > |\mu_4|$ so that (3.42) is unambiguously positive. The sign of (3.41), however, is indeterminate due to uncertainty about the sign and magnitude of μ_3 in situations where the household is rationed on the goods market in the current period.

6.1 An Important Observation

The observations in (3.37)–(3.42) are important. They suggest that the comparative static effects of changes in e and w derived in the fix-price literature – and those derived in the remainder of this book –

can often be interpreted as either temporary changes or permanent changes. As long as *we assume gross substitutability and regressive expectations*, many qualitative results will remain valid.[13] This is true provided we rule out switching between different non-market-clearing regimes as expectations adjust, just as we typically assume that policy changes are small enough that they do not move the economy from one disequilibrium regime to another.

It should be emphasized, however, that the foregoing discussion concerns only price changes and ignores any general equilibrium dependence that they have on current or future profits (incorporated in I). This is consistent with much of the existing fix-price literature that considers profits to be predetermined and hence exogenous, although it differs from recent work on intertemporal models which typically assumes current-period distribution of profits and, in effect, perfect foresight regarding future profit income (see, e.g., Neary and Stiglitz, 1983; Persson, 1982a, 1982b; Persson and Svensson, 1983; Svensson and Razin, 1983). In that context permanent and temporary price changes have effects of different magnitudes on the present value of household income and hence commodity demands and labor supply in the current period. This may cause the current account effects of various policies to differ.

The intertemporal models of open economics are of very recent vintage (as the references in the above paragraph attest) and are likely to play an important role in future research. At this point, however, the literature is insufficiently developed to permit a thorough-going treatment of open-economy fix-price models. Nevertheless, in the following chapters, it is often instructive for the reader to re-examine various issues with the intertemporal framework in mind, thereby gaining further insights.

---

[13] The case in (3.41) is an exception. The effective labor supply function in the presence of goods market rationing on which (3.41) is based, however, never arises in the small open-economy context discussed in this chapter.

PART II

A Two-sector Fix-price Approach

4

The Tradeables-Nontradeables Model: The Fixed Exchange Rates Case

The one-good, fix-price model described in chapter 3 represents a marked improvement over standard open-economy models, which ignore the important difference between notional and effective demands in their specification of non-Walrasian equilibria. Nevertheless, the model has obvious shortcomings. The most important one in the present context is that it allows for non-market-clearing only in the labor market. The "small open economy" assumption insures that the country's aggregate supply of goods can always be sold at the prevailing world price. Consequently, the economy can never experience Keynesian unemployment, which is due to a deficiency of demand for domestic output. Traditional aggregate demand management policies, therefore, have no effect on domestic output or employment.

The main drawback of the simple model of chapter 3 is not that it contains only one *traded* good. Even if this good was disaggregated into, say, importables and exportables, quantity constraints in goods markets would still be ruled out by the small open-economy assumption employed there. The fundamental distinction in a small open economy is instead the one between traded and nontraded goods.[1] The inclusion of a nontraded good opens up the possibility of disequilibrium in the markets for domestic output. All of the possible disequilibrium regimes described by Barro and Grossman (1976), Malinvaud (1977), and others in the closed-economy context (see chapter 2) reappear in a small open-economy context once traded and nontraded goods are distinguished.

This chapter presents a tradeables–nontradeables model of the small open economy. By considering two sectors it raises issues that

[1] The reason that a good is not traded internationally may be transportation costs or other impediments to international trade. See Prachowny (1975).

do not arise in the more common, single-sector framework of chapter 3. Many policies have important effects on the *sectoral* allocation of resources. Some important sectors – including the often large public sector – are "sheltered" or nontraded goods sectors. Kemp (1969) estimates that nontradeables represent more than 50 percent of total production in many highly industrialized countries. The distinction between traded and nontraded goods makes it possible to examine effects of aggregate and relative disturbances as well as internal and external disturbances (cf., Grossman *et al.*, 1982, p. 78). The model described here is, with some differences explained below, the one developed by Neary (1980). It is used to analyze fiscal, exchange rate, and wage–price policies under different disequilibrium regimes.

Some policy problems like the analysis of tariffs or quotas cannot be properly treated in this tradeables–nontradeables framework. For such commercial policies, the distinction between exportable and importable goods is critical. Consequently in chapter 6, where commercial policies are discussed, an exportables–importables model allowing for quantity rationing in the markets for tradeable goods is used. The reader interested in models disaggregating tradeables into exportables and importables is also referred to Cuddington (1980, 1981), Grossman *et al.* (1982), Johansson (1981, 1982a), Johansson and Löfgren (1980, 1981), Lucas (1980), and Steigum (1980).

1 Analytical Preliminaries

1.1 *The Production Sectors*

As in chapter 3, the *small open-economy* assumption employed in this chapter implies that producers of the *traded* good never face sales constraints. They are able to sell any quantity of output they desire at the prevailing world price p_t^*. The domestic-currency price, therefore, equals $p_t = ep_t^*$ where e is the fixed domestic-currency price of foreign exchange. In the case where tradeables producers are also unconstrained in the labor market, their derived demand for labor is obtained from the usual first-order conditions for profit maximization:

$$L_t = L_t(p_t, w), \qquad \partial L_t/\partial p_t > 0, \qquad \partial L_t/\partial w < 0. \qquad (4.1)$$

Substituting (4.1) into the short-run production function yields the *notional* supply of tradeables:

$$Y_t = Y_t(p_t, w), \qquad \partial Y_t/\partial p_t > 0, \qquad \partial Y_t/\partial w < 0. \qquad (4.2)$$

If tradeables producers face a constraint $\bar{L}_t$ on their labor demand, on the other hand, their *effective* output supply is obtained by substituting $\bar{L}_t$ into the short-run production function:

$$\hat{Y}_t = \hat{Y}_t(\bar{L}_t), \qquad \hat{\partial} Y_t / \partial \bar{L}_t > 0. \tag{4.3}$$

The effective supply $\hat{Y}_t$ falls short of the unconstrained profit-maximizing level in (4.2) because firms cannot obtain all the labor they are prepared to hire at prevailing prices. A bar over a variable denotes a quantity constraint; a circumflex denotes an effective supply or demand when the economic agent faces rationing in the labor market.

Like firms in the tradeables sector, producers of *nontraded* goods may or may not face a shortage of labor at prevailing wages and prices. If they perceive no quantity constraints in either the labor or output markets, their derived demand for labor is such that profits are maximized:

$$L_n = L_n(p_n, w), \qquad \partial L_n / \partial p_n > 0, \qquad \partial L_n / \partial w < 0. \tag{4.4}$$

The resulting output relationship when (4.4) is substituted into the production function is the *notional* supply curve:

$$Y_n = Y_n(p_n, w), \qquad \partial Y_n / \partial p_n > 0, \qquad \partial Y_n / \partial w < 0. \tag{4.5}$$

If nontradeables producers face a shortage of labor, *effective* output supply is found by substituting the available quantity of labor $\bar{L}_n$ into the production function:

$$\hat{Y}_n = \hat{Y}_n(\bar{L}_n), \qquad \hat{\partial} Y_n / \partial \bar{L}_n > 0. \tag{4.6}$$

Effective supply falls short of the unconstrained profit-maximizing level of output or notional supply in (4.5) due to rationing in the labor market.

Situations may also occur where producers of *nontradeables* face a sales constraint $\bar{Y}_n$ on final output because domestic demand for nontradeables falls short of their profit-maximizing output level.[2] The *effective* demand for labor $\tilde{L}_n$ is then found by inverting the short-run production function and evaluating it at the point where output equals the sales constraint:

$$\tilde{L}_n = \tilde{L}_n(\bar{Y}_n), \qquad \partial \tilde{L}_n / \partial \bar{Y}_n > 0. \tag{4.7}$$

It never pays to hire more labor than required to produce the amount of (perishable) output demanded in the market.

---

[2] As was pointed out in chapter 2, in the absence of either storable output or, alternatively, a production setup with more than one variable input, firms never face rationing on both the labor and output markets simultaneously. See Muellbauer and Portes (1978) for an intertemporal model of the firm that permits inventory holding of storable output.

It should be pointed out that it is arbitrarily assumed above (for notational simplicity) that nominal wages are equal in the two sectors (i.e., $w_n = w_t = w$) even though the labor market need not clear in the Walrasian sense.

1.2 *Household Behavior*

The maximization problem of the "representative" household takes the same form as in chapter 3, the only difference being that there are now two consumption goods, tradeables and nontradeables, in the current period. In the absence of quantity constraints the utility-maximization problem reduces to:

$$\max U(D_n, D_t, L^s, W'; \theta)$$
$$\text{s.t.} \quad p_n D_n + p_t D_t + W' = wL^s + \pi + W. \tag{4.8}$$

W is defined as initial wealth net of any current-period taxes which the government levies on households. The term $\pi = \pi_n + \pi_t$ now indicates the sum of expected current-period profit (and dividend) income from both tradeables and nontradeables producers. Throughout it will be assumed that expected profit income equals actual profit income.[3] The utility function should be interpreted as a "mixed direct–indirect" utility function where nominal wealth W' is included to capture the desire to save for future consumption. The parameter θ, which will be suppressed henceforth, indicates that the utility function depends on expectations regarding future-period prices and quantity constraints, as discussed in detail in chapter 3.

Commodity demands, labor supply, and saving (i.e., desired wealth accumulation) are derived in the usual manner from (4.8):

$$D_n = D_n(\bar{p}_n, \overset{+}{p}_t, \overset{+}{w}, \overset{+}{W} + \pi),$$
$$D_t = D_t(\overset{+}{p}_n, \bar{p}_t, \overset{+}{w}, \overset{+}{W} + \pi),$$
$$L^s = L^s(\bar{p}_n, \bar{p}_t, \overset{+}{w}, \bar{W} + \pi),$$
$$S = W'(\overset{+}{p}_n, \overset{+}{p}_t, \overset{+}{w}, \overset{+}{W} + \pi) - W. \tag{4.9}$$

Assuming that all commodities including leisure are normal and gross substitutes, the partial derivatives will have the signs indicated in (4.9).[4]

---

[3] In contrast to Dixit (1978) and Neary (1980), we distribute profits in the current period. For a discussion, see chapter 3, section 5.

[4] As discussed in chapter 3, these behavioral functions are not homogeneous or degree zero in the listed arguments because *future* prices are being held constant.

In the case where the household faces a quantity constraint $\bar{L}$ in the labor market, it maximizes the utility function subject to the budget constraint plus the employment constraint $L^s \leqslant \bar{L}$. The resulting behavioral functions – the *effective* demand functions – take the form:

$$\hat{D}_n = \hat{D}_n(\bar{p}_n^{-}, \overset{+}{p}_t, \overset{+}{w}, \overset{+}{W} + \pi, \overset{\pm}{\bar{L}}),$$

$$\hat{D}_t = \hat{D}_t(\overset{+}{p}_n, \bar{p}_t^{-}, \overset{+}{w}, \overset{+}{W} + \pi, \overset{\pm}{\bar{L}}), \qquad\qquad (4.10)$$

$$\hat{S} = \hat{W}'(\overset{+}{p}_n, \overset{+}{p}_t, \overset{+}{w}, \overset{+}{W} + \pi, \overset{\pm}{\bar{L}}) - W,$$

as discussed in chapter 3. Regarding the signs of the partial derivatives in the effective demand functions (4.10), note that an increase in the wage rate w has a positive income effect but no substitution effect when there is a binding constraint on labor supply. The stated signs of the partial derivatives with respect to the constrained employment level $\bar{L}$ assume that all commodities including leisure are net substitutes.[5]

The fact that an increase in the wage rate has an income effect but no substitution effect when the household faces a quantity constraint on the labor market means that the effective behavior functions can be rewritten in the following equivalent form:

$$\hat{D}_n = \hat{D}_n(p_n, p_t, W + \pi + w\bar{L}, \bar{L}) = \hat{D}_t(p_n, p_t, W + Y, \bar{L}),$$

$$\hat{D}_t = \hat{D}_t(p_n, p_t, W + \pi + w\bar{L}, \bar{L}) = \hat{D}_t(p_n, p_t, W + Y, \bar{L}), \quad (4.10a)$$

$$\hat{S} = \hat{W}'(p_n, p_t, W + \pi + w\bar{L}, \bar{L}) - W$$

$$= \hat{W}'(p_n, p_t, W + Y, \bar{L}) - W,$$

where $Y = \pi + w\bar{L}$ denotes nominal national income, i.e., profit and wage incomes have been lumped together. The last argument of each function indicates that a change in the constrained level of employment $\bar{L}$ affects effective demands for goods and wealth also through other channels than a pure income effect, as explained in chapter 3. However, a sufficient condition for this argument to vanish is that labor supply is weakly separable from nontradeables and wealth in the utility function, $U = u(D_n, D_t, W') + v(L^s)$. Then, a change in the level of employment, like a change in the wage rate, only has an income effect. (See appendix A on the microeconomics of rationing for details.) The assumption of weak separability will be employed in the comparative statics in chapters 4–8, as it greatly simplifies

[5] For a detailed discussion of the properties of constrained behavior functions see chapter 3 and appendix A on the microeconomics of rationing.

the calculations while leaving (almost all of) the signs of the effects of policy changes unchanged. We have decided that the increased ease of exposition is well worth the small sacrifice in generality. The summary tables 4.1–4.5 indicate when the results depend on the weak separability assumption.

Given the small-country assumption, the household never faces a constraint on its demand for the traded good. In the market for the nontraded good, however, the consumer may be rationed. When there is a constraint $(D_n \leqslant \bar{D}_n)$ on nontradeables demand but no labor market constraint, the constrained optimization problem yields the *effective* behavioral functions:

$$\tilde{D}_t = \tilde{D}_t(\bar{p}_t, \overset{+}{w}, \overset{+}{W} + \pi - p_n \bar{D}_n, \bar{D}_n),$$

$$\tilde{L}^s = \tilde{L}^s(\bar{p}_t, \overset{+}{w}, \bar{W} + \pi - p_n \bar{D}_n, \bar{D}_n), \qquad (4.11)$$

$$\tilde{S} = \tilde{W}'(\overset{+}{p}_t, \overset{+}{w}, \overset{+}{W} + \pi - p_n \bar{D}_n, \bar{D}_n) - W,$$

with the specified signs on the partial derivatives. Note that when consumption of the nontraded goods is rationed, a change in p_n has only a (negative) income effect. Hence the signs of the derivatives on tradeables demand and saving with respect to p_n are now reversed from what they were in (4.10).

In most real-world situations, one would expect that reduced availability of a rationed good would cause the demand for unrationed substitutes to increase. $\bar{D}_n$ affects the effective demand functions negatively through its effect on *discretionary* (nonlabor) *income* $I = W + \pi - p_n \bar{D}_n$ and via what we call a *gross quantity-substitute* (or complementarity) *effect* $(\partial \tilde{D}_t / \partial \bar{D}_n)_{I=c}$, where $I = c$ emphasizes that discretionary income argument in (4.11) is kept constant (as the use of a *partial* derivative indicates). In general, the partial derivative $\partial \tilde{D}_n / \partial \bar{D}_n$ cannot be unambiguously signed even if the often-used assumption that commodities are net substitutes is employed. If nontradeables are assumed to be weakly separable from all of the other arguments in the utility function, however, this partial derivative equals zero. This assumption is stronger than necessary to obtain the intuitively reasonable case where an increase in the rationed supply $\bar{D}_n$ decreases the demand for the unrationed good $\tilde{D}_t$. This is perhaps reassuring given the severe nature of the assumption. The interested reader should consult appendix A for mathematical details.

Finally, it is possible that the household faces quantity constraints on both its nontradeable demand and labor supply. In this case, utility maximization subject to the budget constraint and the constraints $D_n \leq \bar{D}_n$ and $L^s \leq \bar{L}$ yields the behavioral relations:

$$\tilde{D}_t = \tilde{D}_t(\bar{p}_t, \overset{+}{W} + \pi + w\bar{L} - p_n\bar{D}_n, \bar{D}_n, \bar{L}),$$

$$\tilde{S} = \tilde{W}'(\overset{+}{p}_t, \overset{+}{W} + \pi + w\bar{L} - p_n\bar{D}_n, \bar{D}_n, \bar{L}) - W.$$

(4.12)

The indicated signs of the partial derivatives follow from the assumptions that the goods are normal and net substitutes. Once again, a change in the price of each rationed commodity has only an income effect: an increase in the price of rationed nontradeables decreases demand for other goods, while an increase in the wage rate has only a positive income effect. A small relaxation of the constraint in the nontraded goods market is again assumed to have an unambiguous negative impact on demand for tradeables. Therefore it is innocuous to invoke the weak separability assumption so that the *partial* derivative $(\partial\tilde{D}_t/\partial\bar{D}_n)_{I=c}$ equals zero. Then a rise in $\bar{D}_n$ affects commodity demand only via its negative effect on discretionary income. Analogously, in the comparative statics it is assumed that the partials with respect to $\bar{L}$ are zero. Thus if the constraint on employment is partially relaxed, demand for both tradeable goods and future consumption is stimulated solely due to the resulting increase in discretionary income.

2 The Full-employment Version of the Fixed Exchange Rate Model

Our formal analysis of the model starts by presenting the case where both the markets for labor and nontradeables clear through price adjustments. Although the exchange rate is fixed, the balance of trade need not equal zero in the short run.[6] To see this, we make two observations. First, recall the well-known accounting identities that the trade balance equals either the difference between national income and expenditure[7] or the difference between national saving and investment. Although investment is assumed to be zero in the present context, nothing prevents the household or government

[6] In the *long run*, the trade balance gradually adjusts to zero under either fixed or flexible exchange rates. But here we are not concerned with the international adjustment process. See chapter 3, section 4.

[7] This identity is the focal point for S. S. Alexander's (1952) discussion of the "absorption approach" to the balance of trade.

sectors from being nonzero savers in the short run, at least. Hence the trade balance need not equal zero in every period.[8]

In the fixed exchange rate, flexible wage–price version of the model, the nontradeables prices and the wage rate adjust to simultaneously equate notional supplies and demands in the markets for nontradeable goods and labor:

$$Y_n(p_n, w) = D_n(p_n, p_t, w, W + \pi) + G_n, \tag{4.13a}$$

$$L^s(p_n, p_t, w, W + \pi) = L_n(p_n, w) + L_t(p_t, w). \tag{4.13b}$$

G_n is government expenditure on nontradeables.[9] It should be emphasized that, given our assumption that profits are distributed in the current period, π is not exogenous in (4.13). Rather it equals:

$$\pi = p_t Y_t(p_t, w) - w L_t(p_t, w) + p_n Y_n(p_n, w) - w L_n(p_n, w). \tag{4.13c}$$

The balance of trade in units of foreign currency is found by taking the difference between domestic production and private- plus public-sector consumption of tradeables at equilibrium prices (w, p_n):

$$BT = p_t^* [Y_t(p_t, w) - D_t(p_n, p_t, w, W + \pi) - G_t]$$

$$= \frac{1}{e} [W'(p_n, p_t, w, W + \pi) - W - p_n G_n] - p_t^* G_t. \tag{4.14}$$

By inserting the firms' profit functions into the household budget constraint, we get the second equality in (4.14) relating the trade surplus to the economy's net private plus government saving. Recall that W should be interpreted as initial wealth less current-period taxes levied by the government.

3   Non-market-clearing Situations

Once the open-economy model of chapter 3 is extended to include both traded and nontraded goods sectors, all of the disequilibrium regimes discussed in chapter 2 for a closed economy reappear. In effect, the model just developed is like the single-sector, closed-

---

[8] This is also true under flexible exchange rates provided private capital mobility is not ruled out, as the model in chapter 5 makes clear.
[9] If G_n is changed without changing after-tax wealth in the household's behavioral equations, it is in effect being assumed that the government spending is money-financed.

economy model except that a tradeables sector has been added. This causes few complications, however, because the small-country assumption is employed to ensure that no domestic agent perceives quantity constraints in the tradeables market. Chapter 6 discusses the large-country case.

The market-clearing loci in figure 4.1, delineating the various non-market-clearing regimes, refer to the markets for labor and *nontradeables* (not tradeables). In principle these loci are directly comparable to the borders in figure 2.4 of chapter 2. As before, under *orthodox Keynesian unemployment* (OKU) the market for goods (nontradeables only in the present open-economy context) clears through Walrasian price adjustment, while the labor market is characterized by unemployment (excess supply) given the fixed nominal wage. The *Keynesian unemployment* (KU) fix-price equilibrium has the market for nontradeables clearing through quantity adjustments; the labor market is again in a state of unemployment. Under *classical unemployment* (CU) the firms' profit-maximizing demand for labor determines total employment. (The wage–price vector is such that this demand is insufficient to absorb the forthcoming supply of labor.) Furthermore, the market for nontradeables is in a state of excess demand: effective nontradeables demand (given unemployment) exceeds firms' notional supply.

The disequilibrium regimes characterized by an excess *demand* for labor (i.e., repressed inflation and underconsumption) are more complicated in the present two-sector context than they were in simple one-sector models. When labor is in short supply, some ration-

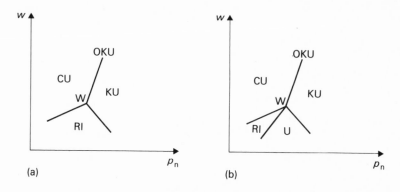

FIGURE 4.1   The different non-market-clearing regimes: (a) and (b) differ due to the influence of the rationing rule when there is an excess demand for labor

ing scheme must evolve to allocate the available labor among producers in the two sectors. Below we will consider alternative schemes and, consequently, have to split figure 4.1 into two parts.

3.1   Unemployment Equilibria

There is a common feature to all of the unemployment regimes described above: the traded goods industry is unconstrained in all markets. Its behavioral functions are given by (4.1) and (4.2). As long as p_t and w are fixed, the profit-maximizing levels of production and employment in the traded goods sector remain unchanged. Matters are different in the nontraded goods sector. Consider the various disequilibrium regimes where there is unemployment in the labor market.

Orthodox Keynesian unemployment

If the price of nontradeable goods is flexible, as it is assumed to be under *orthodox Keynesian unemployment*, the market clears through price adjustment. Consequently, when households are rationed in the labor market, a short-run equilibrium requires that the price p_n equate the notional supply of nontradeables to the *effective* demand (which recognizes the households employment constraint):

$$Y_n(p_n, w) = \hat{D}_n(p_n, p_t, W + \pi + w\bar{L}) + G_n$$
$$= \hat{D}_n(p_n, p_t, W + Y) + G_n. \tag{4.15}$$

In (4.15) and throughout the rest of the book the assumption of weak separability is employed to eliminate the separate influence of the rationed variable(s) on the behavior functions. Once again it should be noted that profits π are distributed in the current period. Thus π is not exogenous but a function of the price vector: $\pi = \pi(p_n, p_t, w)$ as it was in (4.13c). Substituting in for profits yields the second equality in (4.15) which is a function of nominal income:

$$Y = p_n Y_n(p_n, w) + p_t Y_t(p_t, w). \tag{4.16}$$

Given the market-clearing nontradeables price from (4.15) and the fixed wage w and tradeables price p_t, total employment and demand for tradeables are easily determined:

$$\bar{L} = L_n(p_n, w) + L_t(p_t, w), \tag{4.17}$$

$$\hat{D}_t = \hat{D}_t(p_n, p_t, W + Y). \tag{4.18}$$

The balance of trade in terms of foreign currency equals the difference between domestic production and consumption of tradeable goods:

$$BT = p_t^* [Y_t(p_t, w) - \hat{D}_t(p_n, p_t, W + Y) - G_t], \qquad (4.19)$$

valued at p_t^*, the foreign-currency price of traded goods.

Keynesian unemployment

In the *Keynesian unemployment* (KU) case, both w and p_n are assumed to be fixed above their market-clearing levels in the short run. Producers of nontradeables, therefore, face a sales constraint $\bar{Y}_n$ equal to the level of aggregate demand for their product at prevailing prices and wages. Thus, in short-run equilibrium nontradeable output equals:

$$\bar{Y}_n = \hat{D}_n(p_n, p_t, W + \bar{Y}) + G_n. \qquad (4.20)$$

Note that national income $\bar{Y}$ in (4.20) is a function of the fixed price vector and the sales constraint facing producers of nontradeables:

$$\bar{Y} = p_n \bar{Y}_n + p_t Y_t(p_t, w). \qquad (4.21)$$

Total employment equals:

$$\bar{L} = \tilde{L}_n(\bar{Y}_n) + L_t(p_t, w). \qquad (4.22)$$

As before, the trade balance in units of foreign currency equals the difference between domestic supply and demand for tradeables:

$$BT = p_t^* [Y_t(p_t, w) - \hat{D}_t(p_n, p_t, W + \bar{Y}) - G_t]. \qquad (4.23)$$

Classical unemployment

The fact that p_n is fixed in the short run need not necessarily imply that there is an excess *supply* of nontradeables. Depending on the level of wages, the price of tradeables, and initial wealth relative to p_n, there may be an excess demand. If so, we have *classical unemployment* (CU) where both production and employment are determined by the unconstrained profit-maximizing behavior of firms. National income therefore equals:

$$Y = p_n Y_n(p_n, w) + p_t Y_t(p_t, w). \qquad (4.24)$$

Aggregate demand has no effect on output or employment. Households face rationing in both the labor and nontradeables markets:

$$\bar{L} = L_n(p_n, w) + L_t(p_t, w),$$
$$\bar{D}_n = Y_n(p_n, w) - G_n. \qquad (4.25)$$

This, of course, affects their demand for tradeables goods. Hence, the balance of trade (in units of foreign currency) depends on *effective* demand for tradeable goods given these constraints:

$$BT = p_t^*[Y_t(p_t, w) - \tilde{\tilde{D}}_t(p_t, W + Y - p_n \bar{D}_n) - G_t]. \qquad (4.26)$$

3.2   *Repressed Inflation*

Under repressed inflation (RI) both p_n and w are fixed *below* market-clearing levels. Hence households are rationed in the nontradeable goods market but not in the labor market. As mentioned above, when labor is in short supply some rationing scheme must evolve to allocate the available labor among firms in the two industries. The properties of the repressed inflation regime depend on the postulated rationing scheme and whether agents can manipulate the rationing scheme by emitting false market signals, e.g., signals that are inconsistent with their budget constraints.[10]

Excluding the possibility of manipulable rationing schemes, we consider two particular ways of rationing labor among sectors, and therefore also two repressed inflation cases. First, when only producers of nontraded goods are rationed in the labor market, actual employment in that sector equals total labor supply minus the amount demanded by the priority (tradeable goods) sector:

$$\bar{L}_n = \tilde{L}^s(\bar{p}_t, \overset{+}{w}, \bar{W} + \pi - p_n \bar{D}_n) - L_t(\overset{+}{p}_t, \bar{w}), \qquad (4.27)$$

where profits are endogenous: $\pi = \pi(p_n, p_t, w, \bar{L}_n)$. Thus the rationed amount of labor available for nontradeables producers depends on the arguments of $\tilde{L}^s$ and L_t.

An alternative labor market rationing rule is the other extreme case where the nontradeables sector gets priority. Assuming labor supply is at least large enough to meet this demand, only tradeable goods producers face a supply constraint in the labor market. Their rationed quantity of labor equals the remaining supply after meeting labor demand by the tradeables sector:

$$\bar{L}_t = \tilde{L}^s(\bar{p}_t, \overset{+}{w}, \bar{W} + \pi - p_n \bar{D}_n) - L_n(\overset{+}{p}_n, \bar{w}), \qquad (4.28)$$

where the profit function again takes the form $\pi = \pi(p_n, p_t, w, \bar{L}_t)$.

Of course, there are more general cases where *both* tradeables and nontradeables producers are rationed on the labor market in the presence of excess demand. Here matters are more complicated. A rationing rule is needed to specify the allocation of effective labor supply between sectors. From the two special cases studied above it

[10] For details, see chapter 2.

is clear that this allocation will, in general, depend on prices, wages, and initial wealth as well as other factors affecting labor supply (such as quantity constraints on goods markets). Unfortunately, the signs of the effects are indeterminate *a priori*. This may explain why most authors examining the repressed inflation case assume that one of the sectors gets priority, and that the rationing is not so severe that notional demand for labor by that sector exceeds the total available supply. There are, however, a few exceptions. Cuddington (1980) assumes that both sectors are rationed but that an increased goods price causes a reallocation of labor toward that sector. If the supply of labor increases due to a wage increase, *both* sectors are assumed to receive more labor. Johansson (1982a), on the other hand, includes the latter effect but assumes no reallocation of labor rations following relative price changes. One must conclude that the difficult problem of providing a theoretical explanation of why particular rationing rules prevail in given situations remains unsolved in the literature.

Due to the possibility of different labor rationing rules, figure 4.1 has been split into two parts. In figure 4.1a nontradeables producers (and possibly also tradeables producers) are rationed in the labor market. Under "repressed inflation" (RI) in this figure, households are rationed in the nontraded goods sector while at least nontradeables producers are rationed in the labor market.

In figure 4.1b nontradeables producers are assumed to get priority over tradeables producers in the labor market. Furthermore, total labor supply is assumed to be large enough to meet the nontraded sector's demand. Repressed inflation (RI) in this figure represents a situation in which the household is rationed in the market for nontradeables and firms producing tradeables are rationed in the labor market.

3.3 *Underconsumption*

The rationing rule where nontradeables producers get priority in the labor market opens up the possibility of an additional regime, labeled *underconsumption* (U), where households perceive no quantity constraints. Firms' output of nontradeables is limited by the level of aggregate demand defined by (4.29) below, while output of tradeables is limited by the amount of labor available, which is given by the labor rationing rule (4.30). Thus a short-run equilibrium with consistent trading is defined by:

$$\bar{Y}_n = D_n(p_n, p_t, w, W + \pi) + G_n, \tag{4.29}$$

$$\bar{L}_t = L^s(p_n, p_t, w, W + \pi) - \tilde{L}_n(\bar{Y}_n). \tag{4.30}$$

Equations (4.29) and (4.30) must be solved simultaneously using the appropriate profit function $\pi = \pi(p_n, p_t, w, \bar{Y}_n, \bar{L}_t)$ to determine the level of production of nontraded goods and the amount of labor available for the traded goods production after labor demand in the nontradeables sector has been satisfied. Such a situation might more aptly be called "structural imbalance," but we retain the Muellbauer and Portes (1978) label "underconsumption" to avoid introducing new terminology.

4   Fiscal and Wage–Price Policies to Combat Unemployment

The short-run effects of macroeconomic stabilization policies depend critically on whether the labor and output markets are initially in equilibrium or not. Presumably in many cases it is precisely the absence of market clearing that makes policy action necessary. In this section it is demonstrated that fiscal policy as well as policy-induced wage and price changes have quite different effects on aggregate and sectoral output and employment depending on the type of market imbalance prevailing at the time of the policy change.[11] Thus, *it is important for policymakers to accurately diagnose the state of excess supply or demand in the labor and output markets if appropriate policies are to be recommended.*

For the rest of this chapter we concentrate on the regimes where there is unemployment, i.e., an excess supply of labor,[12] as these regimes are the most interesting from an economic and political standpoint. Unfortunately, the number of unambiguous results that can be obtained for cases involving excess *demand* for labor are few, in part due to the effect of different labor rationing rules described above. The reader interested in repressed inflation and underconsumption in open economies, which involve excess demand in the labor market, is referred to Cuddington (1980), Johansson (1982a), Neary (1980), and Steigum (1980).

4.1   *Fiscal Policy*

Keynesian unemployment

Under any type of unemployment regime in the present model the levels of output and employment in the tradeables sector are deter-

[11] It should be emphasized that the comparative static analysis assumes that a policy change is never large enough to move the economy from one type of disequilibrium situation to another.

[12] To avoid being overly taxonomic, the orthodox Keynesian unemployment case is not discussed in the text. The effects of government policies under this regime are, however, included in the various summary tables.

TABLE 4.1   Fiscal policies under different unemployment
regimes

	G_n	G_t
Output of nontraded goods, Y_n		
Orthodox Keynesian unemployment	+	0^a
Keynesian unemployment	+	0^a
Classical unemployment	0	0
Output of traded goods, Y_t		
All unemployment regimes	0	0
Balance of trade		
Orthodox Keynesian unemployment	–	–
Keynesian unemployment	–	–
Classical unemployment	–	–

[a] If financed by lump-sum taxes, government purchases of traded goods will have a contractionary effect.

mined by the firm's profit-maximizing behavior as shown in (4.1) and (4.2). Consequently, aggregate demand management policies such as government expenditure on either nontraded (G_n) or traded (G_t) goods have no effect on the traded goods sector (table 4.1).

In the *nontraded* goods sector when there is Keynesian unemployment, however, the situation is very different, because output depends on the level of aggregate demand. Increased government expenditure on the nontradeable good (financed by money creation) has a stimulative impact effect on private demand in that sector, which gives rise to the familiar multiplier process. From (4.20):

$$\frac{d\bar{Y}_n}{dG_n} = 1 \Big/ \left(1 - \frac{\partial \hat{D}_n}{\partial Y} p_n\right) > 0, \tag{4.31}$$

where the denominator equals one minus the marginal propensity to spend on nontraded goods. The government expenditure multiplier expression in (4.31) equals the usual textbook formula given our assumption of weak separability of labor in the utility function. Without this assumption the denominator would contain an additional term. This is because an increase in employment has two effects: (1) an income effect and (2) an effect on the marginal rate of substitution between consumption and leisure. The assumption that consumption and wealth are weakly separable from leisure/labor ensures that the latter effect vanishes. The multiplier expression then reduces to the textbook formula (4.31).

The reader should also note that the above calculations presuppose that the economy has only one household or a number of identical households. This often-employed assumption in the work on micro-foundations of macroeconomics enables us to ignore income distribution effects. If the model contained many different households, it would be necessary to make detailed assumptions about their marginal propensities to consume in order to sign the effects of government policies that involve income redistribution among households.[13]

It should be fairly obvious that aggregate demand management policies worsen the balance of trade under Keynesian unemployment. Money-financed government expenditure on *tradeable* goods causes a dollar-for-dollar[14] deterioration in the balance of trade:

$$\frac{\mathrm{d}BT}{\mathrm{d}G_t} = -p_t^* < 0. \tag{4.32}$$

As both prices and wages remain unchanged, domestic production of tradeables as well as household demands for both tradeable and non-tradeable goods are unaffected. Thus increased government demand can only be satisfied through increased imports. (Note that tax-financed government spending would affect private demand via taxes T.)

Government outlays on *nontradeable* goods also worsen the external balance. By increasing profit and labor incomes in the nontraded goods sector, government spending stimulates private demand for traded goods, causing the trade balance to deteriorate:

$$\frac{\mathrm{d}BT}{\mathrm{d}G_n} = -p_t^* \left[\frac{\partial \hat{D}_t}{\partial Y} \left(\frac{\mathrm{d}\pi_n}{\mathrm{d}G_n} + w \frac{\mathrm{d}\tilde{L}_n}{\mathrm{d}G_n} \right) \right] = -p_t^* \frac{\partial \hat{D}_t}{\partial Y} \frac{\mathrm{d}\bar{Y}}{\mathrm{d}G_n} < 0. \tag{4.33}$$

Classical unemployment

In the classical unemployment case the levels of output and employment in both sectors are determined by firms' profit-maximizing behavior as shown in (4.24). Consequently, aggregate demand management policies have no effect on either domestic output or employment (in (4.24) and (4.25)).

Although aggregate demand management policies leave production unchanged under classical unemployment, they do affect external balance. Again government expenditure on *traded* goods causes a

---

[13] For a fix-price model of a multihousehold economy, see Johansson (1981).
[14] Assuming the dollar is the foreign currency here.

dollar-for-dollar deterioration in the balance of trade. Matters are more complicated if the government increases its expenditure on nontradeables G_n because this increases the severity of the nontradeable goods shortage perceived by households (assuming government demand gets priority). However, due to the separability assumption, the effect of increased government expenditure on nontradeables is an unambiguous deterioration of the trade balance:

$$\frac{\mathrm{d}BT}{\mathrm{d}G_n} = p_t^* \frac{\partial \tilde{\tilde{D}}_t}{\partial Y} \left(p_n \frac{\mathrm{d}\bar{D}_n}{\mathrm{d}G_n} \right) = -p_t^* \frac{\partial \tilde{\tilde{D}}_t}{\partial Y} p_n < 0. \qquad (4.34)$$

Conclusions regarding fiscal policy

In summary, with the inclusion of a nontraded goods sector in a fix-price model of the small open economy, the effects of aggregate demand management policies may be quite different from those predicted by the simple Dixit model of chapter 3. This is particularly true when considering internal balance, i.e., production and employment.[15] In the simple Dixit model aggregate demand management policies leave production and employment unchanged. The same holds true for the two-sector model only when there is classical unemployment. In the presence of Keynesian unemployment, on the other hand, fiscal policy has a stimulative impact on production and employment – at least if it is directed toward the demand-constrained nontradeables sector. It is indeed critical to determine the prevailing type of market imbalances in order to make appropriate policy recommendations.

The effect of fiscal policy on *external* balance, on the other hand, is less fraught with ambiguity. As can be seen in table 4.1, a fiscal expansion typically worsens the trade balance.

4.2 Exchange Rate Policy

Like the effects of fiscal policy, exchange rate realignment has different effects depending on whether unemployment is Keynesian or classical in nature. In the tradeables–nontradeables framework, devaluation drives up the relative price of tradeables in terms of nontradeables, which in turn affects households' expenditure decisions. In addition devaluation provides a way of reducing the

---

[15] Another aspect of the analysis not further elaborated in this volume would be to consider how effective demands are affected by policy changes – see Malinvaud (1977).

TABLE 4.2   Devaluations under different unemployment
regimes

	P_t
Output of nontraded goods; Y_n	
Orthodox Keynesian unemployment	+
Keynesian unemployment	+
Classical unemployment	0
Output of traded goods, Y_t	
All regimes	+
Balance of trade	
Orthodox Keynesian unemployment	?
Keynesian unemployment	?
Classical unemployment	$+$[a]

[a] Sufficient conditions for a positive sign is a nonpositive trade
balance account in the initial situation.

real product wage in the tradeables sector, thereby stimulating
production and employment in that sector (table 4.2):

$$\frac{dY_t}{dp_t} = \frac{\partial Y_t}{\partial L_t} \frac{dL_t}{dp_t} > 0. \tag{4.35}$$

This, of course, assumes that the nominal wage remains unchanged
as the devaluation drives up the domestic price of tradeables. The
effect of wage indexation on the efficacy of devaluation is investigated in section 4.4 below.

Keynesian unemployment

In the Keynesian case, devaluation also stimulates output in the
nontradeable goods industry – through three channels, as can be
seen by differentiating (4.20):

$$\frac{d\bar{Y}_n}{dp_t} = \frac{\partial \hat{D}_n}{\partial p_t} + \frac{\partial \hat{D}_n}{\partial Y} \frac{d\pi}{dp_t} + \frac{\partial \hat{D}_n}{\partial Y} w \frac{d\bar{L}}{dp_t} \tag{4.36a}$$

$$= \left(\frac{\partial \hat{D}_n}{\partial p_t} + \frac{\partial \hat{D}_n}{\partial Y} \frac{d\pi_t}{dp_t} + \frac{\partial \hat{D}_n}{\partial Y} w \frac{dL_t}{dp_t} \right) \Big/ \left(1 - \frac{\partial \hat{D}_n}{\partial Y} p_n \right) > 0. \tag{4.36b}$$

The effect of an increase in the price of tradeables raises the demand
for nontraded goods, assuming gross substitutes ($\partial \hat{D}_n / \partial p_t > 0$). In

addition, demand for nontradeables is stimulated through the increased profit income generated in the traded goods sector. Finally, demand increases via the marginal propensity to spend on nontradeables following an increase in the employment in the traded goods sector. These impact effects, in turn, give rise to the usual multiplier expansion (as discussed under aggregate demand management policies above).

As is well known, devaluation has an ambiguous effect on the trade balance in the Keynesian unemployment case due to the conflicting influence of substitution and income effects. To see this, differentiate (4.23):

$$\frac{\mathrm{d}BT}{\mathrm{d}p_t} = p_t^* \frac{\partial Y_t}{\partial p_t} - p_t^* \left(\frac{\partial \hat{D}_t}{\partial p_t} + \frac{\partial \hat{D}_t}{\partial Y} \frac{\mathrm{d}\pi}{\mathrm{d}p_t} + \frac{\partial \hat{D}_t}{\partial Y} w \frac{\mathrm{d}\bar{L}}{\mathrm{d}p_t} \right) \gtreqless 0. \qquad (4.37)$$

The first term represents the stimulative effect of the devaluation on production of traded goods. The terms within parentheses concern the effect of devaluation on domestic demand for tradeables. The first gives the negative direct price effect, while the remaining terms reflect the positive demand effect of increased profit and wage income. Thus, the net effect of the devaluation is ambiguous, depending on the relative magnitude of these different price ("elasticities") and income ("absorption") effects.

The foregoing analysis suggests that policymakers should be skeptical about the efficacy, in the short run, at least, of exchange rate adjustment for restoring equilibrium in the trade balance.

Classical unemployment

In the classical unemployment case, devaluation has no effect on nontradeables production.[16] The effect on domestic demand for tradeables again depends on conflicting income and substitution effects. One might, therefore, expect the short-run effect of devaluation to be uncertain, as it was under Keynesian unemployment. It can be shown, however, that the effect of devaluation on the trade balance under classical unemployment is unambiguously positive provided the country initially has a nonpositive trade balance, which is indeed typical when devaluation is being contemplated.

---

[16] This statement is not true once imported intermediate goods are introduced – see section 5 below.

To see this, differentiate (4.26) to get the effect of devaluation on the trade balance:

$$
\frac{\mathrm{d}BT}{\mathrm{d}p_t} = p_t^* \left\{ \frac{\partial Y_t}{\partial p_t} - \left[\frac{\partial \tilde{D}_t}{\partial p_t} + \frac{\partial \tilde{D}_t}{\partial Y} \left(p_t \frac{\partial Y_t}{\partial p_t} + Y_t \right) \right] \right\}
$$

$$
= p_t^* \left\{ \underbrace{\left(1 - \frac{\partial \tilde{D}_t}{\partial Y} \, p_t \right) \frac{\partial Y_t}{\partial p_t}}_{(+)} - \underbrace{\left(\frac{\partial \tilde{D}_t}{\partial p_t} \right)_{\mathrm{comp}}}_{(-)} + \underbrace{\frac{\partial \tilde{D}_t}{\partial Y} (\tilde{D}_t - Y_t)}_{(+)} \right\} > 0.
$$

$$
(4.38)
$$

In the last equality, the first term in parentheses is positive provided the marginal propensity to spend on tradeables is less than unity. To obtain the second and third terms we have decomposed the price effect in a Slutsky substitution effect and an income effect. The second term then represents the substitution effect of a devaluation, which is clearly negative. The devaluation also has a negative income effect. This is reflected in the first part of the third term in (4.38). If domestic consumption of tradeables $\tilde{D}_t$ exceeds domestic production Y_t so that the country initially has a nonpositive trade balance, the third term in (4.38) will be positive. In this case, it is clear that *devaluation unambiguously improves the trade balance under classical unemployment.*[17]

The mechanism behind this result, it should be noted, is more complicated than the one suggested by the simple elasticities approach (cf., Dornbusch, 1975)). That approach gives a complete answer only if it is assumed that profits are not distributed to households in the current period and the marginal propensity to spend on traded goods following from an increase in employment is zero. Then only the first and second ("price") terms in the first equality in (4.38) remain, and the expression is in accordance with the simple elasticities approach.

Conclusions regarding exchange rate devaluation

Once again interesting differences exist in the efficacy of policy under the two unemployment regimes considered above. Devaluation stimulates production of traded goods under all unemployment regimes in a small open economy. Under Keynesian unemployment, production of nontraded goods also rises via the usual multiplier

---

[17] In the Keynesian case treated above it is the positive impact of increased incomes in the nontradeable goods sector on demand for tradeables that causes trouble. In the classical case the nontraded goods sector is unaffected by the devaluation.

process. Hence, devaluation will have a more stimulative impact on national income and employment under Keynesian unemployment than under classical unemployment.

Notable also is the fact that, although the devaluation improves "internal balance" (production and employment), it has an ambiguous impact on "external balance" in the Keynesian unemployment case. Under classical unemployment, on the other hand, devaluation does improve the trade balance. The lack of ambiguity is a consequence of the smaller income effect on domestic demand for tradeables in this case.

4.3   Real Wage Adjustment via Wage-Price Policies

Before turning to the so-called wage indexation problem, we briefly summarize the separate effects of policy-induced changes in the nominal wage rate and the price of nontradeables, holding the exchange rate constant. Each of these policies has some effect on real wages as well as other macroeconomic consequences (table 4.3).

Under classical unemployment, it is clear that a wage hike decreases the profit-maximizing level of production and employment in both sectors; see (4.24) and (4.25).

The same qualitative conclusion emerges under Keynesian unemployment. Here the contractionary effect in the *nontradeables* sector

TABLE 4.3   Real wage rate changes via wage-price policies under different unemployment regimes

	p_n	w
Output of nontraded goods, Y_n		
Orthodox Keynesian unemployment	a	—
Keynesian unemployment	—	—
Classical unemployment	+	—
Output of traded goods, Y_t		
All regimes	0^a	—
Balance of trade		
Orthodox Keynesian unemployment	a	?
Keynesian unemployment	?	$-^b$
Classical unemployment	0^b	$-^b$

[a] The price of nontradeables p_n is endogenous under orthodox Keynesian unemployment.
[b] Weak separability is a sufficient condition for an unambiguous sign.

is due to the negative effect on aggregate demand of reduction in tradeables-sector production and employment caused by the increase in the nominal wage. To see this, differentiate the short-run equilibrium condition (4.20) to get:

$$\frac{d\bar{Y}_n}{dw} = \frac{\partial \hat{D}_n}{\partial Y} \frac{\partial Y_t}{\partial w} p_t \left/ \left(1 - \frac{\partial \hat{D}_n}{\partial Y} p_n\right) \right. < 0. \tag{4.39}$$

In the single-sector closed-economy model of chapter 2, in contrast, a wage change will leave output unaffected under Keynesian unemployment if both profit and labor income are currently distributed to households. When there is rationing in the labor market (unemployment), an increase in the nominal wage has an income effect but no substitution effect on commodity demand. In a one-household, one-sector economy this positive labor income effect is just offset by the decrease in profit income that the wage increase causes. Aggregate demand and production are thus left unchanged by the wage hike when the economy is suffering from Keynesian unemployment.

In a small open economy, in contrast, a cut in the wage stimulates production and employment in all sectors regardless of whether there is classical or Keynesian unemployment.[18]

Consider, next, the effects of a policy-induced increase in the price of nontradeables. Under Keynesian unemployment, the increased price of nontradeables affects nontradeables demand and hence output through two channels. First, there is the negative price effect $\partial \hat{D}_n / \partial p_n$, which tends to reduce output. Second, there is the positive effect brought about by the change in profit income from the nontradeables sector. The sum of these two impact effects, which can be shown to be negative by using the Slutsky decomposition of the price effect, is then magnified by the usual multiplier process. Differentiating the short-run equilibrium condition (4.20):

$$\frac{d\bar{Y}_n}{dp_n} = \left(\frac{\partial \hat{D}_n}{\partial p_n} + \bar{Y}_n \frac{\partial \hat{D}_n}{\partial Y}\right) \left/ \left(1 - \frac{\partial \hat{D}_n}{\partial Y} p_n\right) \right.$$

$$= \left(\frac{\partial \hat{D}_n}{\partial p_n}\right)_{comp} \left/ \left(1 - \frac{\partial \hat{D}_n}{\partial Y} p_n\right) \right. < 0. \tag{4.40}$$

[18] If profits are not distributed in the current period, then a wage cut will *decrease* output of nontradeables *ceteris paribus*. The reason for this is that the wage cut does not result in an increased distributed profit income. For details see Neary (1980) or Malinvaud (1977).

Under the assumption of gross substitutes and normal goods, the numerator is negative.[19] To see this, decompose the price effect $\partial \hat{D}_n / \partial p_n$ into a substitution effect and an income effect. The latter effect (equal to $- \bar{Y}_n \, \partial \hat{D}_n / \partial Y$) is netted out by the term $\bar{Y}_n \, \partial \hat{D}_n / \partial Y$ reflecting increased profit income. Hence, there remains only a negative substitution effect in the numerator of (4.40). This confirms our conclusion that an increase in the price of nontradeables will decrease output and employment in the nontradeables sector (but leaves the tradeables sector unchanged).

The above result is similar to Malinvaud's (1977) conclusion in the closed-economy context: a cut in the real wage brought about by an increase in the price of (nontradeables) output may actually *decrease* aggregate demand thereby reducing national income under Keynesian unemployment.

In the classical case, in contrast, such a cut in the real wage rate brought about by an increase in nontradeables prices unambiguously *increases* aggregate demand by driving up output and hence income from the nontradeables sector.

It should be noted that a considerable difference exists between the impacts of real wage adjustments on internal balance and external balance. These effects are summarized in table 4.3. As a rule, wage and price policies have an unambiguous impact on production and employment. The trade balance is, in contrast, affected in an ambiguous way by wage and price policies due to the often-encountered conflict between income and substitution effects.

4.4 *Devaluation and Wage Indexation*

One of the channels through which devaluation typically operates (see, e.g., section 4.2 above) is by reducing the real wage. This increases international competitiveness, bringing about an unambiguous expansion in the tradeables sector. The effect of devaluation on nontradeables production, on the other hand, depends on whether the economy is suffering from classical unemployment – in which case the real product wage relevant to nontradeables producers and hence production is unchanged – or Keynesian unemployment – where nontradeables production is stimulated via devaluation's effect on nontradeables demand.

---

[19] In fact, it is sufficient to assume net substitutes as the income effects net out in a one-household economy as is shown below. Compare Johansson and Löfgren (1980, 1981) and Lindbeck (1982).

TABLE 4.4   Devaluation in the presence of wage indexation

	$\dfrac{dp_t}{p_t} = \dfrac{dw}{w}$
Output of nontraded goods, Y_n	
Orthodox Keynesian unemployment[a]	?
Keynesian unemployment	+
Classical unemployment	−
Output of traded goods, Y_t	
All regimes	0
Balance of trade	
Orthodox Keynesian unemployment	?
Keynesian unemployment	?
Classical unemployment	+[b]

[a] Note that the price of nontraded goods p_n is endogenous under orthodox Keynesian unemployment.
[b] This sign is obtained if weak separability is assumed and the trade balance is nonpositive initially.

The efficacy of devaluation, it is clear, will depend in part on the vigor with which laborers resist real wage reductions by demanding compensating upward adjustment in nominal wages. One particular form that this *real wage resistance* may take is cost-of-living adjustment or other forms of wage indexation in labor contracts (table 4.4). Of course, even in the absence of such contractual agreements, laborers may demand higher nominal wages to at least partially offset consumer price increases, including those caused by devaluation.

To analyze the effect of compensation claims or automatic indexation on exchange rate policy, suppose that the nominal wage is adjusted upward by the proportion α of the devaluation-induced increase in tradeable goods prices:[20]

$$\frac{dw}{w} = \alpha \frac{dp_t}{p_t}. \tag{4.41}$$

Presumably α is less than unity in most cases for two reasons. First, in the short run, indexation and real wage resistance are often less than 100 percent. Second, laborers care about their real wage defined in terms of some consumption basket (i.e., the real "consumption

[20] Nontradeables prices are assumed to remain constant and hence are omitted from the indexation scheme in (4.41). To treat the case of orthodox Keynesian unemployment where the nontradeables price is endogenous would require that (4.41) be generalized accordingly.

wage"). When the price of tradeable goods rises, the increase in their cost of living depends on the fraction of total expenditure allocated to tradeables. Thus if α is set equal to the expenditure share of tradeable goods in (4.41), the real consumption wage will remain unchanged following devaluation.

In section 4.2 above we implicitly assumed no wage response to devaluation, i.e., $\alpha = 0$. In this section we examine the case where $\alpha = 1$, so that wages rise to such an extent following devaluation that international competitiveness of the tradeables sector is left completely unchanged. It should be emphasized that this case is, in fact, "100-percent-plus" indexation in the usual case where the weight of tradeables in the consumption price index (and hence α) is less than 100 percent. The analysis of other cases where $0 < \alpha < 1$ follows straightforwardly.

Classical unemployment

Consider the classical unemployment case where the supply of goods in each sector is a decreasing function of the real product wage in that sector. When $\alpha = 1$, devaluation leaves the real wage rate and hence production in the tradeable goods sector constant. Output in the nontradeables sector falls, however, because producers face higher wages while their prices, by assumption, remain unchanged. Therefore, a devaluation followed by an equal percentage increase in the nominal wage rate may have a *contractionary* impact on the country's national income:

$$\frac{dY}{dp_t} = Y_t + p_n \frac{\partial Y_n}{\partial w} \frac{dw}{dp_t} \leqslant 0. \tag{4.42}$$

This result stands in sharp contrast to the *stimulative* aggregate output effect of devaluation under classical unemployment in the absence of wage indexation; recall section 4.2 above.

It is, however, possible to show that the trade balance unambiguously improves (if the utility function is weakly separable). Differentiating (4.12) with respect to p_t yields:

$$\frac{d\tilde{D}_t}{dp_t} = \frac{\partial \tilde{D}_t}{\partial p_t} + \frac{\partial \tilde{D}_t}{\partial Y} \left(\frac{dY}{dp_t} - p_n \frac{\partial \bar{D}_n}{\partial w} \frac{dw}{dp_t} \right), \tag{4.43}$$

where the change in the rationed supply of nontradeables equals:

$$\frac{\partial \bar{D}_n}{\partial w} \frac{dw}{dp_t} = \frac{\partial Y_n}{\partial w} \frac{dw}{dp_t} \tag{4.44}$$

from (4.25). Using (4.42) and (4.44), equation (4.43) reduces to:

$$\frac{d\tilde{D}_t}{dp_t} = \frac{\partial \tilde{D}_t}{\partial p_t} + Y_t \frac{\partial \tilde{D}_t}{\partial Y}$$

$$= \left(\frac{\partial \tilde{D}_t}{\partial p_t}\right)_{comp} - (\tilde{D}_t - Y_t) \frac{\partial \tilde{D}_t}{\partial Y} < 0. \tag{4.45}$$

Consequently if the utility function is weakly separable and the country initially has a trade deficit ($\tilde{D}_t - Y_t \geqslant 0$), then *even in the presence of wage indexation* ($\alpha = 1$) *devaluation will unambiguously improve the trade balance:*

$$\frac{dBT}{dp_t} = -\frac{d\tilde{D}_t}{dp_t} > 0, \tag{4.46}$$

just as it did in the absence of wage indexation. Recall (4.38).

Keynesian unemployment

Next, consider the effect of devaluation with 100-percent-plus wage indexation in the Keynesian unemployment case. Recall from section 4.2 above that devaluation (without indexation) stimulates production in both sectors. In section 4.3 above, on the other hand, it was shown that an increase in nominal wage rate decreases production in both sectors. Combining these two effects in a way that reflects $\alpha = 1$ wage indexation in (4.41) is straightforward once it is recognized that such indexation leaves both employment and profit in the tradeables sector unchanged. Hence, of the three channels through which devaluation operated in the absence of indexation (recall (4.36)), only the substitution effect remains:

$$\frac{d\bar{Y}_n}{dp_t} = \left(\frac{\partial \hat{D}_n}{\partial p_t} + \frac{\partial \hat{D}_n}{\partial Y} Y_t\right) \Big/ \left(1 - \frac{\partial \hat{D}_n}{\partial Y} p_n\right)$$

$$= \left(\frac{\partial \hat{D}_n}{\partial p_t}\right)_{comp} \Big/ \left(1 - \frac{\partial \hat{D}_n}{\partial Y} p_n\right) > 0. \tag{4.47}$$

Equation (4.47) establishes that a proportional increase in the exchange rate and the nominal wage rate unambiguously *stimulates* production of nontradeables, given the assumption that all goods are gross substitutes. Note that the substitution effect gives rise to the usual multiplier effects in the nontradeable goods sector.

The effects of 100-percent-plus indexation on the efficacy of devaluation can now be summarized by referring to tables 4.2 and

4.4. First, *devaluation stimulates output in the tradeable goods sector only to the extent that there is less than complete wage indexation. With full (i.e., α = 1) indexation, output is unchanged.*

Second, *the effect of devaluation with and without indexation on the nontradeables sector depends critically on whether the economy is suffering from Keynesian or classical unemployment.* Under Keynesian unemployment, the stimulative effect of devaluation on nontradeables production is reduced (but never eliminated) as the degree of wage indexation rises (compare (4.36) and (4.47)). Under classical unemployment, on the other hand, nontradeables production will actually *fall* if there is wage indexation, whereas it remained unaffected by devaluation in the absence of indexation. Given that some degree of indexation will almost invariably prevail in the real world, one must, therefore, anticipate sectoral conflicts concerning devaluation policy in situations where unemployment is classical in nature. The degree of consensus will be higher during periods of Keynesian unemployment.

5 Oil Price Shocks

Interest in the effects of terms-of-trade changes has increased dramatically in the West since the beginning of the 1970s due to the sharp increase in the price of crude oil. Therefore, it is worthwhile to suggest how the open-economy fix-price framework in this chapter might be extended so as to analyze a rise in the world price of an imported intermediate good.

In the tradeables–nontradeables model used in this chapter there is not much room for terms-of-trade changes because all traded goods are aggregated together. (The terms of trade is defined as the price of exportables relative to the price of importables in foreign currency.) A minor reformulation, however, makes the model capable of handling more interesting cases. Following Steigum (1980) we simply introduce an imported raw material (e.g., oil) R as a second factor of production. The *unconstrained* supply functions for tradeables and nontradeables then become:

$$Y_i = Y_i(p_i, w, p_r), \qquad i = \text{n, t,}$$

$$\partial Y_i/\partial p_i > 0, \qquad \partial Y_i/\partial w < 0, \qquad \partial Y_i/\partial p_r < 0 \qquad (4.48)$$

where p_r is the price of raw materials. Supply of tradeables and nontradeables depends positively on the output price, and negatively on the nominal wage w and the price of raw materials p_r.

If imports of raw materials are rationed (e.g., by an international cartel or domestic import quotas), the relevant supply functions are the *effective* supply functions:

$$\hat{Y}_i = \hat{Y}_i(p_i, w, \bar{R}_i), \qquad i = \text{n, t,}$$

$$\partial\hat{Y}_i/\partial p_i > 0, \qquad \partial Y_i/\partial w < 0, \qquad \partial Y_i/\partial\bar{R}_i > 0, \tag{4.49}$$

where $\bar{R} = \bar{R}_n + \bar{R}_t$ is the total available quantity of imported inputs. A sufficient condition for output to increase when rationing in the raw material market becomes less severe is that labor and raw material are technical complements so that an increase in one input will increase the marginal product of the other input (see appendix A on the microeconomics of rationing, and also Frisch (1965)).

We will not go through all calculations necessary to derive comparative static results but merely indicate some interesting ones; see Steigum (1980) for details. In a small open economy with a fixed exchange rate, an increased foreign-currency price p_r^* of imported raw materials means that the domestic price p_r increases by the same amount. As summarized in table 4.5, a rise in p_r in the absence of rationing of the imported input reduces domestic production of tradeable goods. (Recall the unconstrained behavior functions in (4.48) above.)

Matters are somewhat different in the nontraded goods sector. Under Keynesian unemployment, demand-constrained producers of nontraded goods use *more* labor and less raw materials to produce

TABLE 4.5   Effects of (*1*) an increase in the world price p_r^* of an imported raw material when firms are unconstrained in this market, and (*2*) an increase in the rationed quantity of raw materials $\bar{R}$ when firms are constrained in the raw materials market

	p_r^*	$\bar{R}$
Output of nontraded goods, Y_n		
Orthodox Keynesian unemployment	−	+
Keynesian unemployment	?	?
Classical unemployment	−	+
Output of traded goods, Y_t		
All regimes	−	+
Balance of trade		
All regimes	?	?

the demand-constrained quantity $\bar{Y}_n$ when imported input prices p_r rise. Firms in the unconstrained traded goods sector, in contrast, use *less* labor according to (4.48). Hence the net impact on labor income and, therefore, aggregate demand is ambiguous. In the classical case no such counteracting forces are in operation, explaining the unambiguous fall in production noted in table 4.5. The (symmetrical) outcome of a change in the rationed quantity of imported raw materials can be explained in an analogous way.[21]

Noteworthy is that both changes in the price of imported raw materials (oil) and changes in the rationed quantity in the market for such goods have ambiguous impacts on the trade balance. Although the effect on the volume of imported raw materials is determinate, the net export of tradeable goods may rise or fall. Domestic demand for traded goods tends to shift in the same direction as production (income) leaving us with an ambiguous net impact on the current account.

Finally it should be emphasized that the introduction of imported intermediate goods into the tradeables–nontradeables framework described in this chapter would have important consequences in our analysis of devaluation in section 4.2 above. Whereas exchange rate changes affected the notional supply for tradeables, it previously left the supply function for nontradeables unchanged. With imported inputs whose price is driven up by devaluation, the supply curve for nontradeables will shift upward to the left following devaluation. This will be particularly important in regimes (such as classical employment) where nontradeables output is supply-determined. Furthermore, the profit income from both sectors will be affected negatively by increased raw material prices brought by devaluation (*ceteris paribus*). This, in turn, will affect private-sector commodity demands.

Once the methodology described in this chapter has been mastered, the reader should have no problem exploring the sorts of extensions alluded to here.

6 Concluding Remarks

As the foregoing analysis has demonstrated, the impact effects of various policies (summarized in tables 4.1–4.5) often differ greatly

---

[21] In the Keynesian case firms producing nontraded goods are now rationed in both the goods market and the market for raw materials. Less severe rationing in the raw materials markets implies that firms will use less labor to produce the demand-constrained level of output.

depending on whether the prevailing economic environment is one characterized by classical or Keynesian unemployment. Thus, *it is critical to determine the prevailing type of supply–demand imbalance in the labor and output markets in order to make appropriate policy recommendations.*

Unfortunately, policymakers may often be uncertain about the nature of market imbalances, knowing only the direction in which target variables such as output and the balance of trade deviate from their desired levels. In such circumstances, the *a priori* assignment of policy instruments to targets may be necessary. Tables 4.1–4.5 provide useful information in this regard. A government expenditure increase is seen to cause an unambiguous worsening of the trade balance. Its effect on output may either be positive or zero, but never negative. *A priori*, the effects of real wage rate changes are indeterminate. It appears, therefore, that fiscal policy is a somewhat more precise tool than real wage rate changes: policymakers face little uncertainty about the direction of fiscal policy effects on various variables although their magnitudes are uncertain. The indeterminacy of the effects of real wage rate changes suggest that such instruments should probably be employed infrequently if the objective is to influence domestic output or the trade account.

5

Macroeconomic Stabilisation Policies: Fixed versus Flexible Exchange Rates*

1 Introduction

The extension of the disequilibrium macroeconomics literature to open economies has proved to be extremely useful for analyzing employment, output, and balance-of-trade effects of aggregate demand management, trade, and wage–price policies. As we have seen in chapters 3 and 4 (see also Dixit, 1978; Cuddington, 1980, 1981; Johansson and Löfgren, 1980; Neary, 1980; Steigum, 1980), these writings not only provide a more complete description of Keynesian unemployment, they also enable the analysis of other types of quantity-rationed equilibria when prices fail to adjust instantaneously to clear goods and factor markets.

To date, most fix-price rationing models of open economies suffer from the shortcoming that money is the only asset. Yet, as Muell-bauer and Portes (1978, p. 788) point out, "Even without a market for financial assets, the structure of this class of models is in some respects more complex than that of IS–LM." Their remark pertained to closed economies but seems equally appropriate in the open-economy context. With money as the only financial asset, it is impossible to carefully distinguish monetary and fiscal policies. Consequently, the effects of open market operations and alternative methods of financing fiscal deficits cannot be investigated separately.

In open-economy models the absence of nonmoney financial assets has further implications: the treatment of flexible exchange rate regimes is made somewhat artificial because the exchange rate must adjust to continuously balance the *trade* account rather than

* This chapter is based on Cuddington (1983). It was written while he was a Visiting Research Fellow at the Institute for International Economic Studies, Stockholm.

the sum of the current and capital accounts (see, e.g., Chan, 1978; Dixit and Norman, 1980; Johansson and Löfgren, 1980; Grossman *et al.*, 1982). This implies, according to well-known accounting identities, that national income must equal expenditure each and every period, i.e., net foreign borrowing is zero. Because the constraint that the trade balance continually equal zero is not imposed when analyzing fixed exchange rates, the implicit treatment of the country's intertemporal budget constraint differs between the two regimes. This is inappropriate. A legitimate comparison of the two exchange rate regimes must be based on a symmetric treatment of foreign borrowing opportunities, as Helpman and Razin (1979) have stressed.

Unfortunately, it is a difficult task to integrate multiple asset holdings into a rigorous microtheoretic framework in a way that accurately captures both the intertemporal decision-making process giving rise to consumption and asset demands and the role of money in facilitating transactions (by eliminating the inefficiencies of barter). Disequilibrium theory typically assumes a *monetary economy* where all goods and factors are exchanged for money but are not bartered for each other. In fact the coordination failures that lead to market disequilibrium are often attributed to an assumed inability (or costliness) of carrying out direct barter transactions. What the existing models lack is a distinction between "money," which facilitiates trading, from general stores of value, monetary or nonmonetary. This is because the models contain only a single asset, "money," which is therefore forced to play both roles.

In an effort to embed the insights of fix-price quantity-rationing models in a more conventional and realistic macroeconomic framework, this chapter attempts to treat one simple financial market setup, namely the *perfect capital mobility* case for a small open economy (where the interest rate is exogenously fixed at the world level) in temporary equilibrium. A *cash-in-advance* specification of money demand is employed where money *must* be used in carrying out all expenditures; barter transactions are prohibited. In so doing it employs the tradeables–nontradeables model of chapter 4, which under the Keynesian unemployment regime is closely related to the well-known Mundell–Fleming (M–F) model. It goes beyond the M–F model, however, by explicitly specifying the effects of quantity rationing (i.e., across-market spillover effects) in a *two-sector* economy. This replacement of the conventional assumption that the country specializes in the production of a single internationally differentiated good ("domestic output") with the assumption of two domestic production sectors (either tradeables–nontradeables or exportables–importables) increases the richness of the M–F model considerably.[1]

The model is used to explicitly compare the short-run effects on output and the exchange rate of money as well as bond-financed increases in government spending. Finally, other "disequilibrium" regimes not considered in the M–F era can be analyzed. This is demonstrated here by examining the case of classical unemployment. Other regimes alluded to in earlier chapters (such as repressed inflation, underconsumption, and mixed cases) will not be discussed so as to avoid being unduly taxonomic and keep the chapter to manageable proportions.

2   The Model

2.1   The Production Sectors

Following chapter 4, this chapter assumes two production sectors: tradeables and nontradeables. The price of composite tradeable good is fixed in foreign-currency units for the small country under consideration. Assuming the "law of one price" holds, the domestic-currency price of the tradeable good can be taken to be equal to $p_t = ep_t^*$. Furthermore, the small-country assumption will be taken to imply that domestic tradeable-goods producers never face a sales constraint. Hence, they adjust their demand for labor, the sole variable factor, so as to maximize profits. This gives rise to the usual tradeable goods supply function and associated labor demand in terms of the product wage w/p_t:

$$Y_t = Y_t(w, p_t), \qquad \frac{\partial Y_t}{\partial w} < 0, \qquad \frac{\partial Y_t}{\partial p_t} > 0, \tag{5.1}$$

$$L_t = L_t(w, p_t), \qquad \frac{\partial L_t}{\partial w} < 0, \qquad \frac{\partial L_t}{\partial p_t} > 0. \tag{5.2}$$

Here w is the fixed nominal wage paid to workers. As we discuss only the effects of increasing wages simultaneously in both sectors, it is innocuous, but simplifies notation, to arbitrarily assume that wages are fixed at the *same* level in the tradeables and nontradeables industries.[2]

---

[1] Neary (1980) and Grossman *et al.* (1982), for example, show that the inclusion of nontradeables provides interesting changes in the results from a one-good model even when money is the only asset. See chapter 4.

[2] It might, of course, be interesting to analyze the effects of sector-specific wage policies, but this is not pursued here.

In this chapter, only unemployment (Keynesian and classical) regimes are considered, so firms never face rationing in the labor market. Furthermore, all output is perishable and capital investment is ignored so that firms' decisions involve no intertemporal considerations.

The second sector produces a nontradeable output whose price p_n is fixed in domestic currency. Depending on the level of demand, nontradeable producers may or may not be able to sell the level of output that maximizes profits given p_n and w. In the absence of a sales (or, equivalently, output) constraint, the supply and labor demand functions are analogous to those in the tradeables sector:

$$Y_n = Y_n(w, p_n), \qquad \frac{\partial Y_n}{\partial w} < 0, \qquad \frac{\partial Y_n}{\partial p_n} > 0, \qquad (5.3)$$

$$L_n = L_n(w, p_n), \qquad \frac{\partial L_n}{\partial w} < 0, \qquad \frac{\partial L_n}{\partial p_n} > 0. \qquad (5.4)$$

If nontradeable producers face a sales constraint $\bar{Y}_n$ for their output, on the other hand, labor demand is found by inverting the production function. The *effective* labor demand $\tilde{L}_n$ depends positively on the sales constraint $\bar{Y}_n$ and lies unambiguously below profit-maximizing labor demand as long as the sales constraint is binding:

$$\tilde{L}_n = \tilde{L}_n(\bar{Y}_n), \qquad \frac{\partial \tilde{L}_n}{\partial \bar{Y}_n} > 0. \qquad (5.5)$$

Note that a bar over a variable denotes a quantity constraint, whereas a tilde ($\sim$) indicates the effective demand in the labor market when subject to a quantity constraint in the goods market.

Given the sectoral outputs, national income is defined as:

$$Y = p_n Y_n(w, p_n) + p_t Y_t(w, p_t) \qquad (5.6)$$

in the absence of sales constraints (as in the classical unemployment regime below), and as:

$$\bar{Y} = p_n \bar{Y}_n + p_t Y_t(w, p_t) \qquad (5.7)$$

when there is a nontradeables sales constraint (cf., Keynesian unemployment below).

2.2   The Household Sector

Although firms are assumed to have a single-period decision-making horizon, an intertemporal specification of households' utility maximization is at least implicit. The consumer choice problem has already been discussed in detail in chapters 3 and 4. With our earlier assumption that profit income, as well as labor income, is distributed to households in the current period, all income can be lumped together in the commodity demand functions. This symmetric treatment of wage and profit income in the model is a time-honored practice in simple macroeconomic models, including the Mundell–Fleming model elaborated upon and extended here.

In the presence of quantitative restrictions in the labor market (only), consumers' utility maximization gives rise to the effective demand functions:

$$\hat{D}_n = D_n(\overset{+}{\bar{p}_t}, \bar{p}_n, \overset{+}{\bar{Y}} + W; \theta), \tag{5.8}$$

$$\hat{D}_t = D_t(\bar{p}_t, \overset{+}{\bar{p}_n}, \overset{+}{\bar{Y}} + W; \theta), \tag{5.9}$$

where Y is total income, $Y = w\bar{L} + \pi$, and W is beginning-of-period wealth net of current taxes. The assumption that current period tradeable and nontradeable goods are substitutes has been used to sign $\partial\hat{D}_n/\partial p_t$. θ has been included as an argument of the demand functions to emphasize that expectations about future prices and future quantity constraints are being held constant, although it will subsequently be omitted to simplify notation.[3] The interest rate, which is fixed at the world level throughout, will also be suppressed throughout.

In addition to the effective demand functions in (5.8)–(5.9), utility maximization also yields the derived end-of-period wealth – reflecting the demand for future consumption – and hence a saving function:

$$\hat{S} = \hat{W}'(\bar{p}_t, \bar{p}_n, \overset{+}{\bar{Y}} + W) - W, \tag{5.10}$$

where $0 < \partial\hat{S}/\partial Y < 1$. Assumptions regarding the expenditure function below will be sufficient to guarantee that both $\partial\hat{S}/\partial p_t$ and $\partial\hat{S}/\partial p_n$ are negative.

Rationing on the labor market in the presence of unemployment has no direct effect on consumption demands – just its effect through income – due to our assumption that labor is weakly separable in the

---

[3] As chapter 3 pointed out, the assumption of fixed point expectations regarding the future exchange rate p_t' could be replaced by the assumption of regressive expectations if all consumption goods – present and future – were gross substitutes. Unfortunately, gross substitutability is incompatible with the assumptions on the price derivatives of the saving and expenditure functions (5.10) and (5.13) needed to obtain the usual Mundell–Fleming results. Current-period goods are gross substitutes for each other but not for future consumption. See footnote 8 later.

households' utility function. The demand for tradeable goods, however, will be affected by the quantity constraint arising when there is excess demand in the nontradeables market. When faced with a constraint $\bar{D}_n$ on nontradeables demand in addition to the employment constraint (denoted by double tilde as in chapter 4), tradeables demand and desired wealth accumulation equal:

$$\tilde{D}_t = \tilde{D}_t(\bar{p}_t, \overset{+}{Y} + W - p_n\bar{D}_n), \tag{5.11}$$

$$\tilde{S} = \tilde{W}'(p_t, Y + W - p_n\bar{D}_n) - W. \tag{5.12}$$

In general, an exogenous increase in the available quantity of the rationed nontradeable good has two effects on the demand for tradeables. First, it reduces discretionary income, i.e., the income left over for tradeable goods as well as future consumption after paying for the available quantity of nontradeables. This tends to reduce the demand for unrationed goods. Second, it has a direct effect via the substitutability between the (rationed) nontradeable good and the tradeable good.

The specification of the effective demand equations in (5.11) and (5.12) again assumes that changes in the rationed quantity of nontradables enters *only* via its effect on discretionary income. As discussed in chapters 3 and 4 this ignores the effect due to gross quantity-constrained substitutability or complementarity among goods.

2.3   Households' Financial Asset Holdings

The fix-price quantity-rationing literature has not yet been extended to consider the allocation of wealth between money and other financial assets in a completely satisfactory microtheoretic way. Hool (1980) included both money and bonds in the utility function in an initial attempt to distinguish monetary and fiscal policies in closed-economy temporary equilibrium.[4] The relationship between asset demands and future consumption and the role of money in reducing transactions costs are not, however, made explicit. Rather than waiting for the theoretical solution to these current research problems in monetary economics, the financial sector in this chapter will use the "cash-in-advance" specification of money demand suggested by Clower (1967). A similar approach has recently been employed by Helpman (1981) and Persson (1982a, 1982b).

---

[4] The inclusion of money and nonmonetary assets in the utility function has also been exploited in a thoughtful book by Casson (1981). Kähkönen (1982) includes currency and bank deposits in the utility function in a recent University of Michigan dissertation (published by the Helsinki School of Economics) on credit rationing in general disequilibrium.

Instead of assuming that all wealth takes the form of money holdings as almost all of the temporary equilibrium literature has done, it will be assumed that domestic residents (including the government) can costlessly adjust the composition of their beginning-of-period wealth W, choosing between money and (positive or negative) holdings of an internationally traded bond. The latter's interest rate is exogenously fixed at the world level for the small country under consideration. Following Clower, all current consumption demands by both the government and the private sector *must* be carried out using money. Money is demanded solely for facilitating transactions, not as a store of value, given that money and bonds can be costlessly and immediately exchanged at the beginning of each period before commodity demands are effected.[5] Hence beginning-of-period money demand equals real expenditure; the velocity of circulation is, in effect, fixed at unity by this assumption about the transaction technology. No quantity rationing ever occurs in the financial markets, an assumption that is analogous to the small-country assumption concerning the tradeable goods market.

Using (5.8) and (5.9), expenditure by households and the government[6] in the case where households face no demand constraints equals:

$$\hat{Z} = p_n \hat{D}_n(p_t, p_n, Y + W) + p_n G_n + p_t \hat{D}_t(p_t, p_n, Y + W). \quad (5.13)$$

In what follows, we assume that (current-period) tradeables and nontradeables are substitutes and that the price elasticity of the demand for tradeables is less than unity (in absolute value). These assumptions (are stronger than necessary to) insure that:

$$\frac{\partial \hat{Z}}{\partial p_t} = p_n \frac{\partial \hat{D}_n}{\partial p_t} + \hat{D}_t \left(1 + \frac{p_t}{\hat{D}_t} \frac{\partial \hat{D}_t}{\partial p_n}\right) > 0,$$

$$\frac{\partial \hat{Z}}{\partial p_n} = p_t \frac{\partial \hat{D}_t}{\partial p_n} + \hat{D}_n \left(1 + \frac{p_n}{\hat{D}_n} \frac{\partial \hat{D}_n}{\partial p_n}\right) > 0. \quad (5.14)$$

---

[5] Technically, the constraint that money demand (M) equal expenditure (Z) is added to the representative consumer's utility-maximization problem. Note that money does not yield utility directly. Given our assumption of costless portfolio adjustment at the beginning of each period, money demand is determined recursively after expenditure decisions are made. The implied bond demand equals $W_0 - M$ (...) at the beginning of the period and $W_0 - M$ (...) $+ Y$ at the end of the (first) period. Given that $M = Z$, end-of-period wealth could also be expressed as W plus the trade surplus $Y - Z$.

[6] In what follows, fiscal policy is defined as increased government spending on the *nontradeable* good. It is straightforward, given the small-country assumption, to consider government expenditure on tradeable goods. We do not consider this type of fiscal policy here, however. See chapter 4.

This implies that nominal expenditure rises with a depreciation of the domestic currency.[7] Parenthetically, $\partial \hat{Z}/\partial p_i > 0$ implies that $\partial \hat{S}/\partial p_i < 0$ in (5.10) as stated above.

Given the expenditure function in (5.13) and the assumption that money demand (in terms of nontradeables) just equals upcoming expenditure, it is clear that money demand depends positively on p_n, the exchange rate p_t, income and government spending:[8]

$$\hat{M} = \hat{M}(\overset{+}{p_t}, \overset{+}{p_n}, \overset{+}{Y} + W, \overset{+}{G_n}). \tag{5.15}$$

As mentioned above, it is assumed that in a monetary (as opposed to barter) economy the government requires domestic money balances for transactions purposes just like the private sector does. We return to this point below when discussing the different effects of money and bond-financed government spending.

In the case where households face a quantity constraint on non-tradeables demand, national expenditure equals:

$$\tilde{Z} = p_n \bar{D}_n + p_n G_n + p_t \tilde{D}_t(p_t, Y + W - p_n \bar{D}_n). \tag{5.16}$$

The condition that the demand for tradeables is price-inelastic is sufficient (in fact, in this case, necessary) to insure that:

$$\frac{\partial \tilde{Z}}{\partial p_t} = \tilde{D}_t \left(1 + \frac{p_t}{\tilde{D}_t} \frac{\partial \tilde{D}_t}{\partial p_t}\right) > 0. \tag{5.17a}$$

Note also that:

$$\frac{\partial \tilde{Z}}{\partial p_n} = \left(1 - p_t \frac{\partial \tilde{D}_t}{\partial Y}\right) \bar{D}_n + G_n > 0, \tag{5.17b}$$

$$\frac{\partial \tilde{Z}}{\partial \bar{D}_n} = p_n \left(1 - p_t \frac{\partial \tilde{D}_t}{\partial Y}\right) > 0. \tag{5.17c}$$

The assumption that money demand at the beginning of the period

---

[7] It is noteworthy that $\partial \hat{Z}/\partial p_t$ would be negative not positive under our earlier working assumptions; in chapters 3 and 4 where all consumption goods, present and future, were gross substitutes. In that case, total expenditure on future consumption (current saving) would rise following an increase in the current (but not future) price of tradeable goods. This would make $\partial S/\partial p_t$ *positive*.

[8] It might be pointed out that $\partial \hat{M}/\partial p_t$ is also positive in Dornbusch's (1976a) exchange rate dynamics model. There, this effect is due to the fact that p_t is raised above its long-run level thereby creating expectations of subsequent appreciation of the domestic currency. Because changes in p_t and p_n in the present model are changes in current prices, holding future prices constant, the justification for $\partial \hat{M}/\partial p_t > 0$ here is quite similar in flavor (though not identical) to that in Dornbusch. The specification of money demand is critical in the discussion of the flexible exchange rate case; the appendix discusses the robustness of the analysis to alternative specifications.

just equals upcoming expenditure in (5.16), therefore, implies that it can be written:

$$\tilde{M} = \tilde{M}(\overset{+}{p_t}, \overset{+}{p_n}, \overset{+}{Y} + W, \overset{\pm}{\bar{D}_n}, \overset{+}{G_n}) \tag{5.18}$$

for the case where households are rationed in the nontradeable goods market. Again G_n is included in the aggregate money demand function to reflect government demand for transactions balances in order to carry out its current expenditure plans.

2.4 Monetary Equilibrium under Perfect Capital Mobility

The mechanism whereby monetary equilibrium is attained in open economies differs greatly depending on the exchange rate regime. Under fixed exchange rates, the central bank must buy or sell foreign exchange reserves in exchange for domestic money whenever there is market pressure that would move the exchange rate up or down from its target level. In the perfect capital mobility case, this makes it impossible for the central bank to independently control the money supply (by open market operations, for example). The decision to peg the exchange rate renders the money supply M^s endogenous. The central bank must accommodate completely private money demand.

With flexible exchange rates, on the other hand, the central bank has no obligation to adjust the domestic money supply to keep the exchange rate constant. Hence the money supply is now exogenous. Money market equilibrium and goods market equilibrium are achieved simultaneously by adjustment in income and the exchange rate, as will be discussed below. Money market equilibrium in the Keynesian unemployment case (where households are unconstrained in the goods markets) equals:

$$M^s = \hat{M}(p_t, p_n, Y + W, G_n). \tag{5.19}$$

Under classical unemployment, the relevant condition is:

$$M^s = \tilde{M}(p_t, p_n, Y + W, \bar{D}_n, G_n). \tag{5.20}$$

3 Keynesian and Classical Unemployment Regimes

Having described the quantity-constrained behavior of domestic producers and consumers, the two temporary-equilibrium regimes with unemployment can now be characterized. Emphasis will be placed on flexible exchange rates, as previous analyses have been unable to treat this case adequately. Comparing the resulting equilibrium with earlier characterizations for the fixed exchange rate case is straightforward. As long as the interest rate is fixed by invoking the perfect capital mobility assumption, the fixed exchange rate version of the present model is much like that in chapter 4. In discussing wage and fiscal policies in sections 5 and 6 below, the fixed and flexible exchange rate cases are explicitly compared.

3.1   *Keynesian Unemployment*

Keynesian unemployment is characterized by a deficiency in domestic demand for nontradeables at the prevailing nontradeables price p_n, wage rate w, and temporary-equilibrium exchange rate p_t. Domestic producers limit nontradeables production to the level required to meet total domestic demand:

$$\bar{Y}_n = \hat{D}_n(\overset{+}{p}_t, \bar{p}_n, \overset{+}{\bar{Y}} + W) + G_n, \tag{5.21}$$

where G_n is expenditure on nontradeables by the government. Production of tradeables is always at the unconstrained profit-maximizing level given in (5.1). Substituting (5.21) into (5.7) yields an expression for the Keynesian equilibrium level of national income:

$$\bar{Y} = p_n\hat{D}_n(p_t, p_n, \bar{Y} + W) + p_nG_n + p_tY_t(w, p_t). \tag{5.22}$$

Under *fixed* exchange rates (5.22) alone determines national income. Under flexible exchange rates, however, income and the exchange rate must be simultaneously determined in the goods market (5.22) and the money market (5.19). It is useful to represent equilibrium graphically in (Y, p_t) space to emphasize the close similarity of the present model to the Mundell–Fleming model (figure 5.1). Noting that:

$$\frac{d\bar{Y}}{dp_t} = \left(\frac{1}{1 - p_n(\partial\hat{D}_n/\partial Y)}\right)\left(p_n\frac{\partial\hat{D}_n}{\partial p_t} + p_t\frac{\partial Y_t}{\partial p_t} + Y_t\right) > 0, \tag{5.23}$$

it is clear that the Keynesian goods-market equilibrium locus G_kG_k is upward sloping to the right in (Y, p_t) space, as shown in figure 5.1.

The Keynesian money-market equilibrium locus M_kM_k for the flexible exchange rate case, defined by equating the exogenous money supply to money demand in equation (5.19), is also graphed in figure 5.1. It has a negative slope as long as $\partial\hat{M}/\partial p_t > 0$ and $\partial\hat{M}/\partial Y > 0$ (as discussed above).

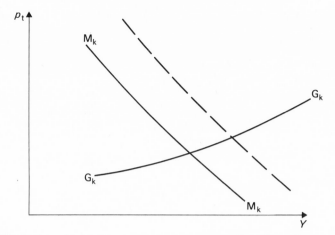

FIGURE 5.1   Keynesian unemployment under flexible exchange rates

3.2   *Classical Unemployment*

Classical unemployment is defined as a situation where the real product wage in the nontradeables sector is too high, so that the profit-maximizing level of output falls short of domestic demand at prevailing wages and prices (w, p_n, p_t):

$$Y_n(w, p_n) < \hat{D}_n(p_t, p_n, Y + W) + G_n. \tag{5.24}$$

Hence households' demand is constrained to the level of output supplied by producers minus that quantity purchased by the government (whose demand is assumed to take priority):

$$\bar{D}_n \equiv Y_n(w, p_n) - G_n. \tag{5.25}$$

National income is just the value of nontradeables and tradeables production:

$$Y = p_n Y_n(w, p_n) + p_t Y_t(w, p_t). \tag{5.26}$$

Differentiating with respect to the exchange rate, it is seen that p_t and Y are again positively related so that the $G_c G_c$ locus is positively sloped in figure 5.2:

$$\frac{dY}{dp_t} = p_t \frac{\partial Y_t}{\partial p_t} + Y_t > 0. \tag{5.27}$$

The money market locus $M_c M_c$, which equates money supply to money demand under flexible exchange rates, is given by equation

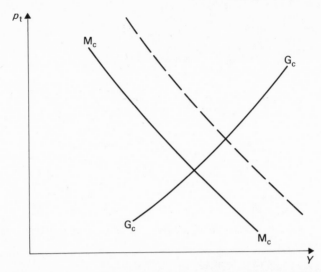

FIGURE 5.2   Classical unemployment under flexible exchange rates

(5.20) when households face a quantity constraint on nontradeables demand, as they do under classical unemployment.

Although figures 5.1 and 5.2 portraying the Keynesian and classical unemployment cases, respectively, are superficially similar, the effects of various policies under the two regimes may differ significantly. This is particularly true for fiscal policy and depends on the method of finance, as we shall see below. The effects of wage and monetary policies, in contrast, differ less between the two unemployment regimes.

For easy reference, the equations that characterize the Keynesian and classical unemployment regimes are summarized in table 5.1. These equations can be used to verify the comparative static results obtained in the remainder of the chapter.

4   Monetary Policy under Flexible Exchange Rates

The effects of an expansionary open-market operation on the exchange rate and national income are easily determined using figures 5.1 and 5.2. Under both Keynesian and classical unemployment, monetary expansion causes the exchange rate p_t to rise (depreciate). The MM

TABLE 5.1   Summary of equations for the Keynesian and
classical unemployment regimes

The Keynesian unemployment regime

$$\bar{Y}_n = \hat{D}_n(p_t, p_n, \bar{Y} + W) + G_n$$
$$Y_t = Y_t(w, p_t)$$
$$\bar{Y} = p_n\hat{D}_n(p_t, p_n, \bar{Y} + W) + p_nG_n + p_tY_t(w, p_t)$$
$$M^s = \hat{M}(p_t, p_n, \bar{Y} + W, G_n)$$
$$BT = Y_t(w, p_t) - \hat{D}_t(p_t, p_n, \bar{Y} + W)$$

The classical unemployment regime;

$$Y_n = Y_n(w, p_n)$$
$$Y_t = Y_t(w, p_t)$$
$$Y = p_nY_n(w, p_n) + p_tY_t(w, p_t)$$
$$\bar{D}_n = Y_n(w, p) - G_n$$
$$M^s = \tilde{M}(p_t, p_n, Y + W, \bar{D}_n, G_n)$$
$$BT = Y_t(w, p_t) - \tilde{D}_t(p_t, Y + W - p_n\bar{D}_n).$$

Notes
    $\partial\hat{M}/\partial G_n$ and $\partial\tilde{M}/\partial G_n$ are positive when government spending is bond- or tax-financed but equal the change in M^s in the case of money-financed spending.
    Under fixed exchange rates, the money supply M^s is endogenous and is recursively determined under either unemployment regime. Under flexible rates, M^s is exogenous while p_t and Y are determined simultaneously by the model.

locus shifts upward to the right.[9] This directly increases the profitability of production in the tradeable goods industry, causing national income to rise.

The effect on nontradeables production, however, differs under the two unemployment regimes. Under Keynesian unemployment, $\bar{Y}_n$ is determined by the level of aggregate demand for nontradeables (5.21). Demand increases following the exchange rate depreciation due to the substitution effect as well as the income effect as tradeable output expands. The ensuing demand-induced stimulation to nontradeables production sets in motion the usual multiplier process.

---

[9] Given the severity of the perfect capital mobility assumption, the open-market operation must technically involve the purchase of bonds from *foreigners*. Domestic residents have no incentive to alter their portfolios, given that the world interest rate is unaffected by the open-market operations of the small country. Having sold bonds in exchange for domestic money, foreigners must turn around and sell unwanted domestic money in the foreign exchange market. This causes the domestic currency to depreciate. (Whether foreigners exchange all or just part of their domestic money for foreign money depends on the assumption regarding currency of invoicing; see the appendix for details.)

Hence under Keynesian unemployment, monetary expansion stimulates both the tradeables and nontradeable sectors.

In the presence of classical unemployment, in contrast, nontradeables output is at the unconstrained profit-maximizing level in (5.3). Exchange rate depreciation has no effect. Monetary expansion, therefore, stimulates only the tradeables industry in this case.

The effects of monetary expansion are summarized in table 5.2. Two things should be noted. First, the balance-of-trade effects are ambiguous in both regimes due to the conflict between the substitution effect (from exchange rate depreciation) and income effect on domestic demand for tradeables goods. Second, the effects of monetary policy are expansionary regardless of whether unemployment is Keynesian or classical in nature. Only the effect on nontradeables production differs (qualitatively) between regimes.

5   Wage Policy: Fixed versus Flexible Exchange Rates

The contractionary effects of a policy-induced rise in the nominal wage are qualitatively the same under Keynesian and classical unemployment for countries with fixed exchange rates. Wage policy under flexible rates, however, is more complicated due to the resulting exchange rate depreciation and, in the classical unemployment case, the tightening of the nontradeable good rationing constraint $\bar{D}_n$. The details follow.

5.1   *Fixed Exchange Rates*

Keynesian unemployment

We first review the fixed exchange rate case to facilitate ease of comparison between the fixed exchange rate case and the flexible exchange rate case to follow. Under both unemployment regimes, a wage increase directly reduces profit-maximizing output of tradeable goods. In the Keynesian unemployment case this causes nontrade-

TABLE 5.2   Monetary expansion under flexible exchange rates

	Y_n	Y_t	y	p_t	BT
Keynesian unemployment	+	+	+	+	?
Classical unemployment	0	+	+	+	?

ables production, which is demand-determined, to fall also (via the usual multiplier process):[10]

$$\frac{d\bar{Y}_n}{dw} = \frac{\partial \hat{D}_n}{\partial Y}\left(\frac{1}{1-p_n(\partial \hat{D}_n/\partial Y)}\right)p_t\frac{\partial Y_t}{\partial w} < 0. \qquad (5.28)$$

Both sectors contract so national income unambiguously falls:

$$\frac{d\bar{Y}}{dw} = p_n\frac{d\bar{Y}_n}{dw} + p_t\frac{\partial Y_t}{\partial w} = \left(\frac{1}{1-p_n(\partial \hat{D}_n/\partial Y)}\right)p_t\frac{\partial Y_t}{\partial w} < 0. \qquad (5.29)$$

In contrast to simple one-good models, one might wonder whether the balance-of-trade effect is uncertain in the two-sector context: Is the drop in domestic demand for tradeables, which is brought about by the fall in national income (5.29), greater or less than the drop in domestic production of tradeable goods? It can be shown that the fall in tradeables production is greater than the induced decline in domestic demand for tradeables. Differentiate the trade balance equation:

$$\frac{dBT}{dw} = \frac{\partial Y_t}{\partial w} - \frac{\partial \hat{D}_t}{\partial Y}\left(p_n\frac{d\bar{Y}_n}{dw} + p_t\frac{\partial Y_t}{\partial w}\right). \qquad (5.30)$$

Substituting (5.28) into (5.30) and using the adding-up constraint:

$$p_n\frac{\partial \hat{D}_n}{\partial Y} + p_t\frac{\partial \hat{D}_t}{\partial Y} + \frac{\partial \hat{S}}{\partial Y} = 1, \qquad (5.31)$$

we find that:

$$\frac{dBT}{dw} = \frac{\partial \hat{S}}{\partial Y}\left(\frac{1}{1-p_n(\partial \hat{D}_n/\partial Y)}\right)\frac{\partial Y_t}{\partial w} < 0. \qquad (5.32)$$

That is, the trade balance unambiguously deteriorates following a wage increase under Keynesian unemployment.

The effects of a wage increase in a fixed exchange rate Keynesian unemployment regime are summarized in table 5.3.

Classical unemployment
The output effects in the classical unemployment case are straight-forward. The wage increase reduces the unconstrained profit-

---

[10] This unambiguous decline in nontradeables output following a wage hike differs from the conclusion in Neary (1980), because he assumes profits are *not* consumed in the current period.

TABLE 5.3   Wage policy

	Y_n	Y_t	Y	p_t	BT
Keynesian unemployment					
Fixed exchange rate	−	−	−	0	−
Flexible exchange rate	?	−	−	+	?
Classical unemployment					
Fixed exchange rate	−	−	−	0	−[a]
Flexible exchange rate	−	?	?	+	?

[a] Weak separability is a sufficient condition to get a negative sign.

maximizing output in both sectors:

$$\frac{dY}{dw} = p_n \frac{\partial Y_n}{\partial w} + p_t \frac{\partial Y_t}{\partial w} < 0. \tag{5.33}$$

As nontradeables output falls, the rationing of this good experienced by the private sector (which characterizes classical unemployment) becomes more severe. From (5.25):

$$\frac{d\bar{D}_n}{dw} = \frac{\partial Y_n}{\partial w} < 0. \tag{5.34}$$

The cross-market spillover effect due to rationing tends to raise the demand for tradeable goods while the fall in income reduces it. It is easy to see (given our weak separability assumption) that the income effect dominates. Substituting the expression for the rationed supply of nontradeables (5.25) directly into the effective demand function for tradeables (5.11) yields:

$$\tilde{D}_t = \tilde{D}_t(p_t, Y + W - p_n \bar{D}_n) = \tilde{D}_t(p_t, p_t Y_t + W + p_n G_n). \tag{5.11'}$$

Hence, domestic demand for tradeables unambiguously falls following the wage increase:

$$\frac{d\tilde{D}_t}{dw} = \frac{\partial \tilde{D}_t}{\partial Y} \left(p_t \frac{\partial Y_t}{\partial w} \right) < 0 \tag{5.35}$$

due to the decline in tradeables production. The reduced income from nontradeable production just nets out against the effect of more severe nontradeables rationing on tradeables demand ($\partial \tilde{D}_t / \partial \bar{D}_n < 0$).

Domestic demand for tradeables falls by only a fraction of the decline in tradeables production, provided the marginal propensity to consume is less than unity. Hence the trade balance necessarily worsens as wages are increased:

$$\frac{\mathrm{d}BT}{\mathrm{d}w} = \left(1 - p_t \frac{\partial \tilde{D}_t}{\partial Y}\right) \frac{\partial Y_t}{\partial w} < 0 \qquad (5.36)$$

when the economy is suffering from classical unemployment. The same conclusion was obtained in the Keynesian unemployment case.

Examining table 5.2, it is noteworthy that wage policy has the same qualitative effects under classical and Keynesian unemployment when the exchange rate is fixed. Consequently, the usefulness of this policy is not reduced by uncertainty about the *type* of unemployment prevailing in the economy. This is an advantage of wage policy under fixed exchange rates. Many policy predictions in the fix-price literature, in contrast, depend crucially on the particular type of non-market-clearing situation.

5.2   Flexible Exchange Rates

Keynesian unemployment
Under Keynesian unemployment, the effects of a wage hike are somewhat different when the exchange rate is flexible rather than fixed. Again, national income falls, but by a smaller amount due to the induced depreciation of the exchange rate: [11]

$$\frac{\mathrm{d}\bar{Y}}{\mathrm{d}w} = \frac{1}{\Delta} p_t \frac{\partial Y_t}{\partial w} < 0, \qquad (5.37)$$

where

$$\Delta \equiv \left(1 - p_n \frac{\partial \hat{D}_n}{\partial Y}\right) + \frac{\partial \hat{M}/\partial Y}{\partial \hat{M}/\partial p_t} \left(p_n \frac{\partial \hat{D}_n}{\partial p_t} + p_t \frac{\partial Y_t}{\partial p_t} + Y_t\right) > 0.$$

This result is obtained by totally differentiating the goods and money market equilibrium conditions (5.22) and (5.19).

The exchange rate depreciation only partially offsets the increase in wages (as the $G_k G_k$ shifts upward to the left). Hence it can be shown that tradeables production in (5.1) unambiguously falls, albeit by less than it would have under fixed exchange rates:

$$\frac{\mathrm{d}Y_t}{\mathrm{d}w} = \frac{1}{\Delta}\left[\left(1 - p_n \frac{\partial \hat{D}_n}{\partial Y}\right) + \frac{\partial \hat{M}/\partial Y}{\partial \hat{M}/\partial p_t}\left(p_n \frac{\partial \hat{D}_n}{\partial p_t} + Y_t\right)\right] \frac{\partial Y_t}{\partial w} < 0.$$

$$(5.38)$$

[11] In figure 5.1, the wage hike causes the $G_k G_k$ curve to shift to the left along an unchanged $M_k M_k$ schedule.

The term in square brackets is smaller than Δ but still positive, as can be confirmed by examining the definition of Δ above.

Nontradeables production, on the other hand, may rise or fall in a flexible exchange rate Keynesian unemployment situation. This is due to the conflict between the contractionary income effect (which was the only effect under fixed exchange rates) and the expansionary substitution effect of the induced exchange rate depreciation:

$$\frac{\mathrm{d}\bar{Y}_n}{\mathrm{d}w} = \left[\underset{(+)}{\frac{\partial \hat{D}_n}{\partial Y}} - \underset{(+)}{\frac{\partial \hat{D}_n}{\partial p_t}} \underset{(+)}{\frac{\partial \hat{M}/\partial Y}{\partial \hat{M}/\partial p_t}} \right] \underset{(-)}{\frac{\partial \bar{Y}}{\partial w}} \gtrless 0. \tag{5.39}$$

The balance-of-trade effect under flexible exchange rates is uncertain for similar reasons:

$$\frac{\mathrm{d}BT}{\mathrm{d}w} = \frac{1}{\Delta} \left[\underset{(+)}{\left(1 - p_n \frac{\partial \hat{D}_n}{\partial Y} - p_t \frac{\partial \hat{D}_t}{\partial Y}\right)} \right.$$

$$\left. + \underset{(+)}{\frac{\partial \hat{M}/\partial Y}{\partial \hat{M}/\partial p_t}} \left(p_n \underset{(-)}{\frac{\partial \hat{D}_t}{\partial p_t}} + p_t \underset{(+)}{\frac{\partial \hat{D}_n}{\partial p_t}} + \underset{(+)}{Y_t}\right) \right] \underset{(-)}{\frac{\partial Y_t}{\partial w}} \lessgtr 0. \tag{5.40}$$

These results are summarized in table 5.3.

Classical unemployment

The effects of a wage rise under flexible exchange rates with classical unemployment are fraught with uncertainty. It is easy to see why diagrammatically. Holding p_t constant in the fixed exchange rate case above, we showed that a wage increase lowers national income. The $G_c G_c$ curve in figure 5.2 shifts to the left. Under flexible exchange rates, however, the $M_c M_c$ curve will also shift due to the effect of worsening shortages of nontradeables $\bar{D}_n$. To elaborate, the wage increase reduces nontradeables (as well as tradeables) production, thereby reducing the rationed supply of the nontradeable good; recall (5.34).[12] Total expenditure and hence money demand (5.20) fall. The exchange rate must depreciate (that is, p_t must rise) at each level of income to keep the money market in equilibrium. So $M_c M_c$ must shift upward to the right.

The net effect on income of the upward shifts in the $G_c G_c$ and $M_c M_c$ is uncertain, although the exchange rate unambiguously

---

[12] In contrast, the effect of a wage increase in nontradeables production was indeterminate *a priori* under Keynesian unemployment with flexible exchange rates. Recall (5.39).

depreciates. The effect on national income can be found by totally differentiating the goods and money market equilibrium conditions (5.20) and (5.26) and solving for:

$$\frac{dY}{dw} = \frac{1}{\Delta'} \left[p_t \underbrace{\frac{\partial Y_t}{\partial w}}_{(-)} + \underbrace{\frac{\partial Y_n}{\partial w}}_{(+)} - \underbrace{\left(\frac{\partial \tilde{M}/\partial \bar{D}_n}{\partial \tilde{M}/\partial p_t} \right)}_{(+)} \left(p_t \frac{\partial Y_t}{\partial w} + Y_t \right) \underbrace{\frac{\partial Y_n}{\partial w}}_{(-)} \right] \gtrless 0,$$

(5.41)

where

$$\Delta' \equiv 1 + \frac{\partial \tilde{M}/\partial Y}{\partial \tilde{M}/\partial p_t} \left(p_t \frac{\partial Y_t}{\partial p_t} + Y_t \right) > 0.$$

This ambiguity is due to the possibility that production of tradeable goods *may* rise in spite of higher wages if the exchange rate depreciation is large enough. Consequently, total income Y may rise or fall under classical unemployment. The trade balance effect is, therefore, also indeterminate.

Examining table 5.3, it is clear that the effects of wage policy are much less certain when the type of unemployment is unknown if the country has a flexible – rather than fixed – exchange rate regime. Some policymakers, particularly those predisposed toward the use of wage policies, may interpret this as a reason for preferring fixed rather than flexible exchange rates. Other interpretations are, of course, possible!

6 Fiscal Policy

Fiscal policy's effect on output as well as its exchange rate effect vary depending on the method of fiscal finance and whether unemployment is Keynesian or classical in nature. Hence a correct diagnosis of the *cause* of unemployment is a prerequisite for appropriate policy recommendation. Whether the country has a fixed or flexible exchange rate is also crucial information, as a quick glance at table 5.3 will reveal.

6.1 *Fixed Exchange Rates*

The effects of fiscal policy under Keynesian and classical unemployment regimes with fixed exchange rates were discussed in chapter 4; see also Cuddington (1980) and Neary (1980). Hence they are only summarized briefly here and in table 5.4. The effects of fiscal expan-

TABLE 5.4   Fiscal policy

	Y_n	Y_t	Y	p_t	BT
Keynesian unemployment					
Fixed exchange rate	+	0	+	0	−
Flexible exchange rate					
Bond-financed spending	+	−	?	−	?
Money-financed spending	+	−	+	−	−
Classical unemployment					
Fixed exchange rate	0	0	0	0	−
Flexible exchange rate					
Bond-financed spending	0	−	−	−	?
Money-financed spending	0	+	+	+	?

sion on the goods market equilibrium loci will be noted to facilitate the discussion of the flexible exchange rate case that follows.

Production in the tradeable goods sector is determined by unconstrained profit maximization. Hence it is unaffected by aggregate demand management policy regardless of whether unemployment is Keynesian or classical as long as the exchange rate is fixed. Under classical unemployment this is also true for the nontradeables sector. Hence a fiscal expansion has no effect on national income and the position of the G_cG_c curve is unchanged. Regardless of whether the government expenditure is on tradeables or nontradeables, the trade balance deteriorates. In the case of government expenditure on nontradeables, this is due to the induced increase in private demand for tradeables as the rationing of nontradeables becomes more severe. We concentrate on government expenditure on nontradeables in what follows.

Under Keynesian unemployment with fixed exchange rates, increasing government expenditure on nontradeables raises aggregate demand. Accordingly, the G_kG_k curve shifts to the right. $\bar{Y}_n$ and Y rise through the usual multiplier process. Finally, the trade balance deteriorates due to the positive marginal propensity to consume tradeables, as is well known.

6.2   Bond-financed Fiscal Policy under Flexible Exchange Rates

The effects of fiscal policy under flexible exchange rates are dramatically different from those under fixed rates. Even the *direction* of the change in national income following a bond- (or tax-) financed increase in government expenditure on nontradeables differs between the Keynesian and classical unemployment regimes. The exchange rate appreciates under both regimes in the short run. Money-financed government spending, on the other hand, causes different sectoral output effects and different exchange rate effects under the two regimes.

To analyze fiscal policy under flexible exchange rates in the present model, it is necessary to recall that money demand depends on government as well as household expenditure. In both the classical and Keynesian unemployment cases, bond-financed government expenditure must be accompanied by an appreciation of the exchange rate at each level of income to maintain money market equilibrium. The mechanism is as follows. The government sells bonds in the world market in exchange for foreign money. Because it needs domestic money for carrying out its expenditure plans, it sells this foreign money for domestic money in the foreign exchange market. The domestic currency must appreciate (i.e., p_t falls) to clear the market. An increase in G_n therefore causes the MM curve in (5.19) or (5.20) to shift downward to the left. This shift in the MM curve must be combined with the effect on the GG curve described above under the fixed exchange rate cases to determine fiscal policy's effects under classical and Keynesian unemployment when the exchange rate is flexible.

Classical unemployment

Under classical unemployment, nontradeables production is determined solely by unconstrained profit maximization at the prevailing product wage w/p_n. Hence it is unaffected by increased government demand under flexible rates just as it was under fixed rates; the $G_c G_c$ curve does not shift.[13] As the government demands more of the nontraded good, however, the rationing faced by the private sector becomes more severe. Total private expenditure falls, but by a smaller amount than government spending rises. Hence, aggregate spending and the demand for money increases.[14] At each level of national income, the exchange rate must appreciate to maintain money market equilibrium. The $M_c M_c$ curve in figure 5.2 shifts to the left.

[13] If imported intermediate goods were used in nontradeables production, output would *fall*. $G_c G_c$ would shift to the left.
[14] Differentiate (5.16) and using (5.17c) to confirm this.

Although government spending on nontradeables has no direct effect on domestic production of nontradeables, the exchange rate appreciation that it causes reduces the profit-maximizing level of output in the *tradeable* goods industry. Consequently national income *falls* following the fiscal expansion:

$$\frac{dY}{dG_n} = -\left(p_t\frac{\partial Y_t}{\partial p_t} + Y_t\right)\frac{\partial \tilde{M}}{\partial G_n}\Big/\left[\frac{\partial \tilde{M}}{\partial p_t} + \frac{\partial \tilde{M}}{\partial Y}\left(p_t\frac{\partial Y_t}{\partial p_t} + \frac{Y_t}{p}\right)\right] < 0.$$

(5.42)

This result (found by differentiating (5.20) and (5.26)) stands in contrast to the Keynesian case below where national income may rise or fall.

The trade balance effect under classical unemployment is indeterminate due to the conflicting influences of exchange rate appreciation and falling income on the domestic demand for tradeables.

Keynesian unemployment

Under Keynesian unemployment, a bond-financed increase in government expenditure on nontradeables may cause either a rise or fall in national income. Employing figure 5.1, the G_kG_k shifts to the right, as we know from the Mundell–Fleming model. Unlike the M–F model where the MM is vertical and unaffected by changes in government spending, however, the M_kM_k curve also shifts (to the left) as the rise in G_n increases the transactions demand for money. The exchange rate must appreciate to maintain financial market equilibrium. If we make the assumption that the transactions elasticity of money demand (empirically around one) is less than the government expenditure multiplier when p_t is held constant (approximately two), M_kM_k would shift to the left by less than G_kG_k shifts to the right. The net effect is then a rise in national income and an appreciation of the exchange rate. If this condition is not satisfied, national income may fall. In the M–F model, in contrast, fiscal expansion under a flexible exchange rate regime has no effect on national output.

The sectoral effects are interesting. The increased government demand for nontradeables brings about the expected increase in $\overline{Y}_n$. Tradeables production, however, *falls* as the exchange rate appreciates. Hence there is a conflict of interest between the two sectors, which may make fiscal expansion politically unpalatable.

The effect on the trade balance, of course, depends on domestic demand for tradeables as well as domestic production. As already mentioned, the induced appreciation of the exchange rate from fiscal expansion ($dp_t/dG_n < 0$) reduces domestic tradeables production. Domestic demand rises due to the usual substitution effect caused by exchange rate appreciation but is also affected by the change in national income. The net effect on the trade account is indeterminate *a priori*:

$$\frac{dBT}{dG_n} = \left(\frac{\partial Y_t}{\partial p_t} - \frac{\partial \hat{D}_t}{\partial p_t}\right) \frac{dp_t}{dG_n} - \frac{\partial \hat{D}_t}{\partial Y} \frac{d\bar{Y}}{dG_n} \lessgtr 0. \tag{5.43}$$
$$\phantom{\frac{dBT}{dG_n} = }\;\;(+)\quad\;\;(-)\quad\;\;(-)\quad\;\;(+)\quad(?)$$

The effects of bond-financed fiscal policy under flexible exchange rates for both classical and Keynesian unemployment are summarized in table 5.4.

6.3 Money-financed Fiscal Policy under Flexible Exchange Rates

The foregoing discussion of bond-financed fiscal expansion noted that the MM curve shifted downward to the left under either Keynesian or classical unemployment. How is the analysis of fiscal policy affected in the case of monetary finance?

Classical unemployment

In the case of money-financed spending, the government's action has no *direct* effect on money market equilibrium. The government simply meets its own increased transactions demand for money by "running the printing press." Consequently the increase in G_n has no *direct* effect in the money market equilibrium (5.20). This can be simply represented by setting $\partial \tilde{M}/\partial G_n = 0$ – or, more precisely, setting $\partial M^s/\partial G_n = \partial \tilde{M}/\partial G_n = 1$. Although money-financed government expenditure has no direct effect on the money market, it has an indirect effect on private-sector money demand in the classical unemployment case. The mechanism is the following. Increased government spending increases the severity of private-sector rationing in the nontradeables market (via (5.25)). As $\bar{D}_n$ falls, so does total expenditure $\tilde{Z}$, thereby leading to a fall in private money demand in (5.20). Consequently, the exchange must depreciate at each level of income in order to clear the foreign exchange market. Thus the $M_c M_c$ curve shifts upward to the right in the case of money-financed government spending in the presence of classical unemployment, whereas it shifted to the left in the case of bond-financed spending.

The $G_c G_c$ curve remains unaffected by government expenditure regardless of whether it is bond- or money-financed. Thus, in stark contrast to the bond-finance case, the exchange rate now *depreciates* because the increased government spending chokes off private spending by increasing the severity of nontradeables rationing. National output falls. As table 5.4 shows, the signs of the sectoral output effects of fiscal expansion are also critically dependent on the method of finance under classical unemployment.

Keynesian unemployment

Under Keynesian unemployment, matters are much more straight-forward. The $M_k M_k$ does not shift in the case of money-financed increases in government spending (because there is no rationing effect via $\bar{D}_n$). The $G_k G_k$ curve shifts to the right, as it did in the case of a bond-financed increase in government spending. Consequently there are fewer ambiguities than in the bond-finance case above.

As in the bond-financed case, money-financed government spending on nontradeables stimulates nontradeables production. The ensuing exchange rate appreciation, however, has a contractionary effect on tradeables production. The latter effect is overpowered by the former under money-financed spending so national income unambiguously rises. This can easily be confirmed diagrammatically: the $G_k G_k$ curve shifts right along an unchanged $M_k M_k$ curve.

The fact that $d\bar{Y}/dG_n$ is positive means that the trade balance unambiguously deteriorates, not only due to increased income but also due to exchange rate appreciation – see (5.43).

Comparison of classical and Keynesian unemployment cases

A comparison of money-financed government spending across the two unemployment regimes proves interesting. Although national output rises in both cases, the exchange rate appreciates with money-financed fiscal expansion under Keynesian unemployment, but depreciates under classical unemployment. Consequently the sectoral output effects differ dramatically across unemployment regimes. Under Keynesian unemployment, government expenditure on non-tradeables stimulates that sector, but the ensuing appreciation has a detrimental output effect on the tradeables sector. Under classical unemployment, increased government expenditure on nontradeables has *no* effect on nontradeables output. It only increases the severity of rationing experienced by the private sector. The resulting exchange rate depreciation, however, causes government spending on non-tradeables to have a *stimulative* effect on the *tradeable* goods sector!

It is impossible, therefore, to predict the effects of fiscal expansion on particular sectors of the economy – even if all government expenditure is only on nontradeables – without first determining whether the economy is suffering from classical or Keynesian unemployment. Moreover, in the classical unemployment case the effects of a fiscal expansion are reversed depending on the method used to finance them.

7 Summary and Conclusions

This chapter has extended the two-sector analysis of macroeconomic policies in temporary equilibrium with quantity rationing by including both money and internationally traded bonds as financial assets. By eliminating the assumption that money is the only asset, an acceptable treatment of flexible exchange rate regimes becomes possible. The effects of monetary policy under flexible rates are summarized in table 5.2. A comparison of wage and fiscal policies under fixed and flexible exchange rates and alternative unemployment regimes (Keynesian versus classical) is undertaken above in sections 5 and 6 and summarized in tables 5.3 and 5.4.

Noteworthy is the dramatic difference in the output effects of fiscal policy depending on the method of finance and whether unemployment is Keynesian or classical in nature. Most strikingly, bond-financed fiscal policy is shown to be *contractionary* under classical unemployment when the exchange rate is flexible due to the adverse effect of exchange rate appreciation on the tradeable goods sector. This is also a possibility, but not the only one, under Keynesian unemployment.

The use of the Mundell–Fleming model, which presumes a simple one-sector Keynesian unemployment structure, if an economy is in fact suffering from classical unemployment would result in major policy errors when fiscal policy is being used. When considerable doubt exists about the prevailing type of unemployment, there is less danger in employing monetary policy when the country has a flexible exchange rate, or wage policy when the country has a fixed exchange rate. The effects of these policies differ less across unemployment regimes than does fiscal policy.

Appendix: Alternative Specifications of Money Demand

The money demand specifications (5.15) and (5.18) are obviously fundamental to this chapter's analysis of the flexible rate regime. Because these equations are somewhat unconventional, at least at first blush, it is important to ask how the results would be affected by the substitution of a standard money demand function and monetary equilibrium defined by:

$$M^s = M(r, Y), \tag{5.44}$$

where r is the domestic interest rate and Y is national income. (The price of nontradeables is constant throughout the chapter, so both M^s and Y could be interpreted as "real" in units of the nontradeable good, if one so desired.)

Comparing (5.44) to either (5.15) or (5.18) suggests three possible channels through which conflicting conclusions might emerge:

(1) Government expenditure enters (5.15) and (5.18) directly but affects (5.44) only via its arguments (r, Y).
(2) Equations (5.15) and (5.18) depend on domestic *expenditure* not income. In addition to implying the inclusion of G_n and $\bar{D}_n$ in the money demand equation, this also leads to the inclusion of the exchange rate e (which equals p_t in the text if we adopt the arbitrary normalization that $p_t^* = 1$) as a determinant of money demand (with a partial derivative whose sign depends on (5.14) or (5.17)).
(3) The domestic interest rate is incorporated in (5.44). It is implicitly fixed at the world level r^* and hence omitted from (5.15) and (5.18).

These issues will be addressed one at a time. Regarding point (1) on government expenditure, it seems natural (in fact, necessary for consistency) to require that *all* market participants – private and government – obtain cash in advance to effect purchases in a Clower-like monetary economy. To free the government from this institutional constraint only makes sense if the government is free to conduct barter transactions, which is contrary to the monetary-economy spirit of the analysis. Even when the government is engaging in money-financed spending, its expenditure alters aggregate money demand but augments money supply by exactly the same amount. Consequently changes in G_n would have no direct effect on the monetary equilibrium. As discussed in detail in the text, the method of finance influences the effect of fiscal expansion under classical (but not Keynesian) unemployment. Both the money- and bond-financed cases are, of course, interesting possibilities.

The second issue (2) involves the choice of expenditure or income as the transactions variable in the money demand function. First, it should be emphasized that the motivation for choosing expenditure is that it is one way to insure that the exchange rate as well as income will enter the money demand functions in (5.15) and (5.18). Hence at one level the issue can be boiled down to the question of whether, having already included income, $\partial M/\partial e \equiv \partial M/\partial p_t$ is positive – as the model in the text prescribes – or zero as in the original Mundell-Fleming specification (5.44). The former yields a negatively sloped MM locus; the latter yields a vertical one. It is, of course, straightforward to examine the limiting case of vertical MM locus, given the analysis in the chapter.

For the short-run context of the fix-price literature, however, Dornbusch's (1976b) extension of the M–F model where $\partial M/\partial e$ is positive produces more realistic results. In his model, this effect is obtained by introducing the expected rate of exchange rate depreciation into the interest rate condition implied by perfect capital mobility to get:

$$M = M(r^* + (e'-e)/e, Y), \tag{5.45}$$

where e' is the expected future-period exchange rate. Replacing (5.15) and (5.18) by (5.45) would obviously leave the entire analysis of the text unaffected (particularly if we confined ourselves to the money-finance case for government expenditure so that $\partial M/\partial G_n = 0$, thereby avoiding issue (1) already discussed above).

The model in this chapter provides an alternative justification for the exchange rate effect on money demand. What our analysis provides that Dornbusch's does not is a multisector generalization of the M–F model, not only for Keynesian unemployment but for classical unemployment as well. Different methods of fiscal finance have then been considered in this context.

At a second level the question of the correct transactions variable can be boiled down to a question of the correct specification of the currency of invoice for various transactions. Presumably nontradeables in each country are invoiced in the local currency. Tradeable goods, on the other hand, may be invoiced in either the buyer's or the seller's home currency. Helpman and Razin (1981) distinguish two extremes: the *B-system* and the *S-system* respectively. Under the B-system, all domestic residents' expenditure (on either domestic or foreign goods) is carried out using the domestic currency. This gives rise to a domestic money demand function depending on domestic expenditure Z, as specified in the text.

In the other institutional setting, the S-system, domestic and foreign residents' demands for domestic money depends on whether the country is a net exporter or importer of tradeable goods. In the case of a net exporter, all domestic expenditure is on domestic goods. Hence domestic residents demand only domestic money. Because domestic sellers under the S-system demand payment in domestic currency, there is a *foreign* demand for *domestic* money to the extent that foreigners import domestic goods. Aggregate *world* demand for *domestic* money, therefore, equals:

$$M = p_n D_n(e, p_n, Y) + e D_t(e, p_n, Y) + e X(e, Y^*),$$
$$M = Z(\overset{+}{p_n}, \overset{+}{e}, Y) + e X(e, Y^*), \tag{5.46}$$

where X is foreign export demand and Y^* is (exogenous) foreign income.

Conversely, when the domestic economy is a net importer of tradeables under the S-system, only domestic residents demand domestic currency:

$$M = p_n D_n(e, p_n, Y) + e Y_t(e, w). \tag{5.47}$$

They also demand *foreign* currency M^*, however, to effect import demand IM:

$$\frac{M^*}{p_t^*} = IM \equiv (D_t - Y_t). \tag{5.48}$$

Under the S-system, therefore, aggregate world demand for domestic money is either (5.46) or (5.47), depending on whether the country is a net exporter or importer of tradeable goods. In either case, as under the B-system employed in the text, money depends positively on both income and exchange rates. In fact, for either (5.46) or (5.47) the necessary condition to insure that $\partial M/\partial e$ is positive is weaker than the one required under the B-system, used in the text (i.e., equation (5.14) or (5.17)).

In sum the analysis of the text appears to be very robust against alternative possible specifications of money demand – either those based on different currency-of-invoice rules within the cash-in-advance setup or a "conventional" but *ad hoc* specification where money demand depends on covered interest rates and national income.

6

The Exportables–Importables Model: Commercial Policies

1 Introduction

Many governments provide incentives to increase domestic output in industries where foreigners presumably have comparative advantage. These "import substitution" policies take various forms, including tariffs, quotas, subsidies, administered wages and prices, and over-valued or multiple exchange rates. (See Bhagwati *et al.* (1978) for a detailed discussion in the context of less-developed countries.) The objective of such policies is to alter the level and composition of domestic output and trade as well as to reduce domestic unemploy-ment. Yet most analyses of import substitution policies are based on models which either implicitly assume full employment or ignore the macroeconomic environment in which policy changes occur. The fact that such government policies deliberately modify or restrict the operation of market forces implies that firms and/or consumers face quantity constraints for labor or output as markets fail to clear. The nature of the non-price-rationing which then evolves determines effective demands and supplies by domestic agents and hence the economy's short-run or temporary equilibrium position. Only once this equilibrium is correctly characterized can the effects of changing various import substitution policy variables be ascertained.

Many policy problems concerning resource allocation and overall development strategy cannot, of course, be properly treated in a single-sector framework (cf. chapter 3). In addressing issues involving trade distortions, the distinction between export and import indus-tries is essential. The present chapter develops a two-sector *export-ables–importables* model for analyzing the effects of exchange rate devaluation, changes in administered prices, tariffs, and import quotas in a country with a package of import substitution policies.

It explicitly recognizes the effects that the rationing of consumers or producers in particular markets has on their effective demands or supplies on *other* markets. This is of obvious importance, for example, in countries where shortages of importable goods due to import quotas and domestic price controls result in a significant deflection of expenditure toward other, nonrationed goods as well as saving for future consumption.

The remainder of this section relates the exportables–importables model, to be described in detail in section 3 below, to the tradeables–nontradeables model used in chapters 4 and 5. Section 2 below briefly elaborates on the phenomenon of import substitution policies in order to provide strong motivation for the analytical framework and policy issues to be discussed in this chapter.

1.1   *The Small Open-Economy Assumption*

The models in chapters 4 and 5 assume that the economy under consideration is a *small open economy* in the sense that: (1) it faces a price of the tradeable good that is fixed in foreign-currency terms p^* and (2) it can buy or sell as much of this good as it wishes at the prevailing world price. Only in the *nontradeable* goods market did the possibility of quantity constraints on supply or demand arise.

There are, however, important situations where one can reasonably expect quantity constraints in the markets for *traded* goods. Even if the economy produces only a single traded good (no nontradeables), and is small in the sense that changes in domestic supply have an imperceptible influence on the world price of its exportable good, domestic producers or consumers may face rationing if the world price is slow to adjust to eliminate *world* excess supply or demand. A good example of such a situation would be a small oil-exporting nation facing a world price and sales constraint imposed by the OPEC oil cartel.

Quantity constraints in tradeable goods markets can also arise in situations where the country in question is not large if it imposes import quotas coupled with domestic price controls. This may result in domestic rationing of the importable good, yet the country might be small in both the importables and exportables markets in the sense that it would, in the absence of such distortionary policies, perceive perfectly elastic world supply or demand curves for these products at prevailing world prices.

Finally, it is important to consider situations where the price of a tradeable good is fixed in terms of the domestic currency in the short run. In such cases, the *domestic* economy typically faces a downward sloping export demand curve rather than the perfectly elastic demand curve assumed in chapters 3–5. This combination of a price fixed in domestic currency and a less than perfectly elastic export demand curve will be referred to as the *large-country assumption*.

The large-country assumption opens up new possibilities in the fix-price context of this volume even if the economy produces only a single, tradeable good. Authors using the large-economy assumption typically take a somewhat different and mixed approach. Cuddington (1980), for example, distinguishes between exportables and importables, assuming that the economy is small and unrationed in the market for the importable good. By admitting the possibility of world excess supply or demand of *exportables* on the other hand, he is able to distinguish both classical and Keynesian unemployment regimes in a model that does not incorporate a nontraded goods sector.[1]

It might be pointed out that the exportables–importables model in Cuddington (1980) is very similar to the tradeables–nontradeables model in Neary (1980) or chapter 4 of this book. If one was to assume that the *foreign* demand for "exportables" in Cuddington was identically equal to zero, that good would, in effect, become the "nontradeable" good in Neary's specification. Cuddington's other good, the importable, then becomes the only tradeable good and performs the same role as the tradeable good in Neary's model. For example, under Keynesian unemployment and fixed exchange rates, government expenditure (on exportables) stimulates exportables output but leaves importables production unchanged in the exportables–importables model. Analogously, in the tradeables–nontradeables model, government expenditure on nontradeable goods causes their output to rise but has no effect on tradeable goods.

In sum, the analysis in chapters 4 and 5 can easily be reworked in an exportables–importables context merely by relabeling nontradeables as exportables (and allowing for foreign demand) and tradeables as importables (retaining the small-country assumption in the latter case). Consequently, there is no need to repeat our earlier analyses of

---

[1] If the economy was also assumed to be small and unrationed in the market for exportables, of course, the model could be collapsed to the single-sector model considered in chapter 3. As long as the relative price of importables in terms of exportables is constant, the goods could be aggregated into a composite tradeable good (according to Hicks' composite commodity theorem).

macroeconomic stabilization policies in the exportables–importables framework.[2]

This chapter explores the effects of commercial policies, in particular "import substitution policies," using the exportables–importables framework. For an analysis of trade distortions this framework is more appealing than that employed in chapters 4 and 5, which lumps all tradeables together. The model to be used is the one developed by Cuddington (1981). It contains two distinct tradeables, labelled exportables and importables respectively. The large open-economy assumption admits the possibility of quantity constraints in the exportable goods markets. Thus no nontraded goods sector is required in order to have the full complement of disequilibrium regimes in the model. The small-country assumption is also relaxed for the importables sector, but in a different way. We assume that the government imposes quantitative restrictions on imports and then rations households' purchases of importables rather than letting prices rise enough to clear the market. The objective of quantitative restrictions on imports may be to provide incentives to increase domestic output in industries where foreigners presumably have comparative advantage. They alter the level and composition of domestic output and employment as well as the foreign trade balance.

2   Import Substitution Policies

As suggested above, various incentives to increase domestic output in industries where foreigners presumably have comparative advantage are omnipresent. As an alternative to promoting traditional exports, which are often labor-intensive, primary-resource, or low-level-technology products, some nations make concerted attempts to foster capital-intensive or technologically advanced, import-competing industries. Besides achieving a preferred industrial mix, import substitution policies are perceived as being at least a partial solution to chronic balance-of-payments deficits. Often, it should be noted, such balance-of-payments difficulties are at least partially caused by domestic authorities' persistence in maintaining an overvalued exchange rate. This exchange rate policy allegedly increases domestic command over foreign goods and dampens domestically

[2] Hoel (1981) and Steigum (1980) use an exportables–importables specification like that in Cuddington (1980), but in addition include a nontraded goods sector à la Neary (1980). Johansson and Löfgren (1980, 1981) also adopt the exportables–importables–nontradeables specification.

generated inflation. Furthermore, any attempt to devalue the exchange rate may be resisted because of the increased burden of external debt denominated in terms of foreign currency that it would entail.

Import substitution policies may take the form of subsidies, tariffs, quotas or quantitative import restrictions (QRs), or other nontariff barriers such as government procurement policy. Sections 3–5 below focus on import quotas combined with stickiness (often policy-induced) of wages and prices. Chapter 7 turns to an analysis of tariff policy under the assumption that the economy is small in the importables market.

The effects of import quotas are especially pernicious because they sever the link between domestic and foreign prices of the importable goods. Although domestic prices differ from world prices in the case of tariff protection, this does not prevent both prices from responding to foreign or domestic changes in supply or demand. With quotas, in contrast, the domestic market for the importable good is effectively separated from the world market. As a consequence the domestic price need not be related to the world price and may, therefore, be more easily manipulated by domestic authorities.

It is, of course, well known from the literature comparing tariffs and quotas that if the (effective) domestic price in the presence of a quota is allowed to adjust to the (protected) market-clearing level (as would occur, for example, if a fixed number of import licenses were auctioned off to the highest bidders), there exists a tariff which would have yielded identical (short-run, static) results to the QR. Unfortunately, in many cases price adjustment ensuring efficient allocation of the restricted supply of importables does not occur. Usually importables' prices are held below the tariff-equivalent level[3] by well-meaning government policy. Consequently, non-price-rationing schemes necessarily emerge. These schemes may be government-mandated rules for allocating the available quantity of importables (whether produced domestically or imported) or rationing may occur informally, for example, through black markets.

The production of traditional exports in these countries is generally more than adequate to meet domestic demand; actual output levels may or may not be limited by the extent of foreign demand, depending on the size of the country and the degree to which it can

---

[3] By tariff-equivalent price is meant the price which would clear the domestic market for importables in the presence of the QR. The statement in the text is quite consistent with a situation where the domestic price exceeds the corresponding world price, the usual effect of protection. See figure 6.1.

influence world prices. In cases where such influence is negligible, the level of world prices and the country's exchange rate relative to domestic wages will determine the level of exportables production. The country's ability to expand employment in traditional export sectors may be limited, particularly if an overvalued exchange rate limits foreign demand.

Sections 3–5 below deal with an economy with the following combination of market distortions. There are quantitative restrictions on imports that are always assumed to be binding. The domestic price of importables is assumed to exceed the world price but is fixed below its protected-market equilibrium level by domestic price controls. Consequently, we are considering only situations where domestic consumers face a quantity constraint in the market for the importable good. Domestic producers of this good can, therefore, always sell their profit-maximizing output level; they face no sales constraint.

Wages are assumed to be fixed above the full-employment level in the short-run time frame under consideration. Possible explanations include government incomes policy, long-term labor contacts or union wage-setting power. With unemployment, neither the domestic exportables nor importables industries ever face quantity constraints on their labor demands.

The non-market-clearing situations just described do not exhaust all possibilities in a three-market (i.e., two goods, labor) framework. Cases of excess demand for labor could be included (see, e.g., Cuddington, 1980), as could cases where there is a domestic excess demand for the good labeled as the "exportable" or a domestic excess supply of the so-called "importable." Obviously the act of labeling one good as the exportable and the other as the importable automatically limits the scope of the investigation.

The objective here is to discuss a couple of situations which are of obvious empirical relevance in an international trade context. In so doing, it should become clear that the approach can be straightforwardly applied to other interesting cases.

3   The Model[4]

3.1   *The Production Sectors*

The model to be developed is a short-run model where prices and wages are fixed. Wages are too high to permit full employment so

---

[4] Sections 3–5 here have been adapted from Cuddington (1981) and have been reprinted with permission from the *Review of Economic Studies*.

firms' demands for labor are always satisfied. The fact that there is an excess supply of labor means that households, never firms, face quantity constraints in the labor market. It is assumed that firms hold no inventories so that output always equals sales.

Producers of the importable good face a domestic-currency price, p_m, which is fixed by government authorities in conjunction with a policy restricting the quantity of imports. This import quota is always assumed to be binding, implying that net domestic demand for the importable good at the prevailing price p_m exceeds the quota. Thus domestic firms are always able to sell their profit-maximizing level of output. Their derived demand for labor is obtained from the usual first-order conditions in a single-period framework:

$$L_m = L_m(p_m, w), \qquad \partial L_m/\partial p_m > 0, \qquad \partial L_m/\partial w < 0. \quad (6.1)$$

Substituting (6.1) into the short-run production function yields the domestic supply of the importable good:

$$Y_m = Y_m(p_m, w), \qquad \partial Y_m/\partial p_m > 0, \qquad \partial Y_m/\partial w < 0. \quad (6.2)$$

Like firms in the importables sector, exportables producers face no shortage of labor. Whether or not they face a sales constraint, however, depends on the nature of foreign demand and the extent to which the foreign-currency price of the export good, p_x^*, is influenced by domestic supply conditions. This will be discussed in greater detail below.

In the case where exportables producers are unconstrained in their output market, profit-maximizing behavior determines labor demand:

$$L_x = L_x(p_x, w), \qquad \partial L_x/\partial p_x > 0, \qquad \partial L_x/\partial w < 0, \qquad (6.3)$$

and the level of output:

$$Y_x = Y_x(p_x, w), \qquad \partial Y_x/\partial p_x > 0, \qquad \partial Y_x/\partial w < 0. \qquad (6.4)$$

Here p_x is the domestic-currency price of exportables and, assuming the absence of export restrictions, equals the foreign-currency price times the exchange rate: $p_x = ep_x^*$.

If, on the other hand, exportables producers face a sales constraint $\bar{Y}_x$ because demand falls short of their profit-maximizing level, their demand for labor will be correspondingly reduced. The constrained labor demand, denoted by a tilde, is found by inverting the short-run production function:

$$\tilde{L}_x = \tilde{L}_x(\bar{Y}_x), \qquad \partial \tilde{L}_x/\partial \bar{Y}_x > 0. \qquad (6.5)$$

3.2   *The Household Sector*

In the present context, we are interested in households' utility maximization in the presence of quantity constraints. Specifically, households face a limited demand for labor, implying the existence of unemployment. Because import quotas are always assumed to be binding (in the current period, but not necessarily in the future), consumers also face quantity constraints in their demand for the importable good. In the market for the exportable good, however, domestic consumers are never rationed; the country is assumed to produce enough of that good so that some is always available for export after meeting domestic demand. Households, therefore, maximize:

$$u(D_x, \bar{D}_m, \bar{L}, W'; \theta)$$
$$\text{s.t.} \quad p_x D_x + W' = W + w\bar{L}_m + w\bar{L}_x + \pi - p_m \bar{D}_m, \quad (6.6)$$

where bars over variables denote quantity constraints. $\bar{L} = \bar{L}_x + \bar{L}_m$ is total employment. $\bar{D}_m$ is the available quantity of the importable good. The constrained optimization problem yields domestic exportable demand and saving functions (conditional on θ, as before):

$$D_x = D_x(\bar{p}_x, \overset{+}{W} + Y - p_m \bar{D}_m),$$
$$S = W'(p_x, W + Y - p_m \bar{D}_m) - W, \quad (6.7)$$

where $Y = \pi + \bar{w}L = p_x Y_x + p_m Y_m$ is national income. The specification implies that tradeables and nontradeables are gross substitutes and that the utility function has a sufficient degree of separability so that $\bar{D}_n$ and $\bar{L}$ affect the behavioral functions only via their effect on discretionary income $W + Y - p_m \bar{D}_m$. As discussed at length in chapters 3 and 4, this greatly simplifies notation and, for the most part, leaves our qualitative results unchanged. Comparative static results whose signs depend on the weak separability assumption are indicated in the summary tables.

4   Classical and Keynesian Unemployment Equilibria

Having described the quantity-constrained behavior of domestic producers and consumers at the prevailing wage and prices, fix-price equilibria in the importables and exportables markets can now be discussed.

    Import supply from foreigners generally depends positively on the foreign-currency price of importables: $I^s(p_m/e)$. It is assumed here, however, that imports are limited to the policy-determined quantity $\bar{I}$ and that this constraint is actually binding in the sense that the domestic effective excess demand for the importable good, $\hat{D}_m - Y_m$, exceeds $\bar{I}$. Given this shortage of importables, domestic producers have no difficulty selling their profit-maximizing level of output:

$$Y_m = Y_m(p_m, w). \qquad (6.8)$$

Domestic consumption of the importable good is limited to this quantity plus the allowable imports from abroad:

$$\bar{D}_m = Y_m(p_m, w) + \bar{I}. \qquad (6.9)$$

Referring to figure 6.1 the import quota is binding whenever the domestic price of the importable lies between $\tilde{p}_m(e)$ and p_m^d. The price p_m^d is the domestic market equilibrium price in the presence of the import quota. It is also the price that would prevail if the quota was replaced by an "equivalent tariff."

It should be emphasized that existence of an import quota does not *necessarily* create a situation where quantity rationing occurs. Quotas by themselves merely alter foreign supply to the domestic market, as shown by the import supply schedule $\bar{I}$ in figure 6.1. It is when prices are not allowed to adjust to their market-clearing levels (because of government pricing policies, for example) that fix-price models with non-price-rationing become appropriate.

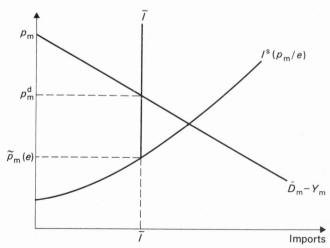

FIGURE 6.1   The domestic market for the importable good in the presence of an import quota

Foreign demand for exportables, X^d, depends negatively on the foreign-currency price p_x^*. In the absence of export restrictions we assume[5] the "law of one price" prevails: $p_x = ep_x^*$. Whether the price of the exportable good is fixed in terms of domestic currency or in terms of foreign currency, however, depends on the size of the domestic economy relative to the rest of the world as well as degree of product differentiation and imperfect competition.

Two situations are particularly relevant to the discussion of import substitution policies which are often accompanied by an overvalued rate.

In the first, the domestic economy is assumed to be able to affect the terms of trade, i.e., the *foreign-currency* price of exportables relative to importables. This is likely if the domestic exportable good is a differentiated product or if the country is a large supplier relative to the size of the world market. In this case, it is reasonable to assume that it is the price in terms of the *domestic* currency, p_x, that is fixed in the short run. Hence, the foreign-currency price varies if the exchange rate is changed. Export demand equals:

$$X^d = X^d(p_x/e), \tag{6.10}$$

implying that the balance of trade in terms of foreign currency is:

$$BT = (p_x/e) \, X^d(p_x/e) - p_m^* \, \bar{I}. \tag{6.11}$$

Given an initially overvalued exchange rate, total (domestic and foreign) demand for the exportable good falls short of the profit-maximizing level of output. Thus exportables production is limited to:

$$\bar{Y}_x = D_x(p_x, W + Y - p_m \bar{D}_m) + X^d(p_x/e). \tag{6.12}$$

This is the typical *Keynesian unemployment* case where output – here, exportables output – is limited by the level of aggregate demand. The derived demand for labor falls short of the unconstrained profit-maximizing level as shown by equation (6.5). Hence total employment equals:

$$\bar{L} = L_m(p_m, w) + \tilde{L}_x(\bar{Y}_x). \tag{6.13}$$

Setting the Keynesian unemployment case aside, it is possible to conceive of situations where the level of output in the exportables

[5] There are undoubtedly real-world examples of situations where domestic producers or their representative distributors fix both the domestic- and foreign-currency prices in the short run. Exchange rate movements would then cause the law of one price to be violated even if it had been satisfied at the time prices were set. Empirically, the law of one price is far from robust. See, for example, Isard (1977) and Kravis and Lipsey (1978).

sector is limited by the profit-maximizing decisions of firms, rather than by aggregate demand, thereby producing *classical unemployment*. In the present context where the domestic-currency price of exportables is fixed, however, classical unemployment would imply that this price is too *low* or, alternatively, that the exchange rate is *undervalued*. Neither of these situations is likely in countries with thoroughgoing import substitution policies. Therefore we treat this case summarily in footnotes. There is, however, a slightly different and more plausible situation where exportables producers face no sales constraint.

This second interesting case occurs when the domestic economy is "small" so that it faces a perfectly elastic demand for exports at the prevailing *foreign-currency* price p_x^*. Notice that it is the foreign-currency price of the exportable rather than the domestic-currency price that is now assumed to be fixed.

Domestic firms produce the profit-maximizing level of output, given the wage w and implied domestic-currency price $p_x = ep_x^*$, with the assurance that any output not sold domestically can always be sold abroad. From (6.4) domestic exportables output equals:

$$Y_x = Y_x(p_x, w). \tag{6.14}$$

The level of employment is limited only because further production is unprofitable given domestic prices, wages and the exchange rate:

$$\bar{L} = L_m(p_m, w) + L_x(p_x, w). \tag{6.15}$$

In contrast to Keynesian unemployment, which results from a deficiency of aggregate demand, unemployment here is caused by excessive nominal wages relative to world prices and the exchange rate. This is a *classical unemployment* situation.[6]

Under classical unemployment the domestic excess supply to the exportable can always be sold to foreigners, whose demand is perfectly elastic at price p_x^*. Hence, actual exports equal:

$$X^s = Y_x(p_x, w) - D_x(p_x, W + Y - p_m\bar{D}_m). \tag{6.16}$$

Figure 6.2 shows the level of export supply for the classical unemployment case where the domestic price p_x lies between p_x^0 and p_x^w. (Above the world-market-clearing price p_x^w, the economy enters the demand-constrained situation of Keynesian unemployment.)

---

[6] Note that when all goods are traded and the exchange rate is fixed, the *orthodox* Keynesian unemployment case could occur if the domestic-currency price p_x could adjust freely to clear the exportable goods market.

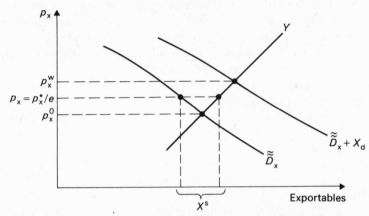

FIGURE 6.2   The exportables market. At prices above p_x^0, the good X becomes an exportable good; p_x^w is the price that clears the world market. At prices such as $\bar{p}_x$ between p_x^0 and p_x^w, the market is characterized by classical unemployment. At prices above p_x^w, there is Keynesian unemployment

Using this expression for export supply, the balance of trade (in foreign currency) under classical unemployment equals:

$$BT = p_x^*[Y_x(p_x, w) - D_x(p_x, W + Y - p_m \bar{D}_m)] - p_m^* \bar{I}. \qquad (6.17)$$

5   The Effects of Import Substitution Policy Changes: Quotas

As many economies are too small to influence world prices and tend to export goods which are relatively homogeneous, one might expect to find a prevalence of classical unemployment rather than Keynesian unemployment. That is, export production and therefore employment will not be limited by aggregate demand, because foreign demand is infinitely elastic at the world price from a small economy's point of view.[7] Instead, domestic firms' demand for labor falls short of the available supply because of an excessive nominal wage relative to output prices.

Yet policy prescriptions are often based, at least implicitly, on standard Keynesian macroeconomic models. Thus it is important to determine the extent to which policy analyses of the two situations

---

[7] This presumes that all goods are tradeables. There are no nontradeables, as there were in chapters 4–5.

TABLE 6.1 Effects of exchange rate devaluation, relaxing import quotas ($\bar{l}$), and increasing the administered price of output in the import-competing industry

	Keynesian unemployment			Classical unemployment		
	e	$\bar{l}$	p_m	e	$\bar{l}$	p_m
Exportables production	+	−	−[a]	+	0	0
Importables production	0	0	+	0	0	+[b]
Volume of exports	+	0	0	?[c]	+[b]	+[b]
Balance of trade (in terms of foreign currency)	?	−	0	?[c]	?	+[b]

[a] Weak separability is a sufficient condition for a negative sign.
[b] Weak separability is a sufficient condition for a positive sign.
[c] The indeterminacy here reflects the well-known possibility of a back-bending export supply curve.

differ. Will policymakers who unwittingly apply Keynesian models, when in fact there is classical unemployment, be giving incorrect policy advice? To provide a partial answer to this question, we consider the effects of several liberalization policies under each type of unemployment. In particular, the effects of exchange rate devaluation, the relaxation of quantitative restrictions on imports, and policy-induced increases in the domestic price of the import-competing good will be examined. For convenient reference, the effect of these policy changes are summarized in table 6.1.

5.1   Keynesian Unemployment

Exchange rate policy

To determine how exchange rate changes affect output, employment, and the trade balance in Keynesian unemployment situations with import restrictions, consider equations (6.8)–(6.13). Exchange rate devaluation increases foreign export demand (6.10) when the selling price is fixed in terms of the domestic currency:

$$\frac{\partial X^{d}}{\partial e} > 0. \tag{6.18}$$

This stimulus to aggregate demand has a multiplier effect on exportables production in the Keynesian case where the level of output is demand-determined. From (6.12):

$$\frac{d\bar{Y}_x}{de} = \left(\frac{1}{1 - p_x\, \partial D_x/\partial Y} \right) \frac{\partial X^{d}}{\partial e} > 0. \tag{6.19}$$

The import-competing industry is unaffected by the devaluation (as long as the import quota remains binding), because the profit-maximizing level of output is already being produced (see equation (6.8)).[8]

National income and employment unambiguously rise following devaluation:

$$\frac{dY}{de} = p_x \frac{d\bar{Y}_x}{de} > 0, \tag{6.20}$$

$$\frac{d\bar{L}}{de} = \frac{d\tilde{L}_x}{d\bar{Y}_x} \frac{d\bar{Y}_x}{de} > 0. \tag{6.21}$$

These changes are due solely to changes in the export sector. Government import restrictions and pricing policy, which break the link between the domestic and foreign price of the importable good, insulate the import-competing sector from the effects of devaluation. As will be seen below, this insulation of the importables sector from the effects of devaluation also occurs under classical unemployment. Thus devaluation policy unaccompanied by other trade liberalization measures has an unambiguous stimulative effect on the export sector to the extent that there are unemployed resources which can be utilized. No contraction in the import-competing sector would be expected, however, at least for small changes in the exchange rate and assuming the import quota remains binding.

The balance-of-trade effect of devaluation in the Keynesian unemployment case with import restrictions depends solely on the price elasticity of foreign demand for the exportable good, ϵ_f. Differentiating (6.11):

$$\frac{dBT}{de} = \frac{p_x}{e} \frac{\partial X^d}{\partial e} - \frac{p_x X^d}{e^2}$$

$$= \frac{p_x X(\epsilon_f - 1)}{e^2} \gtreqless 0 \qquad \text{as } \epsilon_f \gtreqless 1. \tag{6.22}$$

---

[8] As mentioned above, it is assumed that domestic authorities are able to fix the domestic-currency price of the importable good when there is a binding quota. Hence, the law of one price ($p_m = e p_m^*$) will generally *not* hold for this good. Throughout this section the analysis of devaluation presumes that domestic-currency price of importables is unaffected (in equations (6.19) and (6.35) for example). Any devaluation-induced change in the foreign-currency denominated revenue from licensed import sales implicitly accrues to foreign producers rather than the domestic import distributors. Without these assumptions $p_m \bar{D}_m$ in households' budget constraint (6.6) would have to be replaced with $p_m Y_m^S + e p_m^* \bar{I}$ implying that $\partial \bar{D}_m / \partial e$ would not equal zero as assumed here.

If foreign demand for the exportable good is elastic, as it might be if the country was one of many exporters, devaluation would improve the balance of trade. If foreign demand is price-inelastic, devaluation leads to a deterioration in the trade account. By maintaining import quotas (accompanied by importables price controls), the government therefore creates a situation where the trade account will deteriorate following devaluation whenever $\epsilon_f < 1$. Without quotas (but retaining our assumptions about price rigidity), the trade account deteriorates only if $\epsilon_f + \epsilon_d < 1$, where ϵ_d is the price elasticity of domestic import demand. Thus import quotas with importables price controls reduce the effectiveness of exchange rate devaluation. This suggests that any movement away from import substitution policies should not be piecemeal; the interaction of various distortionary policies must be recognized (as we know from the "theory of second best" *à la* Lipsey and Lancaster (1956)).

Changes in the import quota
In contrast to the devaluation of an overvalued exchange rate, the policy of relaxing quantitative restrictions on imports will reduce domestic production of exportables. The argument is as follows. Increasing the quota raises the available supply of the importable good to domestic consumers:

$$\frac{d\bar{D}_m}{d\bar{I}} = 1. \tag{6.23}$$

This follows from (6.9) after it is understood that the domestic production of importables is unaffected as long as the quota, although relaxed, is still binding so that importables producers remain at their profit-maximizing output levels in (6.8). That the quantity constraint on domestic consumption of importables is now less severe implies a reduction in the amount of income previously deflected toward expenditure on exportables or saving when the importable good is in short supply. Hence domestic demand for exportables falls, bringing about a magnified reduction in exportables production via the familiar multiplier process:

$$\frac{d\bar{Y}_x}{d\bar{I}} = \frac{1}{1 - p_x \partial D_x / \partial Y} \frac{\partial D_x}{\partial Y} (-p_m) < 0. \tag{6.24}$$

Exports are unaffected by the relaxation of the import quota:

$$\frac{dX^d}{d\bar{I}} = 0. \tag{6.25}$$

This follows from the fact that the actual level of exports in the Keynesian unemployment case is completely determined by the extent of foreign demand. All determinants of the latter are unaffected by the import quota. Consequently, the balance of trade declines only as a result of the increased expenditure on imports when quotas are relaxed:

$$\frac{\mathrm{d}BT}{\mathrm{d}\bar{I}} = -p_m^* < 0. \tag{6.26}$$

Changes in the administered price of importable goods

When maintaining import quotas, government authorities generally permit the domestic price of importables to remain somewhat above the world price in order to stimulate output in the import-competing sector. However, the price is often held below the level which would equate supply and demand in the protected domestic market, p_m^d, in figure 6.1, presumably to pacify domestic consumers. Hence it is interesting to see the effect that allowing p_m to rise will have on domestic consumption of importables as well as the levels of domestic production and the trade balance, assuming the import quota remains binding.

As expected, an increase in p_m raises the profit-maximizing level of output in the import-competing sector:

$$\frac{\mathrm{d}Y_m}{\mathrm{d}p_m} = \frac{\partial Y_m}{\partial L_m}\frac{\mathrm{d}L_m}{\mathrm{d}p_m} > 0 \tag{6.27}$$

and increases the total quantity $\bar{D}_m$ available to domestic consumers:

$$\frac{\mathrm{d}\bar{D}_m}{\mathrm{d}p_m} = \frac{\mathrm{d}Y_m}{\mathrm{d}p_m} > 0. \tag{6.28}$$

The increase in p_m also reduces the amount of discretionary income that can be spent on exportables or saved for future consumption.

To determine the net effect on domestic demand for exportables, it is helpful to rewrite the effective demand function (6.7) using the expression (6.9) for the available supply of the rationed good:

$$D_x = D_x(p_x, W + Y - p_m\bar{D}_m) = D_x(p_x, W + p_x Y_x - p_m\bar{I}). \tag{6.29}$$

It is then clear that the effect of increased domestic production of the rationed nontradeable good nets out. The increase in the importables price, therefore, has a negative impact effect on the domestic demand for exportables. This causes exportables production, being demand-determined under Keynesian unemployment, to fall:

$$\frac{d\bar{Y}_x}{dp_m} = \left(\frac{1}{1-p_x\,\partial D_x/\partial Y}\right)\left(-\bar{I}\,\frac{\partial D_x}{\partial Y}\right) < 0. \tag{6.30}$$

It might be pointed out that the unambiguous result in (6.30) does depend on our assumption of weak separability. This rules out the *direct* effect of $\bar{D}_n$ on exportables demand, which would cause the exportables production effect to have an indeterminant sign if tradeables and nontradeables are assumed to be gross quantity-constrained substitutes as we call it, i.e., $\partial D_x/\partial\bar{D}_m < 0$ in the general form of the demand function $D_x = D_x(p_x, W + Y - p_m\bar{D}_m, \bar{D}_m, \bar{L})$.

Foreign export demand is, of course, unaffected by a change in the domestic price of importables:

$$\frac{dX^d}{dp_m} = 0. \tag{6.31}$$

Thus as long as the quota is unchanged, raising the domestic price of the importable good has no effect on the foreign currency value of the trade balance:

$$\frac{dBT}{dp_m} = p_m^*\,\frac{d\bar{I}}{dp_m} = 0. \tag{6.32}$$

The fact that the foreign-currency value of imports is unaffected is a consequence of the quantitative restriction on imports which breaks the link between domestic and foreign prices of the importable good, i.e., $dp_m^*/dp_m = 0$.

5.2 Classical Unemployment

Exchange rate policy

The effects of exchange rate depreciation in the classical unemployment case differ somewhat from the Keynesian unemployment case. Again, exportables production and employment are increased, assuming the domestic price of exportables rises with devaluation:[9]

$$\frac{dY_x}{de} = \frac{\partial Y_x}{\partial L_x}\frac{\partial L_x}{\partial p_x}\frac{dp_x}{de} > 0. \tag{6.33}$$

[9] Recall our discussion of the specification of the classical unemployment case at the beginning of section 4 above. If the exportables price was fixed in terms of the domestic currency rather than the foreign currency, exportable production would remain constant.

This time, however, the magnitude of the change in exportables output depends on the price elasticity of domestic supply rather than the elasticity of foreign demand. Output and employment in the import-competing industry are unaffected by devaluation in the presence of import quotas and domestic price controls, as was true in the Keynesian unemployment case. From (6.8):

$$\frac{dY_m}{de} = \frac{\partial Y_m}{\partial L_m} \frac{dL_m}{de} = 0. \tag{6.34}$$

As the foreign-currency price of the exportable is assumed to be fixed, devaluation increases the domestic-currency price, thereby tending to reduce domestic demand for the exportable. This effect coupled with the increase in exportables production does not, however, ensure that the amount of output available for export rises following devaluation because the increased exportables production raises labor and profit income, which tends to raise domestic demand. Hence the net effect on export supply is indeterminate:

$$\frac{dX^s}{de} = \left[\frac{\partial Y_x}{\partial p_x} - \frac{\partial D_x}{\partial p_x} - \frac{\partial D_x}{\partial Y} \left(Y_x + p_x \frac{\partial Y_x}{\partial p_x} \right) \right] \frac{dp_x}{de}$$

$$= \left[\left(1 - p_x \frac{\partial D_x}{\partial Y} \right) \frac{\partial Y_x}{\partial p_x} - \left(\frac{\partial D_x}{\partial p_x} \right)_{comp} - (Y_x - D_x) \frac{\partial D_x}{\partial Y} \right] \frac{dp_x}{de} \gtrless 0.$$

$$\underset{(+)}{} \quad \underset{(+)}{} \quad \underset{(-)}{} \quad \quad \underset{(+)}{} \quad \underset{(+)}{}$$

The fact that export volume may either rise or fall following a devaluation reflects the well-known possibility of a backward-bending export supply curve due to a strong positive income effect from a rise in the exportables price.[10] This is captured by the last term in (6.35).

Changes in the import quota

The effects of relaxing import quotas are also different in the classical unemployment case. From (6.8) and (6.14) it is seen that profit-maximizing levels of production in both industries are unaffected by changes in the import quota as long as prices remain fixed:

$$\frac{dY_m}{d\bar{I}} = \frac{dY_x}{d\bar{I}} = 0. \tag{6.36}$$

---

[10] Even the assumption of a weakly separable utility function cannot resolve the indeterminacy in (6.35).

Increasing the allowable quantity of imports, however, does increase the supply of exports from the domestic economy because it reduces domestic demand:

$$\frac{dX^s}{d\bar{I}} = \frac{-dD_x}{d\bar{I}} = \frac{-\partial D_x}{\partial Y}(-p_m) > 0. \tag{6.37}$$

Nevertheless, the effect on the trade balance in units of foreign exchange is uncertain:

$$\frac{dBT}{d\bar{I}} = p_x^* \frac{dX^s}{d\bar{I}} - p_m^* \gtrless 0. \tag{6.38}$$

Changes in the administered price of importable goods
Increasing the policy-controlled price of the importable good within the domestic economy stimulates importables output and employment, as it did in the Keynesian case:

$$\frac{dY_m}{dp_m} = \frac{\partial Y_m}{\partial L_m} \frac{\partial L_m}{\partial p_m} > 0. \tag{6.39}$$

In the classical unemployment case, however, exportables production remains unchanged at its original profit-maximizing level:

$$\frac{dY_x^s}{dp_m} = 0. \tag{6.40}$$

Contrast (6.30) in the Keynesian unemployment case where the increase in p_m reduces domestic demand and hence production of exportables.

Although domestic production of exportables remains unchanged, domestic export supply will change to the extent that domestic demand for exportables is affected by a change in the price of the importable good. Using (6.29), it is again straightforward to see that discretionary income falls, thereby reducing domestic demand. Hence, export volume rises but, unlike the Keynesian unemployment case, there is no multiplier effect (cf. (6.30)):

$$\frac{dX^s}{dp_m} = \left(-\frac{\partial D_x}{\partial Y}\right)(-\bar{I}) > 0. \tag{6.41}$$

As in the Keynesian unemployment case, the sign of this comparative static result depends on our separability assumption, which insures that $\bar{D}_m$ affects domestic demand for exportables *only* through its effect on discretionary income.

The higher volume of exports in (6.41) insures that the trade balance unambiguously improves when the internal price of importables is increased:

$$\frac{dBT}{dp_m} = p_x^* \frac{dX^s}{dp_m} > 0, \tag{6.42}$$

because there is no effect on imports valued at world prices.

6 Summary

The effects of various trade liberalization policies on the levels and composition of domestic output and the balance of trade have been analyzed for both Keynesian and classical unemployment situations. It has been shown that the impact effects of devaluation, relaxation of import quotas, and raising ceilings on the domestic price of importables often differ depending on whether the economy is suffering from Keynesian or classical unemployment. To facilitate comparison of the policies' effects in these two different situations, the comparative static results obtained in this chapter are summarized in table 6.1.

The table shows that while devaluation of the exchange rate stimulates exportables production under both unemployment regimes, the effects on the volume of exports differ. In the classical unemployment case, the effect on export supply is uncertain *a priori*, as equation (6.35) shows. If the export supply curve is not backward-bending, however, exports will rise, bringing about an unambiguous improvement in the trade account.

In the Keynesian unemployment case, the net effect on countries' ability to earn foreign exchange depends on the elasticity of foreign export demand. The condition for a balance-of-trade improvement following devaluation in the presence of import quotas, it might be noted, is more stringent than the usual Marshall–Lerner condition. Recall (6.22).

The effects of relaxing import quotas, shown under $\bar{I}$ in table 6.1, also differ markedly in the Keynesian and classical unemployment cases. In the former, exportables production will fall, due to the fall in domestic demand in (6.24). Foreign demand remains unchanged. The trade balance unambiguously deteriorates as the import quota is relaxed. In the classical unemployment case, domestic production and employment in both sectors are unaffected by the increase in import quotas. Typically domestic demand for exportable goods falls as more import goods become available. In this case shipments of exports to foreigners increase. As a result, the balance-of-trade effect is uncertain; it depends on the relative magnitudes of foreigners' increased purchases of exports relative to domestic residents' increased expenditure on imports (as the quota is relaxed).

Increasing the administered price of output in the import-competing industry raises domestic output of importables under either Keynesian or classical unemployment. In the Keynesian case, the level of exports and the balance of trade will be unaffected, even though exportables production falls (with the fall in domestic demand). As indicated in table 6.1, exports increase in the classical case. This leads to an improvement in the trade balance.

With the foregoing results in mind, it is useful to return to our initial objective, namely to build a model to aid in the analysis of trade liberalization policies in situations where short-run price and wage rigidities are important, as they are for countries with import substitution policies. For LDCs, many of whom face world-determined prices for their exports and domestically controlled prices and quantitative restrictions on imports, classical unemployment is likely to be more common than Keynesian unemployment. Yet policy analysts often assume, at least implicitly, that they are operating in an environment where standard Keynesian models are appropriate.

This chapter has demonstrated that such an approach may lead to significant policy errors. A prerequisite for correct policy prescriptions is that policymakers first determine whether their unemployment is Keynesian in the sense that it is a consequence of inadequate (world) demand for domestic output; or alternatively, whether the underlying cause of unemployment is classical, i.e., due to excessive real wage demands given the relative productivity of domestic labor.

Once the underlying causes of unemployment are correctly diagnosed, it is possible to choose the correct framework for analyzing the effects of prevailing import substitution policies and the likely effects of trade liberalization. While the need for such an approach would presumably be more readily appreciated when designing macroeconomic stabilization policy (as we do in chapters 4 and 5), it has generally been neglected when the effects of exchange rate, quota, and price control changes are being investigated. The foregoing analysis suggests that the interaction of a multiplicity of domestic market distortions must be explicitly recognized by those considering alternative approaches to economic development if wise policy choices are to be made.

7

Tariff Policy under Fixed and Flexible Exchange Rates

Chapter 6 focused on import quotas, always assuming that the domestic importables price was held below its market-clearing level. The combination of the import quota and the non-market-clearing domestic price created a situation where households were rationed in the market for importable goods. In this chapter the assumptions of import quotas and quantity rationing in the importable goods market are abandoned. Instead we concentrate on another kind of commercial policy, which again is often implemented to promote import substitution, namely tariffs on imports.

The question of how tariffs work in small, fix-price economies has recently been addressed by Chan (1978), Eichengreen (1981), and Johansson and Löfgren (1980, 1981). These authors show that a tariff on imports improves "internal balance" (i.e., raises aggregate output and employment) in a fixed exchange rate economy suffering from unemployment. On the other hand, a tariff worsens internal balance under flexible exchange rates. The latter result is surprising given that it is often argued that tariffs *protect* production and increase employment in sectors facing competition from abroad.

The present chapter considers tariff policy under both fixed and flexible exchange rate regimes in a slightly different context than the small open economies examined by previous authors. The assumption in chapter 6 that the economy is large in the market for its exportables, in the sense that it faces a less than perfectly elastic export demand curve, is retained for the most part.[1] In the importables market, however, the country is "small." Hence in the absence of quantitative restrictions on imports considered in chapter 6, the price of importables is linked to the world price.

[1] For the classical unemployment case, a country that is small in its export market, so that exchange rate changes affect the *domestic-currency* price, is also considered.

More importantly, our treatment of the flexible exchange rate case uses a setup like the model in chapter 5 to incorporate the capital account. Hence the often-employed specification where the exchange rate adjusts to continually keep the *trade* balance rather than the official settlements balance equal to zero can be abandoned. This eliminates the asymmetric treatment of the country's intertemporal budget constraint that has plagued earlier comparisons of fixed and flexible exchange rate regimes.

1   The Model

The analysis of tariffs under fixed and flexible exchange rate regimes with perfectly integrated world capital markets involves a reasonably straightforward modification of the model in chapter 5. Whereas that model distinguished between tradeables and nontradeables sectors within the domestic economy, exportables and importables are distinguished here. This is, of course, a more reasonable disaggregation of goods when import tariffs are being considered.[2]

1.1   *The Production Sectors*

Assuming the country is small in the world market for its importable good, the domestic price of importables p_m will differ from the world price p_m^* only to the extent that the country imposes a tariff on imports. Normalizing so that $p_m^* = 1$:

$$p_m = e(1 + t). \tag{7.1}$$

This relationship holds regardless of whether the exchange rate is fixed or flexible, provided there is no "water in the tariff," i.e., it is not higher than the level where it becomes prohibitive. Furthermore domestic producers of the importable good can always sell their profit-maximizing level of output (given the fixed wage rate) at the prevailing domestic-currency price, as indicated by (7.11) below.

The price of the exportable good for most of our analysis is fixed in units of the domestic currency in the short run. The country is assumed to be "large" in the world market for its exportable good in the sense that it faces a downward-sloping export demand curve ((7.21) below). Given the prevailing domestic wage rate and export-

---

[2] Ideally one might prefer a three-good model distinguishing exportables, importables, and nontradeables as is done in Johansson and Löfgren (1980, 1981). For pedagogic reasons we retain the two-sector setup.

ables price, domestic producers of exportables may or may not face a sales constraint. (The two cases are in (7.19) and (7.12) respectively.) In the classical unemployment case, we briefly consider a second case where the exportables price is fixed in terms of foreign currency rather than domestic currency.

1.2   The Household Sector

The specification of the household sector differs slightly from that in chapter 6 in that households no longer face constraints on their purchases of importables (due to government-imposed import quotas). We continue to assume that households face no constraints on their demand for exportables. In the classical unemployment case, to be described below, this implies that if there is an excess *world* demand for exportables it is always foreigners not domestic consumers that are rationed. That is, we adopt the *rationing rule* that all domestic demand is satisfied before any exportables can be shipped abroad. (As was emphasized in chapter 2, the specification of such rationing rules is important. The temporary equilibrium of the economy depends on them.)

The household's demands for exportables and importables can then be determined by maximizing:

$$U(D_x, D_m, L^s, W'; \theta) \tag{7.2}$$

subject to:

$$p_x D_x + p_m D_m + W' = Y + W + T, \tag{7.3}$$

where $Y = w\bar{L} + \pi$ is national income defined in nominal terms. T is (nominal) tariff revenue, which is assumed to be redistributed to households by the government in the form of lump-sum transfers. (It is straightforward to analyze the case where $T = 0$ to see what happens when the government retains the tariff revenue to finance its expenditures on goods and services.)

The maximization of (7.2) subject to (7.3) yields commodity demand functions of the following form:

$$\hat{D}_x = \hat{D}_x(\overset{+}{p}_m, \bar{p}_x, \overset{+}{Y} + W + T), \tag{7.4}$$

$$\hat{D}_m = \hat{D}_m(\bar{p}_m, \overset{+}{p}_x, \overset{+}{Y} + W + T), \tag{7.5}$$

where households are constrained in the labor market and labor is weakly separable in the utility function so that $\bar{L}$ does not enter (7.4)–(7.5) as a separate argument. Following the analysis in chapter 5, it is assumed that the effective demand functions (denoted by hats when there is an employment constraint) have the above-specified signs on their partial derivatives. Defining nominal expenditure as:

$$\hat{Z} = p_x \hat{D}_x(p_m, p_x, Y + W + T) + p_m \hat{D}_m(p_m, p_x, Y + W + T),$$
(7.6)

we make the additional assumptions (analogous to (5.17) in chapter 5) that:

$$\frac{\partial \hat{Z}}{\partial p_m} = p_x \frac{\partial \hat{D}_x}{\partial p_m} + \hat{D}_m \left(1 + \frac{p_m}{\hat{D}_m} \frac{\partial \hat{D}_m}{\partial p_m}\right) > 0,$$
(7.7)

$$\frac{\partial \hat{Z}}{\partial p_x} = p_m \frac{\partial \hat{D}_m}{\partial p_x} + \hat{D}_x \left(1 + \frac{p_x}{\hat{D}_x} \frac{\partial \hat{D}_x}{\partial p_x}\right) > 0.$$
(7.8)

Equations (7.7) and (7.8) state that an increase in the price of either good is assumed to increase total expenditure. This implies, of course, that saving must fall with a rise in the price of importables or exportables (holding income Y constant).

Following chapter 5, we assume that households' money demand depends positively on expenditure in (7.6). Hence using (7.1), we can write money demand as a function of prices, income, and wealth:

$$\hat{M} = \hat{M}(e(1 + t), p_x, Y + W + T).$$
(7.9)

The specified signs on the partial derivatives:

$$\frac{\partial \hat{M}}{\partial e}, \quad \frac{\partial \hat{M}}{\partial t}, \quad \frac{\partial \hat{M}}{\partial p_x}, \quad \frac{\partial \hat{M}}{\partial Y} > 0$$
(7.10)

follow from the assumptions in (7.7) and (7.8).

2 Classical and Keynesian Unemployment Equilibria

For the sake of clarity and easy reference, the two unemployment regimes described earlier are summarized briefly below.

2.1 Classical Unemployment

Under classical unemployment, domestic producers in both the importables and exportables sectors operate at profit-maximizing output levels:

$$Y_m = Y_m(e(1 + t), w),$$
(7.11)

$$Y_x = Y_x(p_x, w).$$
(7.12)

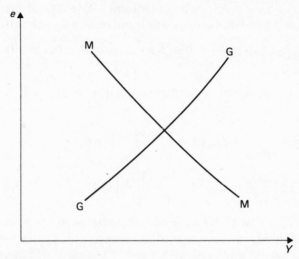

FIGURE 7.1   Short-run equilibrium under flexible exchange rates

National income, therefore, equals:

$$Y = p_x Y_x(p_x, w) + e(1 + t) Y_m(e(1 + t), w). \tag{7.13}$$

Under fixed exchange rates, equation (7.13) alone determines income. As e rises so does Y; this positive relationship is shown by the GG curve in figure 7.1.

Finally money market equilibrium is defined by equating money supply M^s to money demand in (7.9):

$$M^s = \hat{M}(e(1 + t), p_x, Y + W + T). \tag{7.14}$$

If the monetary authority is to keep the exchange rate fixed, it must willingly accommodate all changes in money demand at its target exchange rate through foreign exchange market intervention. Thus the money supply in (7.14) is endogenous (and recursively determined) under a fixed exchange rate regime. This could be represented in figure 7.1 by a horizontal MM locus at the official exchange rate.

Under flexible exchange rates, on the other hand, no such intervention need occur. Hence the money supply is exogenous in this case. Equation (7.14) then indicates a negative relationship between e and Y along the money market equilibrium locus MM in the figure.

Under flexible exchange rates, e and Y must be determined simultaneously (for a given level of tariff revenue T, to be discussed below) using (7.13) and (7.14). The solution is represented graphically as the intersection point of the GG and MM curves.

Given values of (e, Y), the remaining variables of interest under classical unemployment can be specified. Domestic export supply X^s and import demand I^d are defined as:

$$X^s = Y_x(p_x, w) - \hat{D}_x(e(1+t), p_x, Y + W + T), \tag{7.15}$$

$$I^d = \hat{D}_m(e(1+t), p_x, Y + W + T) - Y_m(e(1+t), w). \tag{7.16}$$

The trade balance in units of foreign currency (with $p_m^* = 1$), therefore, equals:

$$BT = \frac{p_x}{e} X^s - I^d. \tag{7.17}$$

Tariff revenue received by the government and redistributed as a lump-sum transfer to households equals:

$$T = et \times I^d. \tag{7.18}$$

The careful reader will note that under flexible rates it is, in general, necessary to solve (7.13), (7.14), *and* (7.18) simultaneously to determine (e, Y). We consider only policy changes around an initial equilibrium where the tariff rate t is zero, thereby avoiding the additional complexities caused by endogenous tariff revenue via (7.18). This will become apparent in the comparative static analyses in later sections of this chapter.

2.2 Keynesian Unemployment

Keynesian unemployment differs from classical unemployment in that exportables production is limited by the extent of aggregate world demand:

$$\bar{Y}_x = \hat{D}_x(e(1+t), p_x, \bar{Y} + W + T) + X^d(p_x/e). \tag{7.19}$$

Domestic producers of importables still operate at profit-maximizing levels. Thus national income equals:

$$\bar{Y} = p_x\hat{D}_x(e(1+t), p_x, \bar{Y} + W + T) + p_xX^d(p_x/e)$$
$$+ e(1+t)Y_m(e(1+t), w). \tag{7.20}$$

Under fixed exchange rates, this equation alone determines national income (for a given tariff revenue T). It indicates a positive relationship between e and $\bar{Y}$, which is shown as the GG locus in figure 7.1 (analogous to the GG locus under classical unemployment).

Under flexible exchange rates, the (aggregate) goods market equilibrium (7.20) and the money market equilibrium condition (7.14) simultaneously determine the exchange rate and national income (for a given T).

Although the level of exports is limited by export *demand* under Keynesian unemployment (so that export supply in (7.15) no longer applies), equation (7.16) still defines import demand:

$$X^d = X^d(p_x/e), \tag{7.21}$$

$$I^d = \hat{D}_m(e(1+t), p_x, Y + W + T) - Y_m(e(1+t), w), \tag{7.22}$$

where tariff revenue again equals (7.18). Hence the trade balance equals:

$$BT = \frac{p_x}{e} X^d\left(\frac{p_x}{e}\right) - I^d \tag{7.23}$$

in the Keynesian unemployment case.

3 Tariffs under Fixed Exchange Rates

Under either classical or Keynesian unemployment with fixed exchange rates, increasing the tariff on imports stimulates the domestic production of importables by driving up the domestic-currency price:

$$\frac{dY_m}{dt} = \frac{\partial Y_m}{\partial p_m} \frac{dp_m}{dt} > 0, \tag{7.24}$$

where $p_m = e(1+t)$. The effect of the tariff on the exportables sector, on the other hand, depends on the type of unemployment being experienced.

3.1 *Classical Unemployment*

In the classical unemployment case, production of exportables (7.12) depends only on the fixed domestic-currency price p_x and wage rate w. Hence, it is unaffected by changes in the tariff. National income nevertheless rises due to the stimulative effect on the domestic production of importables:

$$\frac{dY}{dt} = e(1+t) \frac{dY_m}{dt} + eY_m > 0. \tag{7.25}$$

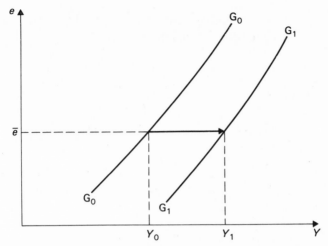

FIGURE 7.2 The effect of a tariff increase on national output under fixed exchange rates regardless of whether unemployment is Keynesian or classical

Thus an increase in the tariff under classical unemployment shifts the GG locus in figure 7.2 to the right.

Although exportables *production* remains unchanged, the volume of exports is affected by the tariff via its effect on domestic demand. (Recall our assumed rationing rule that domestic demand is satisfied before foreign demand.) Both the direct price effect and income effect of the increased tariff contribute to higher domestic demand for exportables, thereby reducing export supply. This is confirmed differentiating (7.15):

$$\frac{\mathrm{d}X^s}{\mathrm{d}t} = -\left[\frac{\partial \hat{D}_x}{\partial p_m}\frac{\mathrm{d}p_m}{\mathrm{d}t} + \frac{\partial \hat{D}_x}{\partial Y}\left(\frac{\mathrm{d}Y}{\mathrm{d}t} + \frac{\mathrm{d}T}{\mathrm{d}t}\right)\right] < 0. \qquad (7.26)$$
$$\quad\;\;\,{\scriptstyle (+)}\;\;\;{\scriptstyle (+)}\qquad{\scriptstyle (+)}\;\;\;{\scriptstyle (+)}\;\;\;{\scriptstyle (+)}$$

Note that the income effect incorporates both the rise in national output in (7.25) and the increased lump-sum transfer of tariff revenue, which differentiating (7.18) with $t = 0$ initially is seen to equal:

$$\frac{\mathrm{d}T}{\mathrm{d}t} = eI^d > 0. \qquad (7.27)$$

The assumption that $t = 0$ initially greatly simplifies our tariff analysis, because it implies that (7.27) can be used under both the fixed or flexible exchange rate cases. This reduces the degree of simultaneity in the model greatly by enabling us to ignore the feed-back effects of endogenous changes in exchange rates and income on tariff revenue and vice versa.

The effect of a tariff increase on import demand depends on its price and income effects on domestic demand, as well as the positive production effect:

$$\frac{\mathrm{d}I^{\mathrm{d}}}{\mathrm{d}t} = \frac{\partial \hat{D}_{\mathrm{m}}}{\partial p_{\mathrm{m}}} \frac{\mathrm{d}p_{\mathrm{m}}}{\mathrm{d}t} + \frac{\partial \hat{D}_{\mathrm{m}}}{\partial Y} \left(\frac{\mathrm{d}Y}{\mathrm{d}t} + \frac{\mathrm{d}T}{\mathrm{d}t} \right) - \frac{\mathrm{d}Y_{\mathrm{m}}}{\mathrm{d}t}. \tag{7.28}$$

By substituting the expressions for $\mathrm{d}Y/\mathrm{d}t$ and $\mathrm{d}T/\mathrm{d}t$ from (7.25) and (7.27) and employing the Slutsky decomposition of the price effect $\partial \hat{D}_{\mathrm{m}}/\partial p_{\mathrm{m}}$, however, equation (7.28) can be written:

$$\frac{\mathrm{d}I^{\mathrm{d}}}{\mathrm{d}t} = \left[\left(\frac{\partial \hat{D}_{\mathrm{m}}}{\partial p_{\mathrm{m}}} \right)_{\mathrm{comp}} - \hat{D}_{\mathrm{m}} \frac{\partial \hat{D}_{\mathrm{m}}}{\partial Y} \right] \frac{\mathrm{d}p_{\mathrm{m}}}{\mathrm{d}t}$$

$$+ \frac{\partial \hat{D}_{\mathrm{m}}}{\partial Y} \left(p_{\mathrm{m}} \frac{\mathrm{d}Y_{\mathrm{m}}}{\mathrm{d}t} + e\hat{D}_{\mathrm{m}} \right) - \frac{\mathrm{d}Y_{\mathrm{m}}}{\mathrm{d}t}$$

$$= \left[\left(\frac{\partial \hat{D}_{\mathrm{m}}}{\partial p_{\mathrm{m}}} \right)_{\mathrm{comp}} - \left(1 - p_{\mathrm{m}} \frac{\partial \hat{D}_{\mathrm{m}}}{\partial Y} \right) \frac{\partial Y_{\mathrm{m}}}{\partial p_{\mathrm{m}}} \right] \frac{\mathrm{d}p_{\mathrm{m}}}{\mathrm{d}t} < 0. \tag{7.29}$$
$$\underset{(-)}{} \qquad\qquad \underset{(+)}{} \qquad \underset{(+)}{} \qquad \underset{(+)}{}$$

Thus, *the tariff unambiguously brings about a reduction in import volume in the classical unemployment case.* Parenthetically, the same result would have been obtained if tariff revenue was not redistributed to households, as can easily be shown by setting $\mathrm{d}T/\mathrm{d}t = 0$ in (7.28).

Even though import volume is reduced by a tariff, the fact that export volume also falls suggests *a priori* that the tariff may or may not move the economy closer to external balance when it has a fixed exchange rate and classical unemployment:

$$\frac{\mathrm{d}BT}{\mathrm{d}t} = \frac{p_{\mathrm{x}}}{e} \frac{\mathrm{d}X^{\mathrm{s}}}{\mathrm{d}t} - \frac{\mathrm{d}I^{\mathrm{d}}}{\mathrm{d}t} \gtrless 0. \tag{7.30}$$
$$\underset{(-)}{} \qquad \underset{(-)}{}$$

Although the balance-of-trade effect is uncertain, tariff policy does nevertheless have an unambiguous, expansionary effect on both output and employment in the import competing sector. Recall (7.24).

3.2 *Keynesian Unemployment*

Under Keynesian unemployment, a tariff hike stimulates production in the exportables, not just the importables, sector:

$$\frac{d\bar{Y}_x}{dt} = \left(\frac{1}{1-p_x\,\partial\hat{D}_x/\partial Y}\right)\left[\frac{\partial\hat{D}_x}{\partial p_m}\frac{dp_m}{dt}\right.$$

$$\left. + \frac{\partial\hat{D}_x}{\partial Y}\left(p_m\frac{dY_m}{dt} + eY_m + \frac{dT}{dt}\right)\right] > 0. \tag{7.31}$$

This stimulus is a result of the tariff-induced increase in domestic demand for exportables. The increase reflects both a price effect toward exportables consumption (as the tariff drives up the price of importables) and an income effect. The income effect can be decomposed into the positive impact of the tariff on profit-maximizing output in the importables sector and the positive transfer of tariff revenue to households (7.27).

As production in *both* the importables and exportables sectors rises under Keynesian unemployment, it is clear that the tariff must raise national income (and employment):

$$\frac{d\bar{Y}}{dt} = p_x\frac{d\bar{Y}_x}{dt} + p_m\frac{dY_m}{dt} + eY_m > 0, \tag{7.32}$$

as long as the central bank keeps the exchange rate fixed. Thus a tariff shifts the GG curve in figure 7.2 to the right under Keynesian unemployment, as it did under classical unemployment. In the latter case, however, this was due solely to expansion in the import-competing sector.

Although domestic demand for exportables rises with an increase in the tariff, *export volume is unaffected in the Keynesian unemployment case* (because p_x/e in (7.21) remains unchanged). Recall that export volume fell in the classical unemployment case (7.26).

Domestic demand for importables may rise or fall because the income and price effects of the tariff hike operate in opposite directions under Keynesian unemployment. Thus, *although importables production unambiguously rises, the net effect on import volume is indeterminate.* Hence the trade balance is again indeterminate *a priori* (just as it was under classical unemployment):

$$\frac{dI^d}{dt} = e\left(\frac{\partial\hat{D}_m}{\partial p_m} - \frac{\partial Y_m}{\partial p_m}\right) + \frac{\partial\hat{D}_m}{\partial Y}\left(\frac{dY}{dt} + \frac{dT}{dt}\right) \gtrless 0, \tag{7.33}$$

$$\frac{\mathrm{d}BT}{\mathrm{d}t} = \frac{-\mathrm{d}I^{\mathrm{d}}}{\mathrm{d}t} \gtreqless 0. \tag{7.34}$$

Parenthetically, the indeterminacy cannot be resolved in this case by substituting for $\mathrm{d}Y/\mathrm{d}t$ and $\mathrm{d}T/\mathrm{d}t$ and employing the Slutsky decomposition of $\partial \hat{D}_{\mathrm{m}}/\partial p_{\mathrm{m}}$, in contrast to the classical unemployment case above.

The effects of imposing a tariff in a fixed exchange rate economy are summarized in table 7.1 for both the classical and Keynesian unemployment cases. The general conclusion emerges that *a tariff will unambiguously raise employment and national income under either regime. The sectoral output effects, however, differ.* Under Keynesian unemployment, the import tariff stimulates production in both the exportables and importables industries, while under classical unemployment only the import-competing sector benefits.

TABLE 7.1   The effects of a tariff increase under fixed exchange rates

	Y_{m}	Y_{x}	Y	X	I	BT
Classical unemployment	+	0	+	−	−	?
Keynesian unemployment	+	+	+	0	?	?

Export volume, on the other hand, is unchanged under Keynesian unemployment, while it falls in the classical unemployment case. In the latter case, we also know that tariffs cause import volume to fall whereas this is uncertain under Keynesian unemployment. The tariff's effects on the trade balance are indeterminate *a priori*. All of this suggests that *the use of a tariff as a protective device designed to stimulate employment and output, particularly in the import-competing sector, is more certain than its efficacy in bringing about external balance.*

4   Tariffs under Flexible Exchange Rates

The effects of tariff increases are greatly complicated in countries with flexible exchange rates. In such cases the short-run exchange rate and national income must be simultaneously determined. Qualitatively, the effect of tariffs can be seen using figure 7.3. As was shown in the fixed exchange rate analysis above. the GG locus shifts

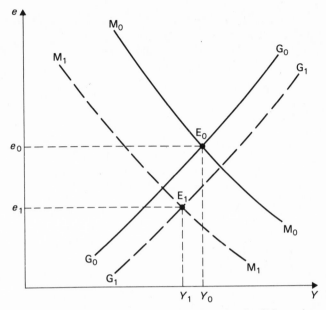

FIGURE 7.3   The effect of a tariff increase under flexible exchange rates

to the right when the tariff is increased. The size of the shift depends on whether unemployment is classical or Keynesian in nature.

Under flexible exchange rates, the effect of tariffs on the money market locus MM must also be considered. It is easy to see from (7.9) that for a given level of the exchange rate and national income, an increase in the tariff would increase money demand:

$$\frac{d\hat{M}}{dt}\bigg|_{Y=Y_0,e=e_0} = \frac{\partial \hat{M}}{\partial t} + \frac{\partial \hat{M}}{\partial Y}\frac{dT}{dt} > 0. \qquad (7.35)$$

This increase in money demand comes from two sources. First, the tariff drives up the domestic price of importable goods. Second, to the extent that tariff revenue is redistributed to households, their disposable income and hence expenditure rises. Thus at each level of national income Y, the exchange rate must appreciate when the tariff is increased if monetary equilibrium is to be maintained. This is shown diagrammatically as a downward shift of the MM locus in figure 7.3.

From the downward shifts of both MM and GG in the figure it is clear that *the short-run equilibrium exchange rate unambiguously appreciates when a tariff is imposed.* Unfortunately this appreciation works in the opposite direction of the tariff itself, making it unclear *a priori* whether the domestic price of importables (7.1) will rise or fall:

$$\frac{dp_m}{dt} = e + \underset{(-)}{\frac{de}{dt}} \gtrless 0. \qquad (7.36)$$

As figure 7.3 suggests, *national income may rise or fall*, in stark contrast to our conclusions for the fixed exchange rate case.

To determine the tariff's effect on national income as well as its sectoral effects requires that each unemployment regime be considered separately.

4.1   *Classical Unemployment*

Under classical unemployment both exportables and importables producers are unconstrained in the labor and output markets. Although the country is small in the world market for *importables*, it is interesting to consider two possibilities in the *exportables* market, as we did in chapter 6. In the first case, the country is large in the exportables market so that *domestic-currency* price p_x is fixed. Hence exchange rate changes affect the *foreign* price $p_x^* = p_x/e$:

$$dp_x/de = 0, \qquad dp_x^*/de < 0. \qquad (7.37a)$$

The second case is that of a small country where the *foreign-currency* price is fixed so that changes in the exchange rate affect the *domestic* price:

$$dp_x/de > 0, \qquad dp_x^*/de = 0. \qquad (7.37b)$$

The large-country case: p_x fixed

Consider the large-country case first. It is simpler than the small-country case for the present analysis of classical unemployment.

The short-run equilibrium conditions are given by (7.13) and (7.14), which for convenience are written here using $p_m = e(1 + t)$:

$$Y = p_x Y_x(p_x, w) + p_m Y_m(p_m, w), \qquad (7.13')$$

$$M^s = \hat{M}(p_x, p_m, Y + W + T(t)). \qquad (7.14')$$

It is assumed that $t = 0$ initially, so that dT/dt is well defined below. Totally differentiating this system yields:

$$
\begin{bmatrix}
1 & -\left(Y_m + p_m \dfrac{\partial Y_m}{\partial p_m}\right) \\[2ex]
\dfrac{\partial \hat{M}}{\partial Y} & \dfrac{\partial \hat{M}}{\partial p_m}
\end{bmatrix}
\begin{bmatrix}
\dfrac{dY}{dt} \\[2ex]
\dfrac{dp_m}{dt}
\end{bmatrix}
=
\begin{bmatrix}
0 \\[2ex]
-\dfrac{\partial \hat{M}}{\partial Y}\dfrac{dT}{dt}
\end{bmatrix}, \quad (7.38)
$$

where the determinant of the matrix, denoted $|A|$, is unambiguously positive. Diagrammatically this is insured by the fact that the GG curve slopes upward and the MM curve slopes downward in figure 7.3. It is now a simple matter to solve for the effect of the tariff on output and the domestic price of importables:

$$
\frac{dY}{dt} = \frac{-1}{|A|}\left(Y_m + p_m \frac{\partial Y_m}{\partial p_m}\right)\frac{\partial \hat{M}}{\partial Y}\frac{dT}{dt} < 0, \qquad (7.39)
$$

$$
\frac{dp_m}{dt} = \frac{-1}{|A|}\left(\frac{\partial \hat{M}}{\partial Y}\frac{dT}{dt}\right) < 0. \qquad (7.40)
$$

It is noteworthy here (see also Johansson, 1981) that if the government did *not* redistribute tariff revenue (i.e., $dT/dt = 0$), the tariff would have no effect on the domestic price of importables and consequently no effect on importables production or national income.

When tariff revenue is redistributed, however, the tariff *reduces* domestic prices in the import-competing sector. Hence the tariff has an *antiprotective* effect causing output and employment in the importables sector (and hence overall, see (7.39)) to fall:

$$
\frac{dY_m}{dt} = \frac{\partial Y_m}{\partial p_m}\frac{dp_m}{dt} < 0. \qquad (7.41)
$$

Exportables production is constant in the large-country case where p_x is unaffected by endogenous changes in the exchange rate (regardless of the tariff redistribution issue).

The direct price effect of the tariff as well as the income effects (due to lower GNP on one hand, but higher tariff revenue redistributions on the other) affect export and import volumes. It can be shown using (7.39) and the definition of $|A|$ above that national income falls by less than tariff revenue rises. Thus disposable income $Y + T$ unambiguously rises with an increase in the tariff provided tariff revenue is redistributed. Consequently the effect on import volume (7.16) is always *positive*, i.e., tariffs *increase* import volume, under classical unemployment with flexible exchange rates:[3]

$$\frac{dI^d}{dt} = \underbrace{\frac{\partial \hat{D}_m}{\partial p_m}}_{(-)} \underbrace{\frac{dp_m}{dt}}_{(-)} + \underbrace{\frac{\partial \hat{D}_m}{\partial Y}}_{(+)} \left(\underbrace{\frac{dY}{dt} + \frac{dT}{dt}}_{(+)} \right) - \underbrace{\frac{\partial Y_m}{\partial p_m}}_{(+)} \underbrace{\frac{dp_m}{dt}}_{(-)} > 0. \qquad (7.42)$$

The tariff causes domestic importables prices to *fall*, thereby increasing domestic demand and reducing domestic production directly. In the case where tariff revenue is redistributed, household disposable income rises, which further stimulates domestic demand.

It must be concluded that tariffs are indeed a poor instrument for increasing importables production or for reducing import volume. Under classical unemployment with flexible exchange rates, tariffs have exactly the opposite effect!

Turning to the effect on export volume (7.15), it appears that the direct price effect of lower importables prices reduces domestic demand for exportables, while the rise in disposable income raises it:

$$\frac{dX^s}{dt} = -\left[\underbrace{\frac{\partial \hat{D}_x}{\partial p_m}}_{(+)} \underbrace{\frac{dp_m}{dt}}_{(-)} + \underbrace{\frac{\partial \hat{D}_x}{\partial Y}}_{(+)} \left(\underbrace{\frac{dY}{dt} + \frac{dT}{dt}}_{(+)} \right) \right] \gtreqless 0. \qquad (7.43)$$

Thus the tariff's effect on export volume is indeterminate.[4]

The small-country case: p_x^* fixed

It turns out that the foregoing tariff analysis under classical unemployment depends in an important way on the assumption that the *domestic* price of exportables is unaffected by tariff-induced changes in the exchange rate. In the small-country case where such changes in exportables prices *do* occur, the appreciation of the exchange rate is much smaller – so much so, in fact, that the domestic price of importables will now rise (rather than fall) when the tariff is imposed. (Recall (7.36).) This causes importables production to rise. The production of exportables, however, falls as the exchange rate appreciates. Hence the total effect on national income is indeterminate, as is the balance-of-trade effect. These effects are summarized in table 7.2, to

---

[3] Note that this is exactly the opposite of the tariff effect on imports under fixed rates. Recall (7.29).

[4] The curious reader might be interested to know that this indeterminacy *cannot* be resolved by using the Slutsky decomposition and the expression for the change in national income in (7.39) or (7.41).

TABLE 7.2 The effects of import tariffs under flexible exchange rates

	Y	e	p_m	Y_m	Y_x	X	I	BT
Classical unemployment								
p_x fixed	−	−	−	−	0	?	+	?
p_x^* fixed	?	−	+	+	−	?	?	?
Keynesian unemployment								
$0 \leqslant \epsilon_f < p_x \partial \hat{D}_x / \partial Y$	?	−	−	−	?	−	?	?
$\epsilon_f = 1$	−	−	0	0	−	−	?	?
$\epsilon_f > 1$	−	−	+	+	−	−	?	?

facilitate a comparison between the large- and small-country cases.[5] Of course, most real-world cases lie between these two extreme cases where exchange rate changes have either no effect or an equal percentage effect on the domestic price of exportables.

4.2 Keynesian Unemployment

Consider next the Keynesian unemployment case for a large country whose exportables producers face a sales constraint $\bar{Y}_x$ determined by domestic plus foreign demand at prevailing prices $(p_x, e(1+t), w)$ and initial wealth, as in (7.19). Under flexible exchange rates, exportables production must be determined simultaneously with the level of the exchange rate.

It was explained above that the imposition of a tariff unambiguously shifts MM downward to the left, while GG shifts downward to the right. Hence, it is clear that the exchange rate must appreciate (i.e., e falls), but the effect on national income is uncertain a priori.

In order to determine the sectoral consequences of the tariff, it is again convenient to write the goods and money market equilibrium conditions (7.20) and (7.14) in terms of Y and p_m rather than Y and e:

$$\bar{Y} = p_x \hat{D}_x(p_m, p_x, \bar{Y} + W + T) + p_x X^d(p_x/e) + p_m Y_m(p_m, w),$$

$$\text{(7.44)}$$

$$M^s = M(p_m, p_x, \bar{Y} + W + T). \qquad (7.45)$$

---

[5] The calculations are straightforward, but tedious. They involve totally differentiating the short-run equilibrium conditions (7.13) and (7.14) using (7.1) to obtain the equilibrium changes in e, p_m, and Y from imposing the tariff.

Total differentiation of this system using (7.36) yields:[6]

$$
\begin{bmatrix}
1 - p_x \dfrac{\partial \hat{D}_x}{\partial Y} & -\left(p_x \dfrac{\partial \hat{D}_x}{\partial p_m} - \dfrac{p_x}{e^2} \dfrac{\partial X^d}{\partial p_x^*} + Y_m + p_m \dfrac{\partial Y_m}{\partial p_m} \right) \\[2ex]
\dfrac{\partial \hat{M}}{\partial Y} & \dfrac{\partial \hat{M}}{\partial p_m}
\end{bmatrix}
\begin{bmatrix}
\dfrac{d\bar{Y}}{dt} \\[2ex]
\dfrac{dp_m}{dt}
\end{bmatrix}
$$

$$
= \begin{bmatrix}
p_x \left(\dfrac{\partial \hat{D}_x}{\partial Y} \dfrac{dT}{dt} + \dfrac{p_x}{e} \dfrac{\partial X^d}{\partial p_x^*} \right) \\[2ex]
- \dfrac{\partial \hat{M}}{\partial Y} \dfrac{dT}{dt}
\end{bmatrix}, \qquad (7.46)
$$

whose determinant $|A|$ is positive definite. Solving for the change in importables prices shows that, in general, they may rise or fall when a tariff is imposed:

$$
\frac{dp_m}{dt} = \frac{1}{|A|} \underbrace{\left(-\frac{\partial \hat{M}}{\partial Y} \right)}_{(+)} \underbrace{\left(\frac{dT}{dt} + \frac{p_x^2}{e} \frac{\partial X^d}{\partial p_x^*} \right)}_{(-)} \gtrless 0. \qquad (7.47)
$$

In the case where tariff revenue is not redistributed to households $(dT/dt = 0)$, however, it is easily seen from (7.47) that importables prices would unambiguously rise. More generally, if the trade balance is initially zero so that $dT/dt = eI^d = p_x X^d$, (7.47) can be written in terms of the price elasticity of foreign export demand ϵ_f:

$$
\frac{dp_m}{dt} = \frac{p_x X^d}{|A|} \left(-\frac{\partial \hat{M}}{\partial Y} \right) \left(1 + \frac{p_x^*}{X^d} \frac{\partial X^d}{\partial p_x^*} \right) = \frac{p_x X^d}{|A|} \left(\frac{\partial \hat{M}}{\partial Y} \right) (\epsilon_f - 1).
$$

$$
(7.48)
$$

If foreign demand is elastic (as it would be for relatively small countries in the world market for the exportable good), the internal price of importables would rise. With an inelastic foreign demand, on the other hand, a tariff will *reduce* the internal price of importables! This, of course, would have an antiprotective effect, causing production in the import-competing sector to fall.

In light of these varying effects on the importables sector, it is interesting to examine the tariff's effects on total output. Price

---

[6] In order to solve this system for p_m and Y, we have used the fact that $p_m = e(1 + t)$ to rewrite the argument of the export function as $p_x/e = p_x(1 + t)/p_m$. This eliminates the need to simultaneously solve for e, which from figure 7.3 clearly appreciates.

effects that impact adversely on the importables sector will stimulate demand for exportables and vice versa. In addition, the redistribution of tariff revenue stimulates domestic demand. Consequently, *national income may, in general, rise or fall when a tariff is imposed in a flexible exchange rate economy suffering from Keynesian unemployment.* This can be confirmed by solving (7.46) for $d\bar{Y}/dt$. As the size of the foreign elasticity of export demand ϵ_f affects the tariff's impact on importable prices, it can be shown that it is also important for the sign of overall output changes, as table 7.2 indicates.

It might also be noted from (7.46) that *national output will unambiguously fall in the case where the government does not redistribute tariff revenue* to the private sector (so that $dT/dt = 0$):

$$\frac{d\bar{Y}}{dt} = \frac{1}{|A|}\left(\frac{p_x^2}{e}\frac{\partial X^d}{\partial p_x^*}\right)\frac{\partial \hat{M}}{\partial p_m} < 0. \tag{7.49}$$

Regarding the tariff's effects on exports, imports, and the trade balance, the tariff-induced appreciation of the domestic currency unambiguously reduces export demand as long as the domestic-currency price of exportables p_x is taken to be fixed, as assumed here. Unfortunately the tariff effect on import volume is indeterminate *a priori* due to the conflict between price, output, and tariff revenue distribution effects. This indeterminacy, of course, also renders the trade balance indeterminate – a recurring result in all of the regimes considered in table 7.2.

5   Concluding Remarks

It is often argued that tariffs protect production and increase employment in sectors facing competition from abroad. The foregoing analysis has demonstrated, however, that if the exchange rate is flexible domestic production of importables may in fact *decrease* when the tariff is imposed on imports. The larger the country is in the world market for exportables, the more likely is this outcome. Moreover, the tariff-induced appreciation of the exchange rate typically causes the production of exportables to fall. All things considered, therefore, tariffs cause national income to fall (or to change in an ambiguous way) regardless of whether the economy is suffering from classical unemployment or Keynesian unemployment. These results suggest that tariffs should not be employed in an economy with flexible exchange rates if the objective is to stimulate domestic production and employment.[7] If the exchange rate is fixed, on the other hand, the general conclusion emerges that a tariff on imports unambiguously raises employment and national income under either classical unemployment or Keynesian unemployment.

The tariff's effect on the trade balance is, in every case, indeterminate *a priori*. This is true under both fixed and flexible exchange rate regimes and under either classical or Keynesian unemployment. One must conclude that the use of a tariff as a protective device designed to stimulate employment and output, particularly in the import-competing sector, is more certain than its efficacy in ameliorating balance-of-payments difficulties.

Finally, it should be pointed out that the efficacy of tariffs under fixed exchange rates will depend on the vigor with which laborers resist real wage reductions by demanding compensating upward adjustment in nominal wages. Recall that the tariff reduces the real wage by raising the domestic price of importables (while the nominal wage is assumed to be fixed). As the analysis of devaluations and compensation claims from trade unions in chapter 4 demonstrates, the outcome will typically depend on the particular form of real wage resistance postulated.

[7] These results are consistent with the results in Johansson and Löfgren (1981), where a similar problem is analyzed in a three-sector model (exportables, importables, and a non-tradeable).

8

Cost–Benefit Rules in General Disequilibrium

1 Introduction

The *efficiency* of macroeconomic policy is most often discussed in terms of its effects on variables like employment, the price level, and external balance rather than in terms of its effect on welfare. This is true, at least in part, because of the difficulty of defining and estimating welfare. Another important reason for the neglect of welfare measures in economic policy analysis is the lack of a satisfactory "link" between the microeconomics of public finance and traditional Keynesian macroeconomics. Whereas public finance theory uses models based on individual optimization, it is ill-equipped to deal with non-market-clearing situations, which lie beyond its Walrasian equilibrium framework. Macroeconomics, on the other hand, focuses on market imblances but its microeconomic underpinning has often been weak. This lack of microeconomic foundations has made it difficult to directly assess the welfare effects of government policies.

In this chapter it is shown how fix-price models can be used to derive project evaluation or cost–benefit rules for situations where there is quantity rationing due to price stickiness in markets for goods and factors. The model employed is the small open-economy model developed in chapter 4. To generate appropriate cost–benefit rules we will follow the tradition in public finance theory of considering state-owned firms that produce marketable goods – either tradeables or nontradeables – using homogeneous labor as the only variable input. Their levels of production are exogenous policy-determined variables so that the value of the marginal product may differ from the wage. These firms, however, like all other agents in the economy, are assumed to take prices as given.

Although this chapter focuses on government *production* activity, it should be clear from the analysis that the setup employed can

167

easily be adapted to the welfare evaluation of fiscal policy, i.e., government *purchases* of privately produced output. This is a major advantage of the microtheoretic approach to open-economy macroeconomics used in this book. It obviates the need for an *ad hoc* evaluation of the efficiency of various macroeconomic policies based on their output, employment or external balance effects. Instead a thoroughgoing welfare assessment based on public finance concepts, as extended here to a disequilibrium framework, is possible. For recent contributions the reader is referred to Bell and Devarajan (1983), Blitzer *et al.* (1981), J. H. Drèze (1982), J. P. Drèze (1982), Johansson (1982a, 1982b), Marchand *et al.* (1983), and Roberts (1982).

2 Cost–Benefit Rules in General Equilibrium

To obtain a reference situation, we begin by deriving shadow pricing rules for situations characterized by continuous market clearing via price adjustment. To do so, consider state-owned firms that produce tradeable and nontradeable goods, respectively, using labor as the sole variable input. The production functions are:

$$Y_{tg} = Y_{tg}(L_{tg}), \tag{8.1}$$

$$Y_{ng} = Y_{ng}(L_{ng}), \tag{8.2}$$

where the t and n subscripts indicate tradeables and nontradeables, as before. The g subscript denotes government (as opposed to private sector) output supply or labor demand. State-owned firms hire labor at the prevailing wage w and sell output at prevailing prices p_n and p_t. Because the levels of public-sector employment L_{ng} and L_{tg} (or equivalently the levels of output Y_{ng} and Y_{tg}) are exogenously determined policy variables, the marginal revenue product of government-employed labor in each sector may exceed or fall short of the wage.

Any profits (or losses) incurred by state-owned firms are assumed to be disposed of (financed) by lump-sum taxes (transfers) T. Hence, the government budget constraint takes the form:

$$T = -[p_n Y_{ng}(L_{ng}) - wL_{ng} + p_t Y_{tg}(L_{tg}) - wL_{tg}], \tag{8.3}$$

where $T > 0$ indicates a lump sum tax; $T < 0$, a transfer payment. This simple specification allows us to concentrate on the market imbalance issue. Later, in section 6 below, we explore the interesting and perhaps more realistic case where public-sector losses are financed by (distorting) taxes on commodities and factors rather than by lump-sum taxes.

In order to focus on efficiency considerations while setting aside matters of equity and income distribution, the commonly employed assumption of a "representative" household is maintained here. As is well known, welfare analysis becomes considerably more complicated when interpersonal utility comparisons must be made. The interested reader is referred to Arrow (1951), Boadway (1974), Smith and Stephen (1975), and Starrett (1979).

The representative household maximizes utility[1] $u(D_n, D_t, L^s, W'; \theta)$ subject to the budget constraint:

$$p_n D_n + p_t D_t + W' = wL^s + W + \pi - T, \tag{8.4}$$

as in section 1 of chapter 4.

To obtain cost–benefit rules in general equilibrium, totally differentiate the utility function of the household and substitute the traditional first-order utility-maximization conditions to obtain:

$$du = \frac{\partial u}{\partial D_n} dD_n + \frac{\partial u}{\partial D_t} dD_t + \frac{\partial u}{\partial L^s} dL^s + \frac{\partial u}{\partial W'} dW'$$
$$= \lambda[p_n \, dD_n + p_t \, dD_t - w \, dL^s + dW'], \tag{8.5}$$

where λ is the marginal utility of money (income). It is useful to rewrite (8.5) in terms of policy instruments. Totally differentiating the household budget constraint gives:

$$p_n \, dD_n + p_t \, dD_t - w \, dL^s + dW'$$
$$= -D_n \, dp_n - D_t \, dp_t + L^s \, dw + d\pi - dT. \tag{8.6}$$

Recognizing the first-order conditions for profit maximization, the total change in private-sector profits equals:

$$d\pi = Y_n \, dp_n - L_n \, dw + Y_t \, dp_t - L_t \, dw. \tag{8.7}$$

Using (8.7) and the government budget constraint (8.3), equation (8.6) can be rewritten as:

$$p_n \, dD_n + p_t \, dD_t - w \, dL^s + dW'$$
$$= (Y_n + Y_{ng} - D_n) \, dp_n + (Y_t + Y_{tg} - D_t) \, dp_t$$
$$+ (L^s - L_n - L_{ng} - L_t - L_{tg}) \, dw$$
$$+ \left(p_n \frac{\partial Y_{ng}}{\partial L_{ng}} - w\right) dL_{ng} + \left(p_t \frac{\partial Y_t}{\partial L_{tg}} - w\right) dL_{tg}. \tag{8.8}$$

[1] Throughout this chapter it is assumed that the utility function possesses a sufficient degree of additive separability to eliminate the separate influence of a rationed variable. See chapter 4 and appendix A.

Given the assumption in this section of continuous market-clearing prices and wages, the first three terms in parentheses equal zero.[2] Because the levels of public-sector employment, L_{ng} and L_{nt}, are policy-determined and need not reflect profit maximization, the last two terms in brackets, reflecting the difference between marginal revenue and marginal cost of public-sector production, need not equal zero.

The change in utility – measured in monetary terms by dividing by the marginal utility of money λ – can now be found by using (8.8) in (8.5):

$$dU = \frac{du}{\lambda} = p_n \, dY_{ng} - w \, dL_{ng} + p_t \, dY_{tg} - w \, dL_{tg}$$

$$= \left(p_n \frac{\partial Y_{ng}}{\partial L_{ng}} - w \right) dL_{ng} + \left(p_t \frac{\partial Y_{tg}}{\partial L_{tg}} - w \right) dL_{tg}. \qquad (8.9)$$

du/λ is an appropriate monetary measure of the change in welfare provided that the changes in the right-hand variables are small enough that the marginal utility of money λ can be treated as constant.[3] This monetary measure of the welfare change – which is a first-order approximation of the change in profits in the public sector – is the standard first-order cost–benefit measure obtained by Boadway (1975, 1978), Boiteux (1956), Harberger (1971), Lesourne (1975), and Starrett (1979), just to mention a few.[4]

Equation (8.9) indicates that the appropriate rule for project evaluation (i.e., evaluating the activity of state-owned firms) would be to *value all outputs and inputs at their domestic (market-clearing) prices*. Using this criterion, it is clear that public-sector production will raise national welfare whenever the marginal productivity of laborers employed in the public sector ($\partial Y_{ng}/\partial L_{ng}$ and $\partial Y_{tg}/\partial L_{tg}$) exceeds that of their private-sector counterparts ($\partial Y_n/\partial L_n = w/p_n$ and $\partial Y_t/\partial L_t = w/p_t$ respectively).

---

[2] The balance of trade need not equal zero in the short run. In the long run, the trade balance gradually adjusts to zero under either fixed or flexible exchange rates. In the present chapter the exchange rate is fixed (i.e., $dp_t = 0$) so that the second term in (8.8) equals zero both in the short run and in the long run.

[3] If the changes are discrete, ΔU is a line integral and the value of ΔU is path-dependent, i.e., depends upon the particular path of integration – see, e.g., Starrett (1979).

[4] Of course, the measures may differ in the sense that different authors include different terms, i.e., consider different problems, but this does not alter the basic similarities.

3   Disequilibrium Cost–Benefit Rules

The assumption of continuous market-clearing prices employed
above in deriving the cost–benefit rules is a strong one. For practical
applications it is invaluable to determine how the shadow pricing
rules are changed by different kinds of market imbalances. The
different disequilibrium regimes will now be considered in the same
order as in the preceding chapters.

3.1   *Orthodox Keynesian Unemployment*

Assume that the nominal wage rate is fixed but that the nontraded
goods price is completely flexible so that there is orthodox Keynesian
unemployment in the economy. The monetary measure of the
welfare change following from a small increase in the level of production of state-owned firms can then be derived in a way analogous to
that used in obtaining (8.9) above.

Due to the constraint in the labor market ($L^s = \bar{L}$) the relevant
first-order conditions for utility maximization are now:

$$\frac{\partial u}{\partial D_i} = \lambda p_i, \qquad i = \text{n, t},$$

$$\frac{\partial u}{\partial L^s} = -\lambda w + \mu, \tag{8.10}$$

$$\frac{\partial u}{\partial W'} = \lambda,$$

where μ is the Lagrange multiplier associated with the constraint in
the labor market. Using these new first-order conditions, equation
(8.5) is replaced by:

$$dU = \frac{1}{\lambda} \left(\frac{\partial u}{\partial D_n} d\hat{D}_n + \frac{\partial u}{\partial D_t} d\hat{D}_t + \frac{\partial u}{\partial \bar{L}} d\bar{L} + \frac{\partial u}{\partial W} d\hat{W}' \right)$$

$$= p_n d\hat{D}_n + p_t d\hat{D}_t - [w - (\mu/\lambda)] d\bar{L} + d\hat{W}'. \tag{8.11}$$

As in section 2 above, the right-hand side of (8.11) can be rewritten
by using a totally differentiated household budget constraint after
substitution for the endogenous changes in private-sector profits and
the taxes needed to subsidize public-sector enterprises.

The resulting monetary measure of the change in welfare equals:

$$dU = p_n \, dY_{ng} - w \, dL_{ng} + p_t \, dY_{tg} - w \, dL_{tg} + (\mu/\lambda) \, d\bar{L}$$

$$= \left(p_n \frac{\partial Y_{ng}}{\partial L_{ng}} - w \right) dL_{ng} + \left(p_t \frac{\partial Y_{tg}}{\partial L_{tg}} - w \right) dL_{tg} + (\mu/\lambda) \, d\bar{L},$$

$$(8.12)$$

where

$$\mu/\lambda = w + (\partial u/\partial \bar{L})/\lambda. \tag{8.13}$$

The welfare measure in (8.12) differs from the one obtained in the general equilibrium case in that a new term reflecting the policy-induced change in *total* employment (private plus public) is now added. This term reflects the fact that the marginal disutility of effort $(\partial u/\partial \bar{L})$ is less than the sticky nominal wage whenever there is unemployment.[5]

Equation (8.12) provides a straightforward rule for evaluating public-sector enterprises under orthodox Keynesian unemployment. *First, evaluate all outputs and inputs of state-owned enterprises at prevailing domestic market prices and assess the firms' profitability on this basis. Second, determine the total policy-induced change in employment in both the private and public sectors ($d\bar{L}$) and evaluate this change at the prevailing wage less any adjustment reflecting household disutility of increased work effort.*

Let us compare this rule with the traditional partial equilbrium rule found in textbooks. The partial equilibrium view, illustrated in figure 8.1, treats all labor employed in a marginal project as coming from the unemployed, and implicitly ignores any effect of increased public-sector employment on employment in the private sector. This means that $d\bar{L}$ is set equal to $dL_{ng} + dL_{tg}$. The welfare evaluation criterion (8.12) then simplifies to:

$$dU = p_n \, dY_{ng} + p_t \, dY_{tg} + \left(\frac{\partial u/\partial \bar{L}}{\lambda} \right) (dL_{ng} + dL_{tg}). \tag{8.14}$$

This says: Value all public-sector output at market prices, but attribute a positive shadow price to the labor hired only to the extent that households perceive disutility from additional employment (i.e., $\partial u/\partial \bar{L} < 0$).

---

[5] The Lagrange expression μ/λ may be interpreted as the amount of compensation that can be taken from the household while leaving it just as well off as it was before the change in employment. See any public finance textbook for a discussion of the *compensating variation* concept.

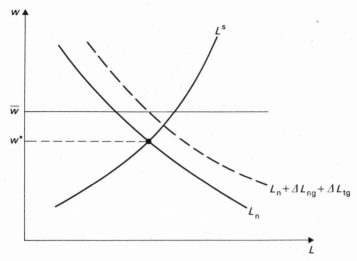

FIGURE 8.1 The partial equilibrium view on the employment effect of an increased demand for labor when the wage rate is fixed above the market-clearing level

Unfortunately this shadow pricing rule based on partial equilibrium analysis is in general incorrect even though the public sector hires only from the pool of unemployed workers. Consider the case of increased public-sector employment in the nontradeables sector.[6] It is easy to see from the short-run equilibrium condition:

$$Y_n(p_n, w) + Y_{ng}(L_{ng}) = \hat{D}_n(p_n, p_t, W + Y - T) \tag{8.15}$$

that even a marginal increase in L_{ng} will increase the supply of non-tradeables, thereby driving down the market-clearing price p_n. This means that increased production by the public firm will displace private supply of nontraded goods (while production of traded goods is unaffected as w/p_t is kept constant). Moreover, the effect on total employment $(d\bar{L}/dL_{ng})$ cannot be signed *a priori*.

Thus, even if the individual supply price of unemployed resources $[-(\partial u/\partial \bar{L})/\lambda]$ is assumed to be zero, the total real opportunity cost

[6] To simplify the exposition we focus here on public-sector firms producing nontradeables. For the most part, when tradeables can be bought and sold without quantity constraints at prevailing world prices, public-sector production of such goods is evaluated at market prices as in section 2 above. The shadow price of labor employed would be the same as that developed in the context of nontradeables production in this section. See section 4 below for an exceptional case.

of public-sector employment may *exceed* the market wage. This would be the case if total employment falls, as can be shown by assuming $\partial u/\partial \bar{L} = 0$, putting $dY_{tg} = dL_{tg} = 0$, and rewriting (8.12) as:

$$dU = p_n \, dY_{ng} - w \, dL_{ng} + w \, d\bar{L}. \tag{8.16}$$

If total employment ($\bar{L}$) decreases, the presence of the last term in (8.16) implies that *profitability calculated at producer prices – which is the general equilibrium rule derived in section 2 above – is not sufficient to insure that a project is socially profitable.* This shadow pricing rule is rather different from the partial equilibrium one discussed above. According to the latter condition a project is always socially profitable if it is profitable measured at producer prices.

3.2 *Keynesian Unemployment*

Under Keynesian unemployment, both the nontradeables market and the labor market experience excess supplies at the prevailing prices and wages. Hence the monetary welfare measure must reflect not only unemployment, as it did under orthodox Keynesian unemployment, but also the fact that *private-sector* nontradeables producers face the sales constraint:

$$\bar{Y}_n = \hat{D}_n(p_n, p_t, W + \bar{Y} - T) - Y_{ng}(L_{ng}). \tag{8.17}$$

The implicit rationing rule is that government-produced nontradeables are sold first so that only private producers are rationed. Consequently, the change in (total) profits due to changes in the sales constraint equals:

$$d\pi = d\pi_n = p_n \, d\bar{Y}_n - w \, d\tilde{L}_n. \tag{8.18}$$

Note that private production of tradeables will remain unchanged as tradeables producers face no quantity constraints and all prices are fixed.

Using (8.12) and (8.18) yields the relevant welfare criterion for evaluating public-sector production of nontradeables under Keynesian unemployment:[7]

$$dU = p_n \, dY_{ng} - w \, dL_{ng} + (\mu/\lambda) \, d\bar{L} + p_n \, d\bar{Y}_n - w \, d\tilde{L}_n. \tag{8.19}$$

Again it is clear that profitability of state-owned firms is not the sole consideration when assessing the social value of increased public-sector employment. As in the orthodox Keynesian unemployment

---

[7] Government production of tradeables goods will be considered in section 4 below.

case, the profitability measure (captured by the first two terms in (8.19)) must be adjusted to the extent that total employment $\bar{L}$ changes. Given that the level of total private- and public-sector production of nontradeables is now demand-determined, the increase in public-sector employment may have an effect on the profitability of private production of nontradeables. Comparing (8.19) to (8.12), we see that there is now an additional term, $p_n \, d\bar{Y}_n - w \, d\tilde{L}_n$, which represents the net change in the profit of privately owned non-tradeables firms due to changes in their sales constraint.

To further examine this expression we can differentiate the short-run equilibrium condition (8.17) with respect to the policy variable Y_{ng}:

$$\frac{d\bar{Y}_n}{dY_{ng}} = -\left(1 - \frac{\partial \hat{D}_n}{\partial Y} p_n\right) \Big/ \left(1 - \frac{\partial \hat{D}_n}{\partial Y} p_n\right) = -1. \tag{8.20}$$

Since there is effective excess supply of nontraded goods only a redistribution of production between the privately owned and the state-owned firm occurs. This result is a counterpart to the famous balanced-budget theorem, i.e., there is a one-to-one relationship between the *decrease* (rather than increase) in the level of production of privately owned firms when the level of *production* (as opposed to demand) by the government increases. This is so because the initial change is on the supply side while the problem is that demand is deficient. The conventional supply–demand figure in figure 8.2, where the price of the goods is fixed above the market-clearing level, illustrates this.

Substituting (8.20) into (8.19), we find that:

$$dU = [-w + (\mu/\lambda)] \, d\bar{L} = \left(\frac{\partial u/\partial \bar{L}}{\lambda}\right) d\bar{L}. \tag{8.21}$$

Due to the crowding-out effects, any change in welfare must follow from differences, if any, in the marginal productivities between privately owned and state-owned firms. Welfare will increase only if state-owned firms are more efficient than private-sector firms so that total employment *decreases* (provided that $\partial u/\partial \bar{L} < 0$ as is usually assumed).

Thus an appropriate rule for project evaluation under Keynesian unemployment could be: *select only public projects that are more profitable, calculated at producer prices, than private-sector projects.* This is a rather restrictive condition in an economy where there is unemployment. It indicates the need for policymakers to ascertain whether or not unemployment is due to productive capacity con-

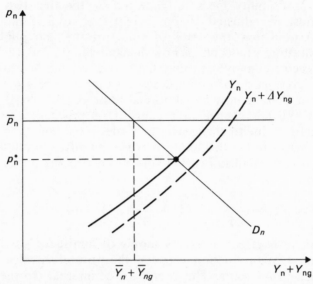

FIGURE 8.2   Illustration of the partial equilibrium effects of increased public-sector supply of nontraded goods when the price of the good is fixed above the market-clearing level

straints or to deficiency of demand for output before adopting a policy that increases public-sector capacity and employment.

3.3   Classical Unemployment

To assess the welfare effect of an increase in government production of nontraded goods under classical unemployment we have to replace both the price of home goods and the wage rate by shadow prices, say $(p_n + v/\lambda)$ and $(w - \mu/\lambda)$ respectively. These shadow prices follow from the household's utility-maximization problem subject to the budget constraint plus the two additional constraints $D_n = \bar{D}_n$ and $L^s = \bar{L}$. The relevant first-order conditions are:

$$\frac{\partial u}{\partial D_n} = \lambda p_n + v, \qquad \frac{\partial u}{\partial L^s} = -\lambda w + \mu, \qquad (8.22)$$

where λ, v, and μ are Lagrange multipliers associated with the budget constraint, the goods market constraint, and the labor supply constraint respectively. v/λ may be interpreted as the difference between the willingness to pay for an additional unit of nontraded goods and the market price. (Picture the conventional supply–demand figure in which the price of the goods is fixed below the market-clearing level.) Regarding the interpretation of the imbalance in the labor market, it is the same as that in the discussion following equation (8.13).

Using the same procedure as before, the monetary welfare measure in the classical unemployment case can be shown to equal:

$$dU = (p_n + v/\lambda)\, dY_{ng} - w\, dL_{ng} + (\mu/\lambda)\, d\bar{L}$$

$$= (p_n + v/\lambda)\, dY_{ng} - (w - \mu/\lambda)\, dL_{ng}. \tag{8.23}$$

Observe that there will be no crowding-out effects in the private sector under classical unemployment, i.e., $dY_n = dY_t = 0$. The reason for this result is that the levels of production of private firms are governed solely by the relative prices, and these are fixed.

Thus, an appropriate rule for project evaluation under classical unemployment is: (a) *use marginal willingness to pay to evaluate rationed goods; and (b) use the supply price of labor* $[-(\partial u/\partial \bar{L})/\lambda = w - (\mu/\lambda)]$ *as a measure of the cost of employing an otherwise unemployed (underemployed) laborer.* In terms of so-called "compensating variations," v/λ and μ/λ may be interpreted as lump-sum payments that leave an individual at his/her initial level of utility after an increase in the consumption of rationed goods and an increase in employment, respectively, evaluated at market prices.

The labor market appears in (8.23) in a way that is consistent with the partial equilibrium view discussed under orthodox Keynesian unemployment above. That is, all labor employed in the marginal project is treated as coming from the unemployed. To point out another similarity with the partial equilibrium approach, assume that the short-run fix-price equilibrium on the home goods market is close to being an unconstrained one so that $v \approx 0$. Then (8.23) generates a rule that coincides with the partial equilibrium rule: Production of a marginal project can be treated as a net addition to the quantity traded so that the prevailing market price measures the benefit.

In other words, if there is classical unemployment it is possible to use the general disequilibrium model to justify the cost–benefit rule which is often advocated on the basis of a partial equilibrium approach.

3.4 *Repressed Inflation and Underconsumption*

The new property of the repressed inflation and underconsumption regimes is that *firms* may be rationed in the factor market. As discussed in chapter 4, the properties of these regimes depend on the kind of rationing scheme that is postulated for allocating the insufficient supply of labor among firms. For instance, if privately owned firms in both sectors, but not the state-owned nontradeable producers, are rationed in the labor market while the household is rationed in the nontraded goods market, the monetary welfare measure can be shown to equal:

$$dU = (p_n + v/\lambda) \left(dY_{ng} + \frac{\partial \hat{Y}_n}{\partial \bar{L}_n} d\bar{L}_n \right) - w(dL_{ng} + d\bar{L}_n)$$

$$+ \left(p_t \frac{\partial \hat{Y}_t}{\partial \bar{L}_t} - w \right) d\bar{L}_t. \tag{8.24}$$

$d\bar{L}_n$ and $d\bar{L}_t$ indicate any change in the rationed supplies of labor to private firms. All privately owned firms now appear in the formula, because they are rationed in the labor market. Hence, the value of their marginal products exceed the wage rate.

Thus, one possible formulation of the project evaluation rules would be: *(a) evaluate the total change – private plus public – in the level of production of rationed nontradeables at the marginal willingness to pay*, which equals $(p_n + v/\lambda)$; *(b) evaluate the net change in labor used in this sector at the market wage; and (c) evaluate output changes in other sectors with the difference between the value of the marginal product and the market wage*. Similar rules can be derived for other variants of the repressed inflation and underconsumption regimes.

4 Government Production of Tradeable Goods

It is of course also possible to use the present model to examine the case when the firm in question supplies (demands) exportables and/or importables. However, in the present context focusing on market imbalances, these cases produce few complications or insights that would modify the results obtained above.

There is, however, an exceptional case. Under Keynesian unemployment and fixed exchange rates, increased government production of traded goods will generate real income-induced multiplier effects in the nontraded goods sector. Formally, by differentiating the equilibrium condition for the nontraded goods market in equation (8.17), one obtains:

$$p_n dY_n = p_n \frac{\partial \hat{D}_n}{\partial Y} (p_t dY_{tg}) \bigg/ \left(1 - p_n \frac{\partial \hat{D}_n}{\partial Y} \right). \tag{8.25}$$

After substitution of (8.25) into the counterpart to the monetary welfare measure (8.19):

$$dU = p_t \, dY_{tg} - w \, dL_{tg} + (\mu/\lambda) \, d\bar{L} + p_n \, d\bar{Y}_n - w \, d\tilde{L}_n^d, \qquad (8.26)$$

the following expression is obtained:

$$dU = p_t \, dY_{tg} \left[1 + \left(p_n \frac{\partial \hat{D}_n}{\partial Y} \right) \Big/ \left(1 - p_n \frac{\partial \hat{D}_n}{\partial Y} \right) \right] - (w - \mu/\lambda) \, d\bar{L}$$

$$= \left[p_t \, dY_{tg} \Big/ \left(1 - p_n \frac{\partial \hat{D}_n}{\partial Y} \right) \right] + \left(\frac{\partial u/\partial \bar{L}}{\lambda} \right) d\bar{L}. \qquad (8.27)$$

So, *the domestic market value of the direct change in output has to be multiplied by the 'textbook' Keynesian multiplier.* There will also be a multiplier effect on employment. *To obtain the welfare cost of increased government production of tradeables, the direct and the income-induced changes in employment* should be multiplied by the supply price of otherwise unemployed laborers.

Cost–benefit analysts have always had difficulty in dealing with macroeconomic issues. This difficulty arose because of the lack of a satisfactory link between microeconomics and Keynesian macroeconomics. For example, empirical studies often include real multiplier effects.[8] Yet these studies are based on the traditional microeconomic model that does not generate real multiplier effects. Equation (8.27) shows that models of the kind used here have the potential for providing a missing link between microeconomics and Keynesian macroeconomics. Equation (8.27), moreover, provides a theoretical rationale for the above-mentioned practice of including real multiplier effects in cost–benefit analysis.

5 On the Shadow Price of Foreign Exchange

The rules derived above provide further support for Boadway's (1978) view that the Little–Mirrlees and Dasgupta–Sen–Marglin project evaluation measures (Little and Mirrlees, 1968; Dasgupta et al., 1972) do not correspond to the net social gain of a project under a fixed exchange rate regime. The *Little–Mirrlees approach* takes as a measure of welfare improvement the net contribution of the project to foreign exchange earnings. It follows straightforwardly from equation (8.27) that such a measure does *not* correspond to the change in welfare. Consider also equations (8.21) and (8.23). In these cases increased public production of nontraded goods leaves produc-

---

[8] See Somers and Wood (1969) and Bohm (1974).

tion of and demand for traded goods unchanged. This means that the net contribution to foreign exchange earnings is zero. Nevertheless, the project certainly affects welfare. Thus the Little–Mirrlees measure is not a comprehensive indicator of welfare changes.

According to the *Dasgupta–Sen–Marglin approach*, nontraded goods are evaluated at domestic willingness to pay while traded goods are evaluated using the shadow exchange rate. Their shadow exchange rate, however, takes account of *direct* project purchases of traded goods only. Because this approach is partial equilibrium, it will not, as a rule, generate the same welfare measure as a general (dis)equilibrium approach. This is most easily seen by introducing a tariff on imports, but we will not elaborate upon this here. The interested reader is referred to Boadway (1978).

Unfortunately the treatment of the foreign exchange constraint by Boadway (1978) and his predecessors does not distinguish clearly between a constraint on the level of the current account deficit due to a limited amount of external borrowing (i.e., "a balance-of-payments constraint") and a constraint on foreign exchange availability for effecting import transactions invoiced in foreign currency. Both types of constraints are often experienced in less-developed countries. Their access to international capital markets may be limited by the foreign bankers concerned with their level of foreign loan exposure. Other times, limits may be imposed by domestic policymakers or foreced upon them by the IMF. Due to persistently overvalued exchange rates and internal price distortions, the foreign exchange needed to purchase imports may also be in short supply.

The most straightforward way of modeling the latter phenomenon in our framework is to assume that the price of the (imported) tradeable goods is fixed in foreign-currency units and that the available quantity of foreign exchange is fixed. Then households in effect face a *quantity* constraint on their demand for tradeable goods. They will maximize utility subject to the budget constraint, the implicit constraint in the market for tradeables (due to the shortage of foreign exchange), and other quantity constraints, if any.

If households are rationed in the market for tradeables and in the labor market, for example, the relevant first-order conditions for utility maximization will read:

$$\frac{\partial u}{\partial D_n} = \lambda p_n, \qquad \frac{\partial u}{\partial D_t} = \lambda p_t + v_t,$$

$$\frac{\partial u}{\partial L^s} = -\lambda w + \mu, \qquad \frac{\partial u}{\partial W'} = \lambda, \tag{8.28}$$

where λ, ν_t, and μ are Lagrange multipliers associated with the budget constraint, the tradeable goods market constraint, and the labor market constraint respectively.

Substitution of (8.28) into the differentiated utility function yields:

$$dU = \frac{du}{\lambda} = p_n \, d\tilde{D}_n + (p_t + \nu_t/\lambda) \, d\bar{D}_t - (w + \mu/\lambda) \, d\bar{L} + d\tilde{W}'.$$
(8.29)

Finally, substitution of the budget constraint into (8.29) will give the following monetary welfare measure if the state-owned firm increases its production of tradeables:

$$dU = (p_t + \nu_t/\lambda) \, dY_{tg} - w \, dL_{tg} + (\mu/\lambda) \, d\bar{L} + p_n \, dY_n - w \, dL_n.$$
(8.30)

Note that privately owned firms producing tradeables are unaffected by government production. Their levels of production are governed by relative prices, which are fixed. Only public-sector production of tradeables increases. This increase is evaluated at the marginal willingness to pay for such goods $(p_t + \nu_t/\lambda)$. Due to the implicit rationing in the traded goods market, however, the marginal willingness to pay exceeds the world market price in domestic currency. Hence, *it is in general illegitimate to use world market prices to evaluate public-sector production (or purchases) of traded goods whose importation is rationed due to lack of foreign reserves.*[9] Moreover, other market imbalances, if present, must be recognized. The cost of otherwise unemployed laborers needed for the production of tradeables is given by the marginal disutility of effort $(-w + \mu/\lambda)$.

We must also take into consideration how the market for non-traded goods is affected. As (8.30) is formulated this market may clear through price adjustments, in which case we could speak of orthodox Keynesian unemployment in this sector, or the price may be fixed such that firms perceive sales constraints ("Keynesian unemployment"). Interestingly, however, production of nontradeables in either case will be unaffected by increased government production of tradeables. To see this, examine the short-run equilibrium condition under "orthodox Keynesian unemployment" where the nontradeables price adjusts to equate the effective demand for nontradeables with the private plus public supply of such goods:

$$Y_n(p_n, w) + Y_{ng} = \tilde{D}_n(p_n, p_t, W + Y - T - p_t\bar{D}_t).$$
(8.31)

[9] See Blitzer *et al.* (1981).

Given the assumption of weak separability employed throughout this chapter, changes in rationed variables will only have income effects. This means that:

$$\frac{\partial \tilde{D}_n}{\partial \bar{D}_t}\, d\bar{D}_t = -\frac{\partial \tilde{D}_n}{\partial Y}\, p_t\, dY_{tg}, \qquad \frac{\partial \tilde{D}_n}{\partial \bar{L}}\, d\bar{L} = \frac{\partial \tilde{D}_n}{\partial Y}\, w\, dL_{tg}. \quad (8.32)$$

Households will use the additional incomes received from government producers in the traded goods sector to buy the increased supply of the rationed goods. Due to the separability condition, the marginal utility of nontradeables and hence consumption of such goods is unaffected by the increased consumption of the rationed goods and the increase in employment. Consequently, there will be no crowding-out or multiplier effects in the nontraded goods sector following increased government production of (rationed) tradeables. The same, of course, holds true under "Keynesian unemployment" in the nontraded goods sector.

The monetary welfare measure to be used when examining government production of rationed tradeables will thus be the same as the measure derived for classical unemployment in section 3.3 above:

$$dU = (p_t + \nu_t/\lambda)\, dY_{tg} - (w - \mu/\lambda)\, dL_{tg}. \quad (8.33)$$

Rationed goods, whether they are traded or nontraded, should be valued at the marginal willingness to pay and not at the market price. The laborers needed for the production of such goods should be treated as coming from the unemployed if there is unemployment in the economy.

6   The Government Budget Constraint

It is well known that the policy variables over which the government has control are of key importance when determining the rules to be used for evaluating the gains from public-sector activities. An instructive examination of this issue in a general equilibrium setting can be found in Boadway (1975). Recently the issue has been examined in fix-price models of closed economies by Johansson (1982b) and Roberts (1982). Here we briefly indicate how the shadow pricing rules can be used when there is *Keynesian unemployment* in an open economy but the government is not limited to nondistorting lump-sum taxes. Three cases will be considered: arbitrarily fixed tax rates, optimal taxation, and money creation.

Suppose that (unit) taxes on goods and labor (b_n, b_t, and b_w respectively) are arbitrarily fixed and that the government is free to use lump-sum taxes T to balance its budget:

$$T = p_n Y_{ng} - wL_n + b_n \hat{D}_n + b_t \hat{D}_t + b_w w \bar{L}. \tag{8.34}$$

The government now obtains revenues from taxation of domestic consumption of goods as well as from a tax on labor income. These tax revenues are used to finance a deficit, if any, of the public sector's production of nontradeables (disregarding here public production of tradeables). Any remaining deficit (surplus) is financed (disposed of) by lump-sum transactions T.

The monetary welfare measure to be used when the government increases its production of nontradeables is similar to the one derived in the Keynesian unemployment case in section 3.2 above:

$$dU = (p_n + b_n)\, dY_{ng} - w\, dL_{ng} + (b_w + \mu/\lambda)\, d\bar{L}$$
$$+ (p_n + b_n)\, d\bar{Y}_n - w\, d\tilde{L}_n. \tag{8.35}$$

The only difference is that producer and consumer prices now differ due to taxes. For welfare evaluation purposes goods are now valued at consumer prices, and not at producer prices, as the marginal willingness to pay for a good equals its purchase price. Labor cost is corrected not only for underemployment but also for the difference between the gross wage rate and the net-of-tax wage rate.

To calculate the effect of changes in public-sector production of nontradeables on private-sector production, use the short-run equilibrium condition:

$$\bar{Y}_n + Y_{ng} = \hat{D}_n(p_n + b_n, p_t + b_t, W + \bar{Y}), \tag{8.36}$$

where the relevant consumer prices have been inserted in the demand function. Differentiation of this expression shows that a change in government production of nontraded goods still crowds out private-sector production:

$$\frac{d\bar{Y}_n}{dY_{ng}} = -\left(1 - \frac{\partial \hat{D}_n}{\partial Y}(p_n + b_n)\right)\Big/\left(1 - \frac{\partial \hat{D}_n}{\partial Y}(p_n + b_n)\right) = -1,$$
$$\tag{8.37}$$

so that the change in welfare again equals:

$$dU = [-w + b_w + (\mu/\lambda)]\, d\bar{L} = \left(\frac{\partial u/\partial \bar{L}}{\lambda}\right) d\bar{L}. \tag{8.38}$$

Thus this case gives the same kind of rule as the lump-sum case considered in section 3.2 above: *The government should only undertake projects that are more profitable, measured at producer prices, than private projects.*

A natural generalization of this analysis would be ·to let tax rates adjust instantaneously to balance the government budget. The shadow pricing rules generated in the variable-tax case are in general extremely difficult to interpret as both prices and profits are affected. Note, however, that *a variable tax on the wage rate works like a lump-sum tax when the household is rationed in the labor market.* What normally distinguishes a lump-sum tax from a tax on a good or a factor is that it has an income effect but no substitution effect. However, if the household is rationed in the labor market, a change in the after-tax wage, like a lump-sum tax, will have only an income effect on demand for unrationed goods. (Recall the discussion in chapter 3, and also appendix A.) *This equivalence between a tax on labor income and a lump-sum tax means that the above cost–benefit rules are valid even if the government uses a variable tax on labor income to balance its budget.* This is an important result as the realism of policy conclusions obtained for the lump-sum tax case often are questioned.

If taxes are imposed in an optimal way in the sense that $dU/db_i = 0$ for a tax "i" as in the *optimal tax* literature (e.g., Sandmo, 1976), some interesting results emerge. For example, assume the government imposes an optimal tax on nontraded goods (with $b_t = b_w = 0$ for simplicity). Rewriting the welfare measure (8.35) using the production functions and the fact that $d\bar{L} = d\tilde{L}_n + dL_{ng}$ gives:

$$dU = \left[(p_n + b_n) - \left(w - \frac{\mu}{\lambda} \right) \middle/ \frac{\partial Y_{ng}}{\partial L_{ng}} \right] dY_{ng}$$

$$+ \left[(p_n + b_n) - \left(w - \frac{\mu}{\lambda} \right) \middle/ \frac{\partial \bar{Y}_n}{\partial L_n} \right] d\bar{Y}_n. \tag{8.39}$$

Keeping public-sector production of nontradeables constant it is obvious from this expression that an optimal unit tax on nontraded goods must fulfill the condition:

$$\frac{dU}{db_n} = \left[(p_n + b_n) - \left(w - \frac{\mu}{\lambda} \right) \middle/ \frac{\partial \bar{Y}_n}{\partial L_n} \right] \frac{\partial \bar{Y}_n}{\partial L_n} \frac{\partial L_n}{\partial b_n} = 0, \tag{8.40}$$

because only private production decisions are affected by changes in the tax rate.

From (8.40) it follows that the optimal tax equals

$$b_n^0 = -\left[p_n - \left(w - \frac{\mu}{\lambda}\right)\bigg/ \frac{\partial \bar{Y}_n}{\partial L_n}\right] < 0. \tag{8.41}$$

The optimal tax is in fact a *subsidy* and equals the difference between the producer price and the "welfare" cost of producing an additional unit.[10] The reason for this is simple. *In an economy where there is unemployment due to deficient demand (i.e., Keynesian unemployment) it is better to subsidize demand than to tax it.*

Given the optimal subsidy (8.41), the project evaluation rule derived above once again applies: *A small public project increases welfare if it is more profitable calculated at producer prices than private projects.* This is so because:

$$dU = \left[(p_n + b_n^0) - \left(w - \frac{\mu}{\lambda}\right)\bigg/ \frac{\partial Y_{ng}}{\partial L_{ng}}\right] dY_{ng} > 0, \tag{8.42}$$

only if the marginal productivity is higher in the public sector than in the private sector ($\partial Y_{ng}/\partial L_{ng} > \partial \bar{Y}_n/\partial L_n$). This follows immediately if (8.41) is inserted into (8.39).

Finally, assume the government prints money to balance its budget (as in chapter 4). To highlight the main point let us follow Roberts (1982) and in addition assume that the government neutralizes any profit in the private sector through a profits tax of 100 percent. The monetary welfare measure then reduces to:

$$dU = (\mu/\lambda)\, d\bar{L}. \tag{8.43}$$

Due to crowding-out effects welfare (and employment) will increase only if the public project is *less* profitable measured at producer prices than private-sector projects: $\partial Y_{ng}/\partial L_{ng} < \partial \bar{Y}_n/\partial L_n$ so that $dL_{ng} > d\tilde{L}_n$ and $d\bar{L} > 0$. Remember that μ/λ is the positive difference between the after-tax wage and the supply price of unemployed laborers. The reason for this "perverse" rule is that all profit incomes are "sterilized" so that only wage incomes matter to households. This result illustrates the potential problems that can arise when it is assumed that current-period profits are not distributed until the following period, as is often done in the fix-price literature. Recall our discussion of the profit distribution issue in chapter 3.

---

[10] It should be emphasized that it is assumed that b_n^0 is not large enough to move the economy from Keynesian unemployment to another type of disequilibrium situation. For a discussion see Marchand, Mintz and Pestieau (1983).

7 Concluding Remarks

An unresolved problem with the disequilibrium framework described here is how the cost–benefit practitioner should determine which regime the economy is experiencing. The foregoing analysis clearly shows that knowledge of the prevailing type of disequilibrium is essential when deciding what kinds of benefits and costs to include. In many instances an examination of the sectors directly affected by a project should give valuable information regarding the nature of market imbalances. In countries like Great Britain and Sweden, for example, the textile, steel, and ship-building industries seem to be working under conditions of Keynesian unemployment; there is "excess output supply" (or more precisely, significant amounts of idle capacity) and a high level of unemployment in these sectors. Often cost–benefit practitioners can identify situations where market imbalances of a particular sort indisputably prevail. Once we admit that the prevailing type of disequilibrium regime can often be identified, there is no doubt also that empirical work on cost–benefit analysis can be greatly improved by an explicit disequilibrium framework.

9

Directions for Future Research

The field of open-economy disequilibrium theory is still young. Hence any claim that this book contains a definitive treatment – the final word – would be presumptuous and premature. Our objective has been to synthesize and integrate the existing work on macroeconomic disequilibrium theory for open economies. In a number of cases, however, this has involved pushing the theory forward in new directions or treating new cases that have escaped earlier investigators but nevertheless seemed worth pursuing. In particular, we have taken pains in chapter 3 to reconcile or at least interpret, to the extent possible, existing work in an explicitly *intertemporal framework*. This raises interesting questions as to whether changes in wages, prices, or other policy-determined variables are permanent or temporary. The intertemporal framework should also facilitate a deeper understanding of the existing literature and of chapters 4–8 in the present book, where intertemporal aspects are typically less explicit.

Second, the role of money has been extensively discussed and the existing open-economy disequilibrium framework has been extended to the case of money and bond holdings under perfect capital mobility. This has facilitated a comparison of fixed and flexible exchange rate regimes with a consistent treatment of the country's intertemporal budget constraint.

In the context of two-sector, open-economy models we have pursued the implications of non-market-clearing in diverse but hopefully realistic and rewarding directions. Macroeconomic stabilization policies have been examined in detail for both fixed and flexible exchange rate economies. An extensive investigation of commercial policies – including those aimed at import substitution, sectoral output and employment objectives, and external balance – has also been carried out. This analysis provides a useful generalization of existing work on tariffs and quotas, which often proceeds in a

Walrasian market-clearing environment. Given that such policies are typically implemented in situations where non-market-clearing is omnipresent, this application of the disequilibrium approach seems particularly fruitful.

Finally, given the microeconomic foundations on which our models are explicitly based, the question of *welfare effects* of various policies naturally arises. The disequilibrium framework has been used in chapter 8 to generate appropriate cost–benefit rules for use in cases where unemployment and idle capacity must be taken into account. These general (dis)equilibrium cost–benefit rules obviate the need to adopt the partial equilibrium rules-of-thumb often employed by practitioners. This should be of interest not only to project analysts but also to students of international economics and public finance.

In spite of these extensions, much remains to be done. The important task of determining – empirically as well as theoretically – whether and why prices are fixed or sticky in the short run remains. There are a few promising attempts to explain slow price adjustments and the existence of non-Walrasian equilibria. The "Leijonhufvud–Alchian" view is that prices adjust slowly, much slower than quantities, due to high information costs (for example), but they continue to adjust as long as markets are not cleared in the Walrasian sense. The contract theoretic explanation of price rigidities is longer run in character. In its present form, however, the theory cannot properly explain *involuntary* unemployment. Solow (1979, 1980) has suggested a number of (not necessarily mutually exclusive) reasons for short-run wage stickiness accompanied by unemployment. One, for example, depends on the presence of government unemployment insurance in the implicit contracts framework. Subsequent work by McDonald and Solow (1981) suggests an alternative explanation based on *efficient* wage bargains between a monopoly union and a single employer.

The theory of *conjectural equilibria*, on the other hand, can generate non-Walrasian *long-run* equilibria. Here, the issue is whether the conjectures are in some sense rational or at least "reasonable," in the sense that all mutually profitable trades are exhausted given reasonable conjectures by economic agents about what would happen if prices or quantities were changed.

In spite of these recent developments there is still no completely satisfactory and generally accepted choice-theoretic basis for the assumption of slow price adjustment in macroeconomic models. Of course, the same can be said of the opposite extreme of instantaneous price adjustment as pointed out in the humorous quotation of Peter Neary:[1]

> The main target for criticism of these models is of course their assumption of fixed prices. *Whenever I am asked "who sets prices?" in such a model I am tempted to reply facetiously that prices are set by a little green man! This is no ordinary little green man, however, but the same one who in many other models moves prices costlessly and instantaneously to their Walrasian or market-clearing levels, except that he's on an off day!* In other words, I know of no macro model which provides a satisfactory choice-theoretic basis for its assumptions about price determination. Devotees of an efficient Walrasian auctioneer do not have a monopoly of virtue in this field, and tend to forget that "tâtonnement" literally means "groping," which may be many things, but is certainly not instantaneous.

In most fix-price models the role of expectations is unclear. This is, at least in part, due to the fact that they focus on a single period, even though it represents only one temporary equilibrium in a sequence of such equilibria. In sections 5–6 of chapter 3, we developed a two-period model of a household that has point expectations about future prices but expects to face no quantity constraints on either goods or labor markets in the future. If the possibility of expected future quantity constraints is introduced, matters become considerably more complicated; the number of possible scenarios increases substantially. Neary and Stiglitz (1983) have shown that the effects of economic policy are very sensitive to the kind of constraints the agents expect to face in the future. Their approach is both interesting and promising in that it shows dramatically the differing effects of expectational errors as opposed to perfect foresight on the current disequilibrium state of the economy. Undoubtedly, a good deal of future research will be concentrated on the formation and role of expectations.

Attempts to model slow price adjustment in markets out of equilibrium typically rely on a *two-time* system. That is, certain prices and quantities adjust *instantaneously*, while other prices adjust only once the first-mentioned price–quantity adjustments have reached a

[1] J. Peter Neary: Comment on "Import competition and macro-economic adjustment under wage–price rigidity" by M. Bruno. Forthcoming in Bhagwati, J. N. and Srinivasan, T. N. (eds) *Import Competition and Adjustment: Theory and Policy*, Proceedings of an NBER Conference held in Cambridge, MA, May 8–11, 1980 (Chicago: Chicago University Press).

short-run equilibrium. A most important question is what governs the long-run adjustments of prices and quantities? Furthermore, does the model converge to a Walrasian full-employment equilibrium. There are a few studies posing such question in non-Walrasian equilibrium models of closed economies, as mentioned in appendix B. However, there seems to be no complete investigations of the dynamics in open economies.[2] Clearly, in such an investigation, the international adjustment process should play a central role. Ideally, exchange rate dynamics should also play a part in the dynamics attributed to short-run fix-price models.

The treatment of adjustment dynamics as the economy moves through a sequence of temporary equilibria over time would benefit from a more thorough investigation of expectations formation. To date, the disequilibrium dynamics for fix-price models have embodied extremely myopic behavior on the part of economic agents. In particular, the adjustment *paths* that various prices follow have no effect on agents' current decisions.

A closely related question to the modeling of expectations and adjustment dynamics concerns the role of financial markets. In chapter 5, we extended the fix-price quantity-constraint models to the perfect capital mobility case. However, the task remains to integrate multiple asset holdings into a rigorous microtheoretic framework in a way that accurately captures both the intertemporal decision-making process giving rise to consumption and asset demands as well as the role of money in facilitating transactions.

Existing fix-price models concentrate on imblances in markets for goods and factors, while the possibility of credit rationing is assumed away. The only treatment of credit rationing using a complete macroeconomic disequilibrium model seems to be Miller (1982) and the recent dissertation by Kähkönen (1982). In the context of less-developed countries as well developed economies with underdeveloped financial markets (Kähkönen's work focuses on the latter), the interactions of non-market-clearing in the goods and financial markets are of critical importance when analyzing the efficacy of stabilization and development policies. Clearly much remains to be done in modeling financial markets, including the possibility of credit rationing, in the general disequilibrium framework.

[2] Chan (1979) provides a discussion of adjustment dynamics for the orthodox Keynesian model where the wage is sticky but output prices are flexible. In both the fixed and flexible exchange rate cases, however, he assumes that both the balance of trade and payments are continuously equal to zero. This model misspecification precludes any discussion of tne international adjustment process.

In the type of models used in this volume the real capital stock is typically fixed and the level of investment is exogenously determined (or ignored completely). This is an understandable simplification as one runs into difficult problems specifying the mechanisms that govern investment when firms perceive constraints on their trading possibilities. Interesting work, particularly on the microfoundations of investment in the presence of anticipated current- and future-period quantity constraints, remains to be done. Endogenizing investment, as a function of these expectations, for example, opens up the possibility of regime switching at given prices. Under Keynesian unemployment firms may scrap equipment to such an extent that the economy moves into a state of classical unemployment as the production potential of an industry is decreased. Technological change may accelerate this process. Given classical unemployment in the initial situation, incentives toward "overinvestment" may move the economy into a Keynesian unemployment situation. Grossman (1972), Malinvaud (1980), Kähkönen (1982), and Steigum (1983), among others, have attempted to model investment decisions in the presence of quantity constraints in markets for final goods and labor. The simulation exercises by Blanchard and Sachs (1982) are also of interest here. These contributions open up interesting and important possibilities for future research.

Useful extensions of welfare theory using disequilibrium models also seem possible. It was demonstrated in chapter 8 that the fix-price framework is a powerful tool when examining welfare consequences of government policies. As disequilibrium theory develops, it should be possible to integrate new and interesting cases into welfare theory. One obvious example is a careful reexamination of the issue of choosing an appropriate social discount rate in a model that explicitly incorporates multiple asset holdings as well as the possibility of credit rationing.

Finally, it should be pointed out that virtually all published work on open-economy disequilibrium theory, including the present book, have dealt with a single economy in an international environment. The difficult job of extending these models to two or more open economies in general disequilibrium has just begun (e.g., Dixit and Norman, 1980; Lori and Sheen, 1982; Owen, 1981). The interaction between a number of fix-price economies, which may be in different disequilibrium regimes, is undoubtedly important. It will force us to pay much more attention to the specification of reasonable (world-wide) rationing rules, which necessarily play a role in resolving market imbalances when prices in world markets fail to adjust instantaneously.

It is our hope that the present book will be useful not only as a synthesis of existing open-economy disequilibrium theory, but that it will also facilitate future research in the related areas – only some of which have been alluded to above – where work remains to be done.

Appendix A
The Microeconomics of Rationing

1 Introduction

This appendix compares the properties of *effective* demand and supply functions with the corresponding properties of *notional* demand and supply functions. Knowledge of how the derivatives of these functions are related to each other is extremely useful when carrying out comparative static analyses in temporary equilibrium models, as well as the analyses of their dynamic and long-run properties.

We will consider both consumer and firm behavior under quantity constraints. The analysis will be conducted in a general setting with n goods and m factors, but we will end the chapter by applying our results to the effective demand functions derived in chapter 2. The general results are used frequently in subsequent chapters.

The first explicit analysis of how the consumer's behavioral functions under rationing are related to the corresponding functions in unrestricted market situations was conducted by Tobin and Houthakker (1950–51). They studied the utility-maximization problem in the presence of what Samuelson (1947) calls *auxiliary constraints*, i.e., constraints that are just on the verge of binding at the initial point from which changes at the initial consumer demand are measured. This situation is depicted in figure A.1a. The ellipses of figure A.1a can be interpreted either as isoprofit curves for a firm or as indifference curves based on the consumer's utility function where the usual budget restriction has been substituted into the "argument set" by solving for the possible consumption of, say, commodity x in terms of commodity y. The free market optimum is at $A(x^*, y^*)$ and, hence, a constraint where $\bar{y} = y^*$ would be auxiliary or non-biting at the prevailing prices.

193

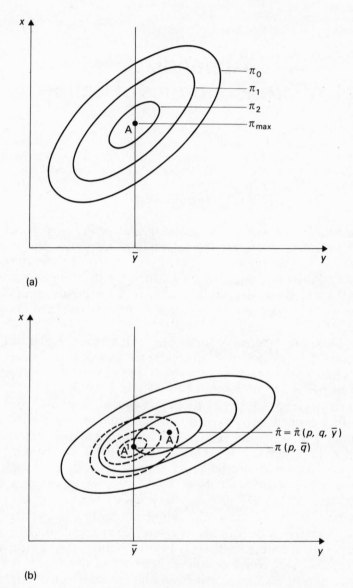

(a)

(b)

FIGURE A.1   (a) The auxiliary constraint approach and (b) the virtual price
approach

The use of auxiliary constraints is, of course, a serious limitation of the analysis, but was used because the derivatives in which Tobin and Houthakker were interested are more easily compared if they are evaluated at a common point. A smart way to make such comparisons under more general conditions where the optimum under rationing is allowed to deviate from the free market optimum, as in figure A.1b, would be the following: construct *shadow* or *virtual* prices, such that an unconstrained agent would choose, at these prices, the same consumption vector as he chooses at prevailing *market* prices in the presence of specified quantity constraints $y = \bar{y}$. Compare the derivatives of the *effective* demand functions evaluated at *market* prices (p, q) to the corresponding derivatives of the *unconstrained* or *notional* demand functions evaluated at the *virtual* prices $(p, \bar{q})$. The broken indifference (or isoprofit) curves in figure A.1b are the indifference curves under virtual prices.[1] Note that the peak of the virtual profit hypersurface coincides with the constrained demand vector A'.

This innovative approach was first exploited in the present context by Neary and Roberts (1980).[2] We reproduce their main results below.

2   A Virtual Price Approach to Consumer Theory under Conditions of Rationing

All good ideas do not always work! A fundamental problem with the virtual price approach is to show that a virtual price vector exists and, given that it exists, how it is related to the actual price vector. Toward this end, Neary and Roberts (1980) start by introducing the utility function:

$$U = U(x_1, \ldots, x_m, y_1, \ldots, y_n) = U(x, y), \qquad (A.1)$$

where $x = (x_1, \ldots, x_m)$ is a vector of goods freely chosen and $y = (y_1, \ldots, y_n)$ is a vector of goods for which the consumer faces a quantity constraint. Let $p = (p_1, \ldots, p_m)$ and $q = (q_1, \ldots, q_n)$ be the prices associated with the unconstrained and constrained demands respectively, and let I be the lump-sum income of the household.

---

[1] $\bar{q}$ are virtual prices associated with the vector of goods subject to quantity constraints $y = \bar{y}$. x is the vector of unrationed goods whose prices are p.
[2] The first to use virtual prices was Rothbarth (1940–41), who used them in an analysis of the measurement of real income under rationing.

The problem of the household under conditions of rationing is to maximize the utility function (A.1) subject to the budget constraint:

$$px + qy = I, \tag{A.2}$$

and the quantity constraint on demand: $y = \bar{y}$. Maximization yields a vector of constrained demands $(\tilde{x}, \bar{y})$. Given that the utility function is strictly quasi-concave and continuous, Neary and Roberts prove the following important result: *Any demand vector (x, y) can be supported with suitable prices, and the particular price vector associated with x, which supports the demand vector ($\tilde{x}, \bar{y}$) in a free market, coincides with the price vector faced by the household when x is chosen subject to the condition that y is fixed at $\bar{y}$.* In other words, a virtual price vector does, in fact, exist. Furthermore, the virtual price vector $(\bar{p}, \bar{q})$ which generates the demands $(\tilde{x}, \bar{y})$ satisfies the condition that $\bar{p} = p$, while $\bar{q} \neq q$ in general. (p, q) is the vector of market prices.

In order to relate the derivatives of the behavioral functions under conditions of rationing to the corresponding unconstrained derivatives, it is convenient to define constrained and unconstrained versions of the *expenditure function*. The *unconstrained expenditure function* commonly employed in duality theory equals:

$$e(p, q, u) = \min_{x,y} [px + qy; u(x, y) \geq u]. \tag{A.3}$$

This function defines the minimum expenditure necessary to achieve a specified utility level u, given the price vector (p, q). The corresponding *quantity-constrained expenditure function* is defined by:

$$\tilde{e}(p, q, u, \bar{y}) = \min_{x} [px + q\bar{y}; u(x, \bar{y}) \geq u]. \tag{A.4}$$

The reader should note that the constrained expenditure function (A.4) is defined only for values of x where it is possible to find an x such that $u(x, \bar{y}) \geq u$. Following Neary and Roberts, we assume that such an x can always be found.

From a well-known result, often referred to as Shephard's lemma, we know that:[3]

$$\tilde{e}_p(p, q, u, \bar{y}) = \tilde{x}^c(p, q, u, \bar{y}), \tag{A.5}$$

$$\tilde{e}_q = \bar{y}, \tag{A.6}$$

where $\tilde{x}^c = (\tilde{x}_1^c, \ldots, \tilde{x}_m^c)$ is the vector of compensated *effective* demand functions, obtained by differentiating the *constrained* ex-

---

[3] See, e.g., Varian (1978) for a detailed discussion.

penditure function with respect to p. Differentiation with respect to price vector for rationed goods, q, yields the vector of demand constraints $\bar{y} = (\bar{y}_1, \ldots, \bar{y}_n)$.

2.1   Derivatives with Respect to Quantity Constraints

To derive the partial derivatives of the expenditure function with respect to the vector of imposed demands (i.e., quantity constraints $\bar{y}$), we use the fact that the constrained expenditure function $\bar{e}$ may be related to the unconstrained expenditure function (A.3) when the latter is evaluated at the virtual price vector. We have:

$$\bar{e}(p, q, u, \bar{y}) = p\bar{x}^c(p, q, u, \bar{y}) + q\bar{y}$$
$$= px^c(p, \bar{q}, u) + qy^c(p, \bar{q}, u)$$
$$= e(p, \bar{q}, u) + (q - \bar{q})\bar{y}, \tag{A.7}$$

where

$$\bar{y} = y^c(p, \bar{q}, u) \tag{A.8}$$

are the n equations that implicitly define the virtual prices $\bar{q}$ as functions of prices on the unconstrained goods p, quantity constraints $\bar{y}$, and utility level u.

Differentiating (A.7) with respect to $\bar{y}$ yields:

$$\bar{e}_y = (e_q - \bar{y})\frac{\partial \bar{q}}{\partial \bar{y}} + (q - \bar{q}), \tag{A.9}$$

where:

$$(e_q - \bar{y}) = \begin{bmatrix} (e_{q_1} - y_1) & \cdots & 0 \\ 0 & \cdots & (e_{q_n} - \bar{y}_n) \end{bmatrix}_{(n \times n)}$$

and $q = [q_1, \ldots, q_n]'$ and $\bar{q} = [\bar{q}_1, \ldots, \bar{q}_n]'$ are the vectors of market and shadow prices, respectively, for the rationed goods y. When the partial derivative e_q is evaluated at virtual prices, we get $e_q = \bar{y}$; recall (A.5) above. Hence equation (A.9) reduces to:

$$\bar{e}_y = q - \bar{q}. \tag{A.9a}$$

This says: if a good y_i is rationed, i.e., in short supply, so that the shadow price to the consumer $\bar{q}$ exceeds the market price q, then the level of expenditure required to maintain an initial utility level u will fall when the severity of rationing is reduced, i.e., $\bar{e}_{y_i} = q_i - \bar{q}_i < 0$.

Moreover, at the rationed consumption point we have the following relationship between the constrained and unconstrained versions of the *compensated* demand curves:

$$\tilde{x}^c(p, q, u, \bar{y}) = x^c(p, \bar{q}, u).$$ (A.10a)

Also (repeating (A.8) for reference):

$$\bar{y} = y^c(p, \bar{q}, u).$$ (A.10b)

Differentiation of (A.10) with respect to $\bar{y}$ yields a relationship between the derivatives of the constrained and unconstrained (compensated) demand functions:

$$\tilde{x}_y^c = x_q^c \frac{\partial \bar{q}}{\partial \bar{y}},$$

$$e = y_q^c \frac{\partial \bar{q}}{\partial \bar{y}} \qquad \text{where} \quad e = [1 \ldots 1]_{n \times 1}'.$$ (A.11)

The reader should note that the components of (A.11) are vectors and matrixes. To save space the definitions of these entities are put in a separate section at the end of the appendix. Solving (A.11) for $\tilde{x}_y^c$, one obtains the effect on the compensated demand for unrationed goods of a change in the quantity constraints:

$$\tilde{x}_y^c = x_q^c (y_q^c)^{-1} e.$$ (A.12)

This is a very general formula but for the case when only one good is rationed (i.e., $n = 1$), it reduces to:

$$\frac{\partial \tilde{x}^c}{\partial y_1} = x_q^c (y_q^c)^{-1} = \left[\frac{\partial x_1^c}{\partial \bar{q}_1} \Big/ \frac{\partial y_1^c}{\partial \bar{q}_1}, \ldots, \frac{\partial x_m^c}{\partial \bar{q}_1} \frac{\partial y_1^c}{\partial \bar{q}_1} \right]'.$$ (A.13)

Take the ith component of the vector in (A.13):

$$\frac{\partial x_i^c}{\partial \bar{y}_1} = \frac{\partial x_i^c}{\partial \bar{q}_1} \Big/ \frac{\partial y_1^c}{\partial \bar{q}_1}.$$ (A.13a)

From the concavity of the expenditure function we know that[4] $\partial y_1^c / \partial \bar{q}_1 < 0$. If the rationed good y_1 and the unrationed good x_1 are net substitutes (complements) then, by definition, $\partial x_i^c / \partial \bar{q}_1 > 0$ ($\partial x_i^c / \partial \bar{q}_1 < 0$). Thus (A.13a) tells us that a relaxation of the severity of rationing of y_1 will reduce (increase) the *compensated* demand for x_i if x_i and y_1 are net substitutes (complements).

The above discussion pertains to the case where there is only one constraint. In the case of several quantity constraints, it is difficult

[4] The substitution effect of a change in the own price of the good is (almost everywhere) negative.

to make such clearcut statements because a change in a single quantity constraint will (in general) alter the shadow price of *all* rationed goods, making the signs of the derivatives in (A.13) indeterminate *a priori*.

So far we have only discussed the effect of changing quantity constraints on compensated demand functions. Our ultimate interest is in the *uncompensated* demand functions. Fortunately there is a simple relationship between the compensated (Hicksian) and uncompensated (Marshallian) demand functions. When income in the uncompensated demand function is set equal to the minimum expenditure needed to reach utility level u, given prices (p, q) and imposed restrictions $y = \bar{y}$, the function will equal the corresponding compensated demand function. That is:

$$\tilde{x}^c(p, q, u, \bar{y}) = \tilde{x}(p, q, \tilde{e}(p, q, u, \bar{y}), \bar{y}) \tag{A.14}$$

where the absence of a "c" superscript denotes an uncompensated demand function. Differentiation with respect to $\bar{y}$, therefore, yields a relationship between the compensated and uncompensated demand derivatives:

$$\tilde{x}^c_y = \tilde{x}_I \tilde{e}_y + \tilde{x}_y, \tag{A.15}$$

where the absence of a "c" superscript again denotes an uncompensated demand function. (Using (A.9a) and rearranging, one gets:

$$\tilde{x}_y = x^c_y - \tilde{x}_I \tilde{e}_y = x^c_y + \tilde{x}_I(\bar{q} - q). \tag{A.16}$$

The first term of (A.16) is a substitution effect, which according to (A.13a) is negative for the case where there is a single rationed good and goods x and y are substitutes. Latham (1980) calls this term the *compensated cross-quantity effect*. The second term is an income effect, and $\tilde{x}_I > 0$ for normal goods. Moreover, for proper rationing[5] the virtual price of the rationed good exceeds the market price $(\bar{q} > q)$. Hence, the income effect is positive for normal goods. *In other words, the income and substitution effects work in opposite directions in the case of net substitutes.*

To be able to sign the derivative in (A.16) in a case when goods are net substitutes, one might assume that the income effect is small or, what amounts to the same thing, that one is close to the free market equilibrium $(\bar{q} = q)$.[6] Both the income and quantity-substitu-

---

[5] That is, for cases where the consumer is forced to consume less – not more – of the good than would be demanded in unconstrained situations.

[6] Intuitively one might say that the income effect is more likely to dominate for large displacements from the free market equilibrium $(\bar{q} \geqslant q)$. This is, however, not quite correct, because one does not know in what directions the terms x^c_y and $\tilde{x}_I$ move when one moves away from the unrationed equilibrium.

tion effects work in the same direction when: (1) the unrationed goods are net complements for the rationed goods and both goods are normal, or (2) the household is rationed in the labor market (unemployed) and leisure and normal goods are net substitutes. In the latter case this is true because the household is forced, in an unemployment equilibrium, to buy too much leisure so that $\bar{q} < q$. We will return to this case below when discussing the magnitude of the marginal propensity to consume out of different kinds of income.

The formula (A.16) is incomplete in one respect. The uncompensated derivatives $\tilde{x}_y$ are not fully characterized in terms of unconstrained functions and derivatives because the constrained income effects, $\tilde{x}_I$, are left in the formula. To eliminate this derivative, note that the constrained uncompensated demands $\tilde{x}$ equal the unconstrained uncompensated demands x, when evaluated at the virtual prices $(p, \bar{q})$ and at the minimum expenditure necessary to reach utility level u when presented with these virtual prices:

$$\tilde{x}(p, q, I, \bar{y}) = x(p, \bar{q}, I + (\bar{q} - q)\bar{y}). \tag{A.17}$$

The virtual price vector is defined by the equations:

$$\bar{y} = y(p, \bar{q}, I + (\bar{q} - q)\bar{y}). \tag{A.18}$$

Differentiating (A.17) with respect to I gives:

$$\tilde{x}_I = [x_q + x_I\bar{y}]\frac{\partial\bar{q}}{\partial I} + x_I = x_q^c\frac{\partial\bar{q}}{\partial I} + x_I. \tag{A.19}$$

To understand the last equality of (A.19) one must recognize that $x_q + x_I\bar{y}$ is equal to the matrix of *compensated* price derivatives, because the income effects in x_q net out against the income effects $x_I\bar{y}$. (Compare, e.g., equation (A.23) below.)

Analogously, by differentiating (A.18) we obtain:

$$0 = (y_q + y_I\bar{y})\frac{\partial\bar{q}}{\partial I} + y_I = y_q^c\frac{\partial\bar{q}}{\partial I} + y_I, \tag{A.20}$$

so that the effect of an increase in expenditure on the virtual prices equals:

$$\frac{\partial\bar{q}}{\partial I} = -y_I(y_q^c)^{-1}. \tag{A.21}$$

This can then be used in (A.19) to get the relationship between the expenditure derivatives of the effective and notional demand functions (where the latter are evaluated at virtual prices):

$$\tilde{x}_I = x_I - x_q^c y_I (y_q^c)^{-1}. \tag{A.22}$$

The second term on the right-hand side of (A.22), in general, has both positive and negative components. In the case of only one rationed good, however, the interpretation of (A.22) is straightforward: the income effect on the effective demand for an unrationed good $\tilde{x}_I$ is magnified (reduced) in relation to the income effect in a free market evaluated at virtual prices provided that the goods are normal and net substitutes (net complements) so that $\partial x^c / \partial \bar{q} > 0$ ($\partial x^c / \partial \bar{q} < 0$).

2.2 Price Derivatives

Finally, let us compare the *price* derivatives of the constrained and unconstrained demand functions. Differentiating (A.14) with respect to p and q yields:

$$\tilde{x}_p^c = \tilde{x}_p + \tilde{x}_I \tilde{e}_p = \tilde{x}_p + \tilde{x}_I \tilde{x}, \tag{A.23a}$$

$$\tilde{x}_q^c = \tilde{x}_q + x_I \bar{y}. \tag{A.23b}$$

Equation (A.23b) can be simplified once it is recognized that $\tilde{x}_q^c = 0$. That is, changes in the prices of the rationed goods do not affect demands for unrationed goods when utility is held constant. (This can be seen by noting that $\tilde{e}_{pq} = \tilde{e}_{qp}$ and examining (A.6).) Thus, an increase of a price of a rationed good has only an income effect on the demand for nonrationed goods:

$$\tilde{x}_q = -x_I \bar{y}. \tag{A.24}$$

For example, if the price of leisure (i.e., the wage rate) increases when the household is unemployed, this will increase labor income and induce increased consumption of normal goods. (Note that the demand for leisure changes in the opposite direction to the supply of labor.)

To relate the own-price derivatives of demand for unrationed goods in (A.23a) to the corresponding derivatives of the rationed demand functions, differentiate (A.17) with respect to p:

$$\tilde{x}_p = x_p + (x_q + x_I \bar{y}) \frac{\partial \bar{q}}{\partial p} = x_p + x_q^c \frac{\partial \bar{q}}{\partial p}. \tag{A.25}$$

By making use of how the virtual price is defined, we can differentiate (A.18) to get:

$$y_p + (y_q + y_I \bar{y}) \frac{\partial \bar{q}}{\partial p} = y_p + y_q^c \frac{\partial \bar{q}}{\partial p} = 0 \qquad (A.26)$$

and solve for:

$$\frac{\partial \bar{q}}{\partial p} = -(y_q^c)^{-1} y_p.$$

Substituting this into (A.25) yields a relationship between the price derivatives of the (uncompensated) effective and notional demand functions:

$$\tilde{x}_p = x_p - x_q^c (y_q^c)^{-1} y_p = x_p + \tilde{x}_q^c y_p. \qquad (A.27)$$

The last equality follows from (A.12). The reader is reminded that the comparisons between the derivatives in (A.27) only hold when the right-hand derivatives of the notional demand functions are evaluated at *virtual* prices.

2.3   A Digression on Separability

A special case referred to repeatedly in chapters 4–8 is the case when the utility function is assumed to be weakly separable in the rationed goods, i.e., there exists a monotone transformation of the utility function such that

$$U(x, y) = u(x) + u(y). \qquad (A.28)$$

In the presence of binding constraints $y = \bar{y}$, the budget constraint can be usefully written as:

$$px = I - q\bar{y} = I', \qquad (A.29)$$

where I' is suitably labeled *discretionary income*. It is easy to show that the maximization of the utility function (A.28) subject to the budget constraint (A.29) results in effective demand functions of the form:

$$\tilde{x} = \tilde{x}(p, I - q\bar{y}) = \tilde{x}(p, I'). \qquad (A.30)$$

As was shown above, changes in the price vector q have only an income effect, here embedded in the discretionary income term. The same is true for changes in the quantity constraints. (Note that

$u(x)$ and thus also $\partial u/\partial x$ is independent of $\bar{y}$.) Differentiation of (A.30) with respect to $\bar{y}$ yields:

$$\tilde{x}_y = \tilde{x}_{I'} \frac{\partial I'}{\partial \bar{y}} = -q\tilde{x}_{I'}. \tag{A.31}$$

Moreover, for the case of only one rationed good, it was shown in discussing (A.22) that:

$$\tilde{x}_{I'} > \tilde{x}_I > 0, \tag{A.32}$$

provided goods x and y are normal and net substitutes. Hence it follows that $\tilde{x}_y < 0$. That is, *a relaxation of a quantity constraint reduces the demand for goods that are net substitutes for the rationed good when the utility function is weakly separable in the rationed good*. In the absence of weak separability in the rationed goods, (A.30) would be replaced by $\tilde{x}(p, I - q\bar{y}, \bar{y}) = \tilde{x}(p, I', \bar{y})$ with the concomitant difficulty of signing the *partial* derivative $\partial\tilde{x}/\partial\bar{y}$. In the text we generally assume weak separability, thereby insuring that a relaxation of a quantity constraint reduces the demand for unrationed goods. See, e.g., the discussion in chapter 4 regarding the assumption $\partial\tilde{D}_t/\partial\bar{D}_n < 0$. Although this assumption is restrictive, it considerably simplifies the calculations in the text. For the most part, similar qualitative conclusions would be obtained if the goods were assumed to be *gross quantity substitutes*, defined as a negative direct effect of $\bar{y}$ on effective demands, i.e., $d\tilde{x}/d\bar{y} < 0$.

3 A Virtual Price Approach to Production Theory under Conditions of Rationing

The above analysis of the properties of consumer demand functions under rationing is easily applied to firm behavior. This section briefly relates the properties of the firm's constrained output supply and factor demand functions to the corresponding unconstrained functions.

We start by defining a vector c, which describes a production plan:

$$c = [c^1, c^2] = [c_1^1, \ldots, c_m^1; c_1^2, \ldots, c_n^2]. \tag{A.33}$$

Positive entries in the vector denote outputs and negative entries denote inputs. The vector has been split into two subvectors c^1 and c^2 where c^1 is a vector of unconstrained inputs and outputs and c^2 is a vector of potentially constrained inputs and outputs.

We start by defining the *profit function* under a constraint-free regime:

$$\Pi(p, q) = \underset{c}{\text{Max}} \, [pc^1 + qc^2; \, c \in C] \qquad (A.34)$$

when C is a strictly convex, compact production possibility set. The frontier of this set may be thought of as an implicit production function. A well-known duality theorem called Hotelling's lemma[7] states that the partial derivative of the profit function with respect to a particular price yields the corresponding output supply function if positive or factor demand function if negative:

$$\Pi_p = c^1(p, q), \qquad \Pi_q = c^2(p, q). \qquad (A.35)$$

We also define the *constrained profit function*:

$$\hat{\Pi}(p, q, \bar{c}^2) = \underset{c}{\text{Max}} \{pc^1 + qc^2; \, c \in C \text{ and } c^2 = \bar{c}^2\}. \qquad (A.36)$$

Differentiating with respect to p and q and using Hotelling's lemma for the derivative with respect to p, we obtain:

$$\hat{\Pi}_p = \hat{c}^1(p, q, \bar{c}^2), \qquad \hat{\Pi}_q = \bar{c}^2, \qquad (A.37)$$

where $\hat{c}^1$ is a vector of *effective* output supply/input demand functions and $\bar{c}^2$ is a vector of imposed inputs and outputs (i.e., quantity constraints) facing the firm.

Assume a virtual price vector $(p, \bar{q})$ exists.[8] In the problem

$$\Pi(p, q, \bar{c}^2) = \underset{c^1}{\text{Max}} \, pc^1 + q\bar{c}^2 = p\hat{c}^1(p, q, \bar{c}^2) + q\bar{c}^2, \qquad (A.38)$$

the choice of c^1 will be independent of q (because the choice set from which c^1 is chosen is independent of q). $q\bar{c}^2$ is a net fixed cost (or revenue) for given q. More formally, note that

$$\hat{\Pi}_{pq} = \frac{\partial \hat{c}^1}{\partial q} = \hat{\Pi}_{qp} = 0$$

from the well-known Young's theorem of continuous functions. Hence, to convince the profit-maximizing firm to choose the vector $(\hat{c}^1, \bar{c}^2)$ in the absence of quantity constraints one should keep p at its initial level and set q appropriately. The virtual price $\bar{q}_j$ will be

---

[7] The proof of Hotelling's lemmas is analogous to the above-mentioned Shephard's lemma.
[8] This can, of course, be formally proved given appropriate assumptions on the production function, in particular that it is strictly concave.

equal to the market price q_j, plus the Lagrange multiplier corresponding to the sales or input constraint in the jth market.[9]

Given the virtual price vector $(p, \bar{q})$ and the definition of the profit function, it will hold by definition that:

$$\hat{\Pi}(p, q, \bar{c}^2) = \Pi(p, \bar{q}) + (q - \bar{q}) \bar{c}^2, \tag{A.39}$$

where the virtual price vector $\bar{q}$ is implicitly defined by:

$$\Pi_q = c^2(p, \bar{q}) = \bar{c}^2. \tag{A.40}$$

Using Hotelling's lemma, differentiation of (A.39) at the virtual price vector yields:

$$\hat{\Pi}_p = \hat{c}^1(p, q, \bar{c}^2) = \Pi_p + (\Pi_q - \bar{c}^2) \frac{\partial \bar{q}}{\partial p} = \Pi_p = c^1(p, \bar{q}). \tag{A.41}$$

Note that $\Pi_q = \bar{c}^2$, when Π_q is evaluated at virtual prices.

3.1   The Effect of Relaxing Constraints

The effect on effective supplies/demands $\hat{c}^1$ of relaxing the ration in the nth market is found by differentiating the first derivative of the profit function in (A.41) with respect to $\bar{c}_n$, and noting that the virtual price vector $\bar{q}$ depends on $\bar{c}_n$. In vector notation, this second derivative of the profit function equals:

$$\frac{\partial \hat{c}^1}{\partial \bar{c}_n^2} = \Pi_{pq} \frac{\partial \bar{q}}{\partial \bar{c}_n^2}. \tag{A.42}$$

(See the final section below for definitions of matrices.) By making use of the implicit definition of the virtual prices in (A.40) we can evaluate the vector $\partial \bar{q} / \partial \bar{c}_n^2$:

$$\frac{\partial \bar{q}}{\partial \bar{c}_n^2} = \Pi_{qq}^{-1} e_n \qquad \text{where} \quad e_n = [0, \dots, 1]_{n \times 1}'. \tag{A.43}$$

Substituting (A.43) into (A.42) yields

$$\frac{\partial \hat{c}^1}{\partial \bar{c}_n^2} = \Pi_{pq} \Pi_{qq}^{-1} e_n, \tag{A.42a}$$

where all elements are evaluated at the virtual price vector $(p, \bar{q})$. In general, the elements of (A.42a) can be positive or negative.

---

[9] For a binding sales constraint this multiplier will be negative, while for an input constraint it will be positive.

3.2   The Effects of Price Changes

Differentiation of (A.41) with respect to p_j yields the effect of price change on *effective* output supplies/factor demands:

$$\frac{\partial \hat{c}^1}{\partial p_j} = \Pi_{pp_j} + \Pi_{pq} \frac{\partial \bar{q}}{\partial p_j}. \tag{A.44}$$

Again the implicit definition of virtual prices (A.40) is used to get an expression for the change in virtual prices:

$$\frac{\partial \bar{q}}{\partial p_j} = -\Pi_{qq}^{-1}\Pi_{qp_j}. \tag{A.45}$$

Substituting (A.45) into (A.44) we get:

$$\frac{\partial \hat{c}^1}{\partial p_j} = \Pi_{pp_j} - \Pi_{pq}\Pi_{qq}^{-1}\Pi_{qp_j}. \tag{A.44a}$$

Equations (A.44a) and (A.42a) are very general expressions from which it is a bit difficult to distill any easily interpretable results. We will therefore consider the special case where only a single output or input constraint, the nth, is binding. We can then write (A.44a) as

$$\frac{\partial \hat{c}^1}{\partial p_j} = \frac{\partial c^1}{\partial p_j} - \frac{\partial c^1}{\partial q_n} \frac{\partial c_n}{\partial p_j} \left(\frac{\partial c_n}{\partial \bar{q}_n} \right)^{-1}. \tag{A.44b}$$

From production theory it is well known that $\partial c_n/\partial \bar{q}_n > 0$.[10] If we introduce the definition that two outputs are complements (substitutes) if $\partial c_i/\partial p_j = \partial c_i/\partial p_i > 0$ (< 0) we can come up with the following result: *The difference between the effect on output i of a change in the price of output j under a free market – the free market derivatives being evaluated at virtual prices – and under rationing* ($\partial c_i/\partial p_j - \partial \hat{c}_i/\partial p_j$) *is positive if output i is complementary to the rationed output and the rationed output is complementary to output j.* Moreover, the effect of an increase in price j on the *effective* supply of good j is smaller than on the *notional* supply. That is, supply is less elastic under rationing than in a free market. These results follow directly from equation (A.44b), the convexity of the profit function, and the above definition of complements and substitutes.

A similar analysis can be carried out for two inputs (and mixed cases of multiple inputs and outputs) if one remembers that inputs are defined negative outputs. This means that two inputs i and j are

[10] This follows from the convexity of the profit function in prices.

complements if $-\partial c_i/\partial p_j > 0$. The derivative $\partial c_i/\partial p_j$ tells us what happens to the demand for input i if the jth input price is decreased. Hence, as the observant reader will already have discovered, the statement in the previous paragraph regarding difference between two derivatives also holds for inputs.

Finally, from (A.42a) the following result can be obtained when there is only one rationed factor: If the supply of the rationed factor is increased, the use of complements (substitutes) to the rationed factor will increase (decrease).

4   A First Application

This section returns to the household behavioral functions derived in chapter 2, and relates the derivatives of the effective demand functions to the corresponding notional (unconstrained) demand functions. When the household was constrained in the labor market, the demand for goods was shown to be the effective demand function (2.20):

$$\hat{D} = \hat{D}\left(Y, \frac{M}{p}, \bar{L}\right), \tag{A.46}$$

where $y = \pi/p + (w/p)\bar{L}$ is real income.

If we start by expressing the marginal propensity to consume from (real) income in terms of the free market derivatives evaluated at virtual prices, the general expression in (A.22) can be written in the present context as:

$$\frac{\partial \hat{D}}{dY} = \frac{\partial D}{dI} - \left(\frac{\partial D}{\partial \omega}\right)_{u=k}\left(\frac{\partial L^s}{\partial \omega}\right)_{u=k}^{-1} \frac{\partial L^s}{\partial I}, \tag{A.47}$$

where $I = \pi/p$. $(\partial D/\partial \omega)_{u=k}$ and $(\partial L^s/\partial \omega)_{u=k}$ are compensated price derivatives. If leisure and goods are net substitutes so that $(\partial D/\partial \omega)_{u=k} > 0$ and normal goods so that $\partial D/\partial I > 0$ and $\partial L^s/\partial I < 0$ both terms in the right-hand member of (A.47) are positive. Hence the marginal propensity to consume is larger under rationing than in unconstrained situations.[11]

In a similar manner the marginal propensity to save can be shown to be positive and larger under rationing than in a free market provided that real balances and leisure are net substitutes and normal goods. Moreover, from the budget constraint (2.13) with the employ-

---

[11] Note that $(\partial L^s/\partial \omega)_{u=k} > 0$ from the convexity of the expenditure function.

ment constraint $L^s = \bar{L}$ it follows that the marginal propensities to consume and save sum to unity:

$$\frac{\partial \hat{D}}{\partial Y} + \frac{\partial \hat{m}^d}{\partial Y} = 1. \tag{A.48}$$

If we define the marginal propensity to consume from real wage income as:

$$MPC_\omega = \frac{\text{increase in real consumption}}{\text{increase in real wage} \times \text{number of hours}} = \frac{\Delta \hat{D}}{\bar{L} \Delta \omega},$$

it follows immediately that *the propensity to consume from real wage income equals the marginal propensity to consume from lump-sum income*:

$$\frac{\partial \hat{D}}{\partial Y} = \frac{\partial \hat{D}}{\partial Y} \frac{\partial Y}{\partial \omega} \frac{1}{\bar{L}}.$$

The marginal propensity to consume from an increased real wage income due to an increased level of employment, on the other hand, is defined as:

$$MPC_{\bar{L}} = \frac{\text{increase in real consumption}}{\text{increase in number of hours} \times \text{real wage}} = \frac{\Delta \hat{D}}{\omega \Delta \bar{L}}.$$

By differentiation of (A.46) with respect to $\bar{L}$, we find:

$$\frac{1}{\omega} \frac{d\hat{D}}{d\bar{L}} = \frac{\partial \hat{D}}{\partial Y} + \frac{\partial \hat{D}}{\partial \bar{L}} \frac{1}{\omega} = MPC_{\bar{L}}. \tag{A.49}$$

The second term in (A.49) is the difference $MPC_{\bar{L}} - MPC$. It expresses the change in consumption that would result if employment was increased while total real income was kept constant. The reason why consumption may change when employment increases even when all relative prices and total real income are held constant is that employment may affect the marginal utilities of goods and money balances. If it does not, one would expect the household to work more without changing its consumtpion/saving pattern. This will be the case (implying that the last term of (A.49) is zero) if consumption and money balances are weakly separable from leisure in the households utility function (see the numerical example below).

Another way to express $MPC_{\bar{L}}$ would be to use the general expression equation (A.16) to get:

$$\frac{1}{\omega} \frac{\partial \hat{D}}{\partial \bar{L}} = \left[\left(\frac{\partial \hat{D}}{\partial \bar{L}} \right)_{u=k} + (w - \bar{w}) \frac{\partial \hat{D}}{\partial I} \right] \frac{1}{\omega}. \tag{A.50}$$

From equation (A.12) it follows that the first term on the right-hand side of (A.50) is positive if and only if consumption and leisure are net substitutes. The virtual wage $\bar{w} = w - (\gamma/\mu)$ is smaller than the actual wage w so the second term is positive if consumption is a normal good. In a loose sense one could argue that the second term is more likely to dominate the first term the larger is the displacement from the unrationed equilibrium, i.e., for sufficiently low values of $\bar{w}$. (The reason why this statement is somewhat vague is that the magnitudes and signs of the terms $(\partial \hat{D}/\partial \bar{L})_{u=k}$ and $\partial \hat{D}/\partial \bar{I}$ depend also on where the unrationed equilibrium is situated. Without specific information about the utility function it is impossible to determine the nature of this influence.)

Under repressed inflation the household in chapter 2 maximizes the utility function (2.12) subject to the budget restriction (2.13) and binding quantity constraints on the demands for particular goods. The resulting effective supply function for labor and flow demand for real balances can be written:

$$\tilde{L}^s = \tilde{L}^s \left(\frac{w}{p}, \frac{\pi}{p}, \frac{M}{p}, \bar{D} \right),$$

$$\tilde{m}^d = \tilde{m}^d \left(\frac{w}{p}, \frac{\pi}{p}, \frac{M}{p}, \bar{D} \right). \tag{A.51}$$

Direct application of (A.16) and (A.12) yields the marginal propensity to work (MPW_y):

$$\omega \frac{\partial \tilde{L}^s}{\partial \bar{D}} = \omega \left[\left(\frac{\partial \tilde{L}^s}{\partial \bar{D}} \right)_{u=k} + (\bar{p} - p) \frac{\partial \tilde{L}^s}{\partial I} \right]$$

$$= \omega \left[\left(\frac{\partial L^s}{\partial p} \right)_{u=k} \bigg/ \left(\frac{\partial D}{\partial p} \right)_{u=k} + (\bar{p} - p) \frac{\partial \tilde{L}^s}{\partial I} \right]. \tag{A.52}$$

In this case, the substitution and income effects work in opposite directions provided that consumption and leisure are normal and net substitutes. The substitution effect tends to increase labor supply while the income effect (which loosely speaking increases with the displacement from the unrationed equilibrium) tends to decrease labor supply. The sign of $\partial \tilde{L}^s/\partial \bar{D}$ in (A.51) is uncertain. Compare the discussion in connection with equation (A.16) above.

4.1   A Numerical Example

A numerical example may help to further illuminate the discussion in section 4 above. Assume that the household possesses the following utility function:[12]

$$u = (1 - L^s) D\left(\frac{M}{p} + m^d\right),$$

(A.53)

which is maximized subject to the budget constraint:

$$I + \omega L^s - D - m^d = 0,$$

(A.54)

where $I = \pi/p$ is real profit income. The maximization problem yields the following unconstrained behavioral functions:

$$D = \frac{1}{3}\left(\omega + I + \frac{M}{p}\right),$$

$$m^d = \frac{1}{3}\left(\omega + I - \frac{2M}{p}\right),$$

(A.55)

$$L^s = \frac{2}{3} - \frac{1}{3\omega}\left(I + \frac{M}{p}\right).$$

When the same household is constrained in the labor market, its effective demand for goods and flow demand for money balances (saving) can be written:

$$\hat{D} = \frac{1}{2}\left(I + \omega \bar{L} + \frac{M}{p}\right),$$

$$\hat{m}^d = \frac{1}{2}\left(I + \omega \bar{L} - \frac{M}{p}\right).$$

(A.56)

Finally, if the household is constrained in the market for goods, its effective supply of labor and effective flow demand for cash are given by the following behavioral functions:

$$\tilde{L}^s = \frac{1}{2}\left[1 + \frac{1}{\omega}\left(\bar{D} - I' - \frac{M}{p}\right)\right],$$

$$\tilde{m}^d = \frac{1}{2}\left[\omega - \bar{D} + I' - \frac{M}{p}\right].$$

(A.57)

From the equations above, it is possible to confirm that all goods are normal and net substitutes.

---

[12] In light of our discussion in section 2.3 above, it might be noted that this utility function is separable in L, D, and m. This is easily seen by taking a logarithmic transformation of the original utility function: $\ln u = u^* = \ln D + \ln (1 - L^s) + \ln (M/P + m^d)$.

If we start by comparing (A.55) and (A.56) it is easily seen that:

$$0 < \frac{\partial D}{\partial I} = \frac{1}{3} < \frac{\partial \hat{D}}{\partial I} = \frac{1}{2}. \tag{A.58}$$

That is, *the income derivative of the notional demand function for goods is smaller than the income derivative of the effective demand function*, which should be expected from the discussion regarding equation (A.31). Moreover:

$$\frac{\partial \hat{D}}{\partial I} + \frac{\partial \hat{m}^d}{\partial I} = MPC + MPS = 1 \tag{A.59}$$

in accordance with (A.48) and

$$MPC = MPC_{\bar{L}} = MPC_\omega = \tfrac{1}{2}$$

due to the additive separable utility function.

The reader is invited to go through some of the remaining implications that follow from rationing theory by comparing the properties of the effective demand and supply functions in (A.57) to the properties of the corresponding notional functions in (A.55). Note, however, that the utility function from which the behavioral functions here are derived is additively separable so that a relaxation of the constraints will only have an income effect.

5 Definition of Matrices

In section 2 above we start the analysis by differentiating equation (A.10). The relevant matrixes are:

$$x_q^c = \begin{bmatrix} \dfrac{\partial x_1^c}{\partial \bar{q}_1} & \cdots & \dfrac{\partial x_1^c}{\partial \bar{q}_n} \\ \vdots & & \vdots \\ \dfrac{\partial x_m^c}{\partial \bar{q}_1} & \cdots & \dfrac{\partial x_m^c}{\partial \bar{q}_n} \end{bmatrix}_{(m \times n)},$$

$$y_q^c = \begin{bmatrix} \dfrac{\partial y_1^c}{\partial \bar{q}_1} & \cdots & \dfrac{\partial y_1^c}{\partial \bar{q}_n} \\ \vdots & & \vdots \\ \dfrac{\partial y_n^c}{\partial \bar{q}_1} & \cdots & \dfrac{\partial y_n^c}{\partial \bar{q}_n} \end{bmatrix}_{(n \times n)},$$

$$\frac{\partial \bar{q}}{\partial \bar{y}} = \begin{bmatrix} \dfrac{\partial \bar{q}_1}{\partial \bar{y}_1} + \ldots + \dfrac{\partial \bar{q}_1}{\partial \bar{y}_n} \\ \vdots \qquad\qquad \vdots \\ \dfrac{\partial \bar{q}_n}{\partial \bar{y}_1} + \ldots + \dfrac{\partial \bar{q}_n}{\partial \bar{y}_n} \end{bmatrix}_{(n \times 1)} .$$

$$\tilde{x}_y^c = \begin{bmatrix} \dfrac{\partial \tilde{x}_1^c}{\partial \bar{y}_1} + \ldots + \dfrac{\partial \tilde{x}_1^c}{\partial \bar{y}_n} \\ \vdots \qquad\qquad \vdots \\ \dfrac{\partial \tilde{x}_m}{\partial \bar{y}_1} + \ldots + \dfrac{\partial \tilde{x}_m}{\partial \bar{y}_n} \end{bmatrix}_{(m \times 1)} .$$

In section 3 above some of the relevant matrixes are:

$$\Pi_{pq} = \begin{bmatrix} \dfrac{\partial c_1^1}{\partial \bar{q}_1} & \cdots & \dfrac{\partial c_1^1}{\partial \bar{q}_n} \\ \vdots & & \vdots \\ \dfrac{\partial c_m^1}{\partial \bar{q}_1} & \cdots & \dfrac{\partial c_m^1}{\partial \bar{q}_n} \end{bmatrix}_{(m \times n)} ,$$

$$\frac{\partial \bar{q}_2}{\partial \bar{c}_n^2} = \begin{bmatrix} \dfrac{\partial \bar{q}_1}{\partial \bar{c}_n} \\ \vdots \\ \dfrac{\partial \bar{q}_n}{\partial \bar{c}_n} \end{bmatrix}_{(n \times 1)} ,$$

$$\Pi_{qq} = \begin{bmatrix} \dfrac{\partial c_1^2}{\partial \bar{q}_1} & \cdots & \dfrac{\partial c_1^2}{\partial \bar{q}_n} \\ \vdots & & \vdots \\ \dfrac{\partial c_n^2}{\partial \bar{q}_1} & \cdots & \dfrac{\partial c_n^2}{\partial \bar{q}_n} \end{bmatrix}_{(n \times m)} ,$$

$$\Pi_{pp_j} = \begin{bmatrix} \dfrac{\partial c_1^1}{\partial p_j} \\ \vdots \\ \dfrac{\partial c_m^1}{\partial p_j} \end{bmatrix}_{(m \times 1)} .$$

Appendix B
Quantity Adjustments,
Price Adjustments,
and Long-run Equilibrium*

1 Introduction

In this appendix we will consider the following questions: Given that the mixed fix-price, flex-price equilibria studied in the foregoing chapters are *short-run* equilibria, what governs the *long-run* adjustments of prices and quantities? Under what conditions will long-run state of the model, which is reached when all prices are allowed to vary, coincide with the Walrasian equilibrium?

In the traditional Walrasian model the tâtonnement process in prices is governed by a measure of the market imbalances that Clower (1965) called the *notional* excess demand functions. In deriving agents' notional supply and demand functions, it is assumed, roughly speaking, that the desired level of transactions at ruling prices can actually be carried out. As is well known, this is true if and only if prices happen to be general equilibrium prices.

This appendix uses Clower's alternative excess demand concept, "*effective* excess demand," as a measure of market imbalance, and analyses how the stability properties of a long-run tâtonnement process in prices governed by effective excess demands is related to the traditional excess demand process. We will also ask how the stability of short-run *quantity* adjustment is related to the stability of the effective excess demand process. The analysis is carried out in a simple closed-economy setting due to the technical problems involved in a more general approach.

It should be emphasized that it is far from self-evident that the effective excess demand measure is the most appropriate specifica-

* We wish to thank Seppo Honkapohja for helpful comments on this appendix.

tion of price adjustments when the economy is in disequilibrium. There is a fundamental problem with the Clower effective excess demand concept introduced in chapter 2. As Svensson (1980) has shown, the effective excess demand vector may violate the budget constraint so that the vector of excess demands is not feasible. The agent "promises," in other words, to transact more than he can afford.

Although it is a bit unclear how this fact might influence the appropriateness of using the concept as a force behind price adjustment, one would ideally like to get rid of this property in one way or another. Svensson suggests an interesting stochastic general equilibrium version of rationing theory.

An alternative approach would be to explicitly model the price-setting behavior of unions, industries, and government. This route is, e.g., taken in Benassy (1976a), Löfgren (1977, 1982), and Hall and Lillien (1979). Still another possibility would be to pursue Arrow's (1959) insight that markets which do not clear cannot be perfectly competitive, and attempt to model the price and quantity decisions taken by firms and households subject to their conjectures about supply and demand schedules. We are then back to the theory of conjectural equilibrium discussed to some extent in chapter 2.

1.1 *The Long-run Stability of the Effective Excess Demand Process*

As was mentioned in chapter 2, the standard way to model slow price adjustment in markets out of equilibrium is to use a "two-time" system. That is, certain prices and quantities are assumed to adjust instantaneously, while other prices adjust only once the first set of price–quantity adjustments have moved the economy to a short-run or "momentary" equilibrium. Stability analysis of this kind was, to our knowledge, first carried out by Veendorp (1975). For a model economy consisting of two consumers and three commodities, where one of the commodities serves as the medium of exchange, he showed[1] that: If the *notional* excess demand functions have the property of gross substitutability, then both the price mechanism based on the *notional* excess demand functions and the price mechanism based on the *effective* excess demand functions will be locally asymptotically stable. Veendorp also made the very optimistic conjecture that a sufficient condition for the local stability of a price

[1] As Laroque (1981) has pointed out, Veendorp's proof has its flaws but can be corrected, thereby salvaging his result.

mechanism based on the *effective* excess demand functions is that a price adjustment process based on the notional excess demand functions is stable. This conjecture, however, proved to be wrong, as Löfgren (1977, 1979) showed in a slightly more general model incorporating production.

To prove that the long-run price dynamics is asymptotically stable under the above-sketched effective excess demand process, given stable short-run dynamics, is rather difficult and cumbersome. In principle, you have to prove that *within* each regime the adjustment process is stable. In addition, it must be stable as the economy moves from one regime to another. This introduces problems due to the nondifferentiability and discontinuity of the differential equations describing the adjustment process at the boundaries between regimes.

Fortunately, there exist some general results that can be used. Ito (1979) has suggested that the discontinuities can be dealt with by defining a so-called *Filippov solution* and together with Honkapohja[2] has proved some useful general results. Their main theorem shows that a sufficient condition for global stability under regime switching is that one be able to find a *continuous* Liapunov function for the whole state space.[3]

However, this really does not reduce the difficulties to any considerable extent, as the number of subregimes that have to be investigated increases very fast as the number of markets increases (number of subregimes = 2^{n-1} where n = the number of markets). To prove that the long-run price adjustment process is locally *unstable* is in a sense easier. It suffices to show that there exists a neighborhood in the interior of a regime, where at least one adjustment trajectory leaves independently of the proximity of the starting point to the Walrasian equilibrium.[4]

2 The Stability of Fix-price Equilibrium[5]

Consider the so-called Barro–Grossman model of a closed economy consisting of one household (or N-identical) and one firm (or F-identical), two commodities, and money. As was pointed out in chapter 2, one can distinguish three different kinds of disequilibrium regimes: (1) Keynesian unemployment with effective excess supply

[2] See Honkapohja and Ito (1983).
[3] It may be pieced from different functions regime by regime.
[4] This line is pursued in Löfgren (1979).
[5] For a related investigation of the stability of quantity adjustments, see Eckalbar (1981).

in both the labor market and the market for goods; (2) classical unemployment with effective excess supply of labor; and (3) repressed inflation with effective excess demand in both markets. The real wages, real balance configurations (ω, M/p) generating the respective regimes were shown in figure 2.4. The fix-price equilibria are determined by:

$$\bar{Y} = \hat{D}\left(\bar{Y}, \frac{M}{p}, \bar{L}\right), \tag{B.1a}$$

$$\bar{L} = \tilde{L}(\bar{Y}), \qquad\qquad (\omega, p) \in \text{K-region}; \tag{B.1b}$$

$$Y = Y(\omega), \tag{B.1c}$$

$$L = L(\omega), \qquad\qquad (\omega, p) \in \text{C-region}; \tag{B.1d}$$

$$\bar{L} = \tilde{L}^s\left(\omega, \frac{M}{p}, \frac{\Pi(\bar{L})}{p}, \bar{Y}\right), \tag{B.1e}$$

$$\bar{Y} = \hat{Y}(\bar{L}), \qquad\qquad (\omega, p) \in \text{R-region}. \tag{B.1f}$$

The equations in (B.1) have been discussed at some length in chapter 2. Equation (B.1e) states that the supply of labor in fix-price equilibrium coincides with the supply of labor that results from the maximization of utility subject to the budget constraint, plus the perceived constraint in the goods market.[6] Equation (B.1f) means that the supply of goods equals the supply which results from the use of the available labor, $\bar{L}$.

The fix-price equilibria are clearly functions of the real wage rate and real balances. The questions addressed in this section are: (1) under what conditions does a fix-price equilibrium exist and (2) does a small perturbation from the initial fix-price equilibrium generate an adjustment process that converges to the fix-price equilibrium?

We will start with (ω, M/p) combination in the region of classical unemployment. From equations (B.1c)–(B.1d) it is clear that a *unique* fix-price equilibrium in the region of classical unemployment will exist once it is recognized that the firm's unconstrained maximization problem has a unique solution.[7] Strict concavity and continuity of the production function are sufficient to guarantee this. Given that the fix-price equilibrium exists, there is no short-run adjustment problem because, at the prevailing real wage rate, the

---

[6] The household perceives a binding constraint on its demand for goods under repressed inflation because effective demand exceeds effective supply.

[7] The functions $L(\omega)$ and $Y(\omega)$ are the firm's notional demand and supply functions.

firm's maximizing behavior determines the fix-price equilibrium once and for all: $Y = Y(\omega)$, $L = L(\omega)$.

The same cannot be said, however, for equations (B.1a) and (B.1b), which characterize Keynesian unemployment. Here we can define an adjustment process under fixed prices by recursively putting:

(i) $\quad \bar{Y}_{n+1} = \hat{D}\left(\bar{Y}_n, \dfrac{M}{p}, \bar{L}_n\right),$ \hfill (B.2a)

(ii) $\quad \bar{L}_{n+1} = \tilde{L}(\bar{Y}_{n+1}),$

where n denotes the moment of time (not "n" for "nontradeables" as it did in the main text).

By substitution for $\bar{L}_n$ the adjustment process can be reduced to:

$$\bar{Y}_{n+1} = \hat{D}\left(\bar{Y}_n, \frac{M}{p}, L(\bar{Y}_n)\right) = h\left(Y_n; \frac{M}{p}\right). \tag{B.3a}$$

Analogously the adjustment process for the R-region ((B.1e) and (B.1f)) can be formulated as:

(i) $\quad \bar{L}_{n+1} = \tilde{L}^s\left(\omega, \dfrac{M}{p}, \dfrac{\Pi(\bar{L}_n)}{p}, \bar{Y}_n\right),$ \hfill (B.2b)

(ii) $\quad \bar{Y}_{n+1} = \hat{Y}(\bar{L}_{n+1}),$

which can be collapsed to:

$$\bar{L}_{n+1} = \tilde{L}^s\left(\omega, \frac{M}{p}, \frac{\Pi(\bar{L}_n)}{p}, \bar{L}_n\right) = g\left(\bar{L}_n; \omega, \frac{M}{p}\right). \tag{B.3b}$$

Fix-price equilibria are defined as the fixed points:

$$Y^* = h(Y^*), \qquad L^* = g(L^*). \tag{B.4}$$

The logic behind the adjustment process (B.2a) is the following. The firm's production in period $n+1$ is determined from effective demand in the same period, which in turn is a function of the firm's production decisions in period n. Employment in period $n+1$ is (via the production function) determined from the demand side as soon as the production decision is made.

In the same manner, the system (B.3b) states that the supply of labor in period $n+1$ is determined by the production decision of the firm in the previous period, which in turn was constrained by the supply of labor in the same period. As soon as the household's supply decision is made, production is given by the production function.

It is fairly easy to show that if $h(\bar{Y}; M/p)$ is a contraction,[8] then there exists a unique fix-price equilibrium, $Y^* = h(\bar{Y}^*; M/p)$, and the adjustment process (B.3a) converges to the fix-price equilibrium. The function $h(\bar{Y}, M/p)$ is indeed a contraction provided that the marginal propensity to consume $h_{\bar{Y}} = \partial D/\partial \bar{Y}$ lies in the interval:[9]

$$0 < h_{\bar{Y}} < 1.$$

Analogously, the fact that $g(\bar{L}; \omega, M/p)$ is a contraction will guarantee a unique fix-price equilibrium in the region of repressed inflation. Moreover $g(\bar{L}; \omega, M/p)$ is a contraction provided that $(0 < g_{\bar{L}} < 1)$. The interpretation of this is that increasing the use of labor by one unit, which increases production of goods by $F_L(\bar{L}) = d\bar{Y}/d\bar{L}$, causes the future supply of labor to increase by less than one unit.[10] (If the utility functions are additively separable it can be shown that the condition $0 < g_{\bar{L}} < 1$ is equivalent to the marginal propensity to save along the constrained saving function $\dot{m}^d$ being larger than zero and less than one (see Löfgren, 1977, p. 109).)

The adjustment process in quantities can alternatively be formulated in terms of differential equations rather than difference equations by assuming that:

$$\dot{Y} = \theta[h(\bar{Y}; M/p) - \bar{Y}], \qquad \theta > 0,$$
$$\dot{L} = \tau[g(\bar{L}; \omega, M/p) - \bar{L}], \qquad \tau > 0, \qquad (B.5)$$

where $\dot{Y}$ and $\dot{L}$ are the derivatives of production and employment, respectively, with respect to time. Although it will not be demonstrated here, it can be shown that the fact that $0 < h_{\bar{Y}} < 1$ and $0 < g_{\bar{L}} < 1$ guarantees stability of the continuous-time adjustment process in (B.5).

To sum up, the quantity adjustment process governing the adjustment toward the short-run fix-price equilibria in the simple Barro–

[8] Definition of a contraction: Let X be a metric space, with metric d; if h maps X into X and there is a positive number $c < 1$ such that

$$d(h(Y_1)h(Y_2)) \leqslant cd(Y_1, Y_2)$$

for all $(Y_1, Y_2) \in X$, then h is said to be a contraction of X into X. A metric space is simply a set whose elements are called *points* (e.g., the set of real numbers $Y \geqslant 0$) with the property that for any two points (Y_1, Y_2), there is an associated real number $d(Y_1, Y_2)$ called the *distance* from Y_1 to Y_2.

[9] If $h(Y; M/p)$ is not differentiable at a certain point, right-hand and left-hand derivatives will always exist due to the fact that a function which is a contraction must be continuous. The sufficient condition on the marginal propensity to consume can then be stated in terms of left-hand and right-hand derivatives.

[10] Note that for a contraction, it is sufficient that $|h_y| < 1$, $|g_L| < 1$. Hence the marginal propensities to consume and to save could be positive or negative and still satisfy the stability condition.

Grossman model[11] is stable if the mappings of effective demands into effective demands are contractions. A sufficient condition for this in the region of Keynesian unemployment is that the marginal propensity to consume is less than one. In the region of repressed inflation a similar condition on the marginal propensity to save can be derived.[12] In the region of classical unemployment, no quantity adjustment takes place, so stability follows trivially from the firms' optimization problem.

The fact that the above-mentioned mappings under Keynesian unemployment and repressed inflation are contractions also guarantees the uniqueness of the fix-price equilibrium. Uniqueness of equilibrium in the classical unemployment region requires strict concavity of the production function.

3 Price Adjustments in the Barro–Grossman Model: Notional versus Effective Demand Processes

This section is organized as follows: In section 3.1 below we set out the Barro–Grossman model and derive the properties of its effective demand and supply functions. Section 3.2 then begins with a definition of Walrasian equilibrium under the traditional excess demand hypothesis. It is shown that the model is locally asymptotically stable under this price adjustment process. Then the *effective* excess demand hypothesis is formulated for the three possible regimes. Although the model is stable under the traditional excess demand process, it is shown that instability may arise in the region of repressed inflation when the *effective* excess demand specification is employed. Finally, section 3.3 deals with problems of discontinuity in the adjustment dynamics, which arise on the border between the Keynesian unemployment and repressed inflation regions.

3.1 *The Formal Properties of the Effective Demand Functions*[13]

The Barro–Grossman model consists of one household and one firm. If the household perceives that it can sell all the labor it wishes and

---

[11] Barro and Grossman (1971).

[12] This condition is not in any simple manner related to the marginal propensity to consume as the effective demand (consumption) function is derived subject to no other restriction than the budget constraint, while the effective flow demand for cash is derived subject to the budget constraint and the binding restriction on demand in the market for goods.

[13] This section is based on Löfgren (1979).

purchase all the commodities it demands at the existing price sector, its decision problem is as follows:

$$\text{Maximize} \quad U = U\left(D, L^s, \frac{M}{p} + m^d\right)$$

$$\text{s.t.} \quad \pi + \omega L^s - D - m^d = 0$$

where D = notional demand for the composite commodity,
L^s = notional supply of labor,
m^d = notional flow demand for real balances,
π = Π/p = real profit,
M/p = initial holdings of real balances,
ω = w/p = real wage rate,
p = price level,
w = nominal wage rate.

The utility function is assumed to be strictly concave and twice continuously differentiable. The partial derivatives of the utility function have the following signs:

$$\frac{\partial U}{\partial D} = U_1 > 0, \qquad \frac{\partial U}{\partial L^s} = U_2 < 0, \qquad \frac{\partial U}{\partial m^d} = U_3 > 0.$$

Under the foregoing assumptions, the behavioral equations of the household become differentiable functions of the parameters m, ω, and π.[14] To simplify later comparisons between the partial derivatives of the notional behavior functions, the behavioral functions may be written in total differential form:

$$dD = D_1\, d\omega + D_2(d\pi + L_0^s\, d\omega) + D_3\, d_m,$$

$$dL^s = L_1^s\, d\omega + L_2^s(d\pi + L_0^s\, d\omega) + D_3\, d_m, \qquad \text{(B.6)}$$

$$dm^d = m_1^d\, d\omega + m_2^d\,(d\pi + L_0^s\, d\omega) + m_3^d\, dm.$$

The first term captures the substitution effect, i.e., the effect on the choice variable of an increase in the real wage rate provided that the household obtains an income compensation so that it remains on the same indifference curve. The second term is the income effect, and the third term is the real balance effect. The parameter L_0^s denotes the value of the labor supply before a parameter shift, and should not be regarded as an argument (of the behavioral function) in the usual sense of the word.

---

[14] Except possibly at single points.

Assumption 1
It is assumed that leisure, goods, and real balances are all net sub-stitutes and normal goods.

This implies the following signs of the partial derivatives:

$$D_1, D_2, D_3 > 0,$$
$$L_1^s > 0, \; L_2^s, \; L_3^s < 0,$$
$$m_1^d, m_2^d > 0, \; m_3^d < 0.$$

Moreover, it can be shown that:

(i) $D_2 = D_3$,

(ii) $L_2^s = L_3^s$,

(iii) $m_3^d = m_2^d - 1$.

The first and second results imply that an increase in real profit and an increase in initial holdings of real balances affect the demand for commodities and the supply of labor to the same extent. This is quite natural as both cause the household's holdings of real cash balances to increase.

If the household perceives a constraint in the labor market, the derivation of the behavioral equations is analogous to that above except that an upper limit on the supply of labor is added. The behavioral equations, written as differentials, will have the following properties:

$$d\hat{D} = \hat{D}_1 \, d\omega + \hat{D}_2(d\pi + \bar{L} \, d\omega$$
$$+ \omega \, d\bar{L}) + \hat{D}_3 \, dm + \hat{D}_4 \, d\bar{L}, \qquad \hat{D}_1 = \hat{m}_1^d = 0,$$

$$d\hat{m}^d = \hat{m}_1^d \, d\omega + \hat{m}_2(d\pi + \bar{L} \, d\omega$$
$$+ \omega \, d\bar{L}) + \hat{m}_3^d \, dm + \hat{m}_4^d \, d\bar{L}, \qquad \hat{D}_2 = \hat{D}_3 > 0, \qquad \text{(B.7)}$$

$$d\hat{L}^s = d\bar{L}, \qquad \hat{m}_3^d = \hat{m}_2^d - 1 < 0,$$

$$\hat{m}_2^d + \hat{Y}_2^d = 1.$$

The hat ($\hat{}$) denotes household choice variables under involuntary underemployment. The fourth term in the first and second behavioral equations is due to the fact that a change in the volume of employ-ment affects both the marginal utility of commodities and the marginal utility of real cash (see appendix A).[15] The total effect on

---

[15] As the main result of this chapter is unaffected by the signs of the derivatives D_4 and m_4^d, the signs of this argument are unspecified. As is pointed out in appendix A, these derivatives will be zero if the utility function is additively separable.

the choice variables of an increase in $\bar{L}$ can be determined by a proposition from rationing theory:[16]

$$\frac{\partial \hat{D}}{\partial \bar{L}} = \omega \hat{D}_2 + \hat{D}_4 = \frac{D_1}{L_1^s} > 0,$$

which holds in the neighborhood of the *unconstrained* (free market) consumption point.

The fact that $\hat{m}_2^d + \hat{D}_2 = 1$ can be derived by partial differentiation of the budget constraint with respect to π. That is, the sum of the marginal propensity to save and the marginal propensity to consume equals one.

Next we derive the household's behavioral functions for the case were it perceives a binding constraint in the goods market. The behavior equations (where the choice variables are denoted by a tilde in this case) can be written in total differential form as:

$$d\tilde{L}^s = \tilde{L}_1^s \, d\omega + \tilde{L}_2^s (d\pi + L_0^s \, d\omega$$
$$- d\bar{Y}) + \tilde{L}_3^s \, dm + \tilde{L}_4^s \, d\bar{Y}, \qquad \tilde{L}_1, \tilde{m}_1^d > 0,$$

$$d\tilde{m}^d = \tilde{m}_1^d \, d\omega + \tilde{m}_2^d (d\pi + L_0^s \, d\omega \qquad \qquad \text{(B.8a)}$$
$$- d\bar{Y}) + \tilde{m}_3^d \, dm + \tilde{m}_4^d \, d\bar{Y}, \qquad \tilde{L}_2^s = \tilde{L}_3^s < 0,$$

$$d\tilde{D} = d\bar{Y}, \qquad \qquad \tilde{m}_3^d = \tilde{m}_2^d - 1 < 0.$$

The fourth term in the first two behavioral equations is analogous to the fourth term in the equations above. From rationing theory, the following local propositions can be derived:

$$\frac{\partial \tilde{L}}{\partial \bar{Y}} = -\tilde{L}_2^s + \tilde{L}_4^s = \frac{L_1^s}{D_1} > 0,$$

$$\frac{\partial \tilde{m}^d}{\partial \bar{Y}} = -\tilde{m}_2^d + \tilde{m}_4^d = \frac{m_1^d}{D_1} > 0.$$

Our earlier assumptions suffice to determine the effects on the choice variables of an increased supply of the rationed (composite) commodity. The fourth argument will be disregarded in what follows by invoking the separability assumption referred to in footnote 15. By differentiating the budget constraint with respect to π, the following useful result is obtained:

$$1 + \omega \tilde{L}_2^s = \tilde{m}_2^d.$$

[16] See appendix A.

We are now ready to deal with the firm's decision problem under the different regimes. In the absence of quantity constraints, the firm will maximize profits:

$$\pi = Y - \omega L$$

subject to the production function:

$$Y = F(L),$$

where Y is the supply of the composite commodity and L is the demand for labor. The production function is assumed to be strictly concave, twice continuously differentiable, and increasing in its argument. Profit maximization yields the well-known labor demand and associated output supply equations:

$$L = L(\omega), \qquad L_1 < 0,$$
$$Y = Y(\omega), \qquad Y_1 < 0. \tag{B.9}$$

If the firm perceives a constraint on its sales volume $(\bar{Y})$, it maximizes profit by choosing the optimum quantity of labor to produce that level of output.[17] The resulting *effective* labor demand function equals:

$$\tilde{L} = F^{-1}(\bar{Y}) = \tilde{L}(\bar{Y}), \qquad \partial \tilde{L}/\partial \bar{Y} > 0,$$
$$Y = \bar{Y}. \tag{B.10}$$

Finally, if the firm perceives a constraint in the labor market, its behavior is described by the effective output supply function and the labor constraint:

$$\tilde{Y} = F(\bar{L}) = \tilde{Y}(\bar{L})$$
$$L = \bar{L}. \tag{B.11}$$

3.2 Price Mechanisms and Stability

Price adjustment based on notional excess demands
The Walrasian equilibrium (W-equilibrium) is determined by the following equations system:

$$D = D(\omega, \pi, m),$$
$$L^s = L^s(\omega, \pi, m),$$

---

[17] Following Barro and Grossman (1971), it is assumed that the composite good is non-storable.

$$Y = Y(\omega),$$
$$L = L(\omega),$$
$$D = Y,$$
$$L = L^s,$$
$$\pi = Y - \omega L.$$

(B.12)

If the system is out of equilibrium, an application of the traditional (i.e., notional) excess demand hypothesis implies the following price mechanism:

$$\dot{p} = f(D - Y), \qquad f(0) = g(0) = 0,$$
$$\dot{w} = g(L - L^s), \qquad f' > 0, \ g' > 0,$$

(B.13)

where $\dot{p} \equiv dp/dt$ and $\dot{w} \equiv dw/dt$ are rates of change with respect to time.

Linearization of (B.13) in a neighborhood of the W-equilibrium (w^*, p^*) gives:[18]

$$\dot{p} = \left(D_1 \frac{\partial \omega}{\partial p} + D_3 \frac{\partial m}{\partial p} - Y_1 \frac{\partial \omega}{\partial p} \right)(p - p^*)$$
$$\quad + \left(D_1 \frac{\partial \omega}{\partial w} - Y_1 \frac{\partial \omega}{\partial w} \right)(w - w^*),$$

$$\dot{w} = \left(L_1 \frac{\partial \omega}{\partial p} - L_1^s \frac{\partial \omega}{\partial p} - L_3^s \frac{\partial m}{\partial p} \right)(p - p^*)$$
$$\quad + \left(L_1 \frac{\partial \omega}{\partial w} - L_1^s \frac{\partial \omega}{\partial w} \right)(w - w^*).$$

(B.14)

It is assumed that $f'(0)$ and $g'(0)$ equal one. There is no generality lost by this assumption, as it can be shown that the properties of the system imply local stability independent of the *speeds* of price and wage adjustment.

The stability concepts used in this appendix are as follows.

Definition
Let (p^*, w^*) be the Walrasian equilibrium of the nonlinear system (B.13). Then (p^*, w^*) is said to be stable in the sense of Liapunov if given any $\epsilon > 0$ there exists $\delta > 0$ such that:

---

[18] $D_2 \left(\dfrac{\partial \pi}{\partial \omega} + L_0^s \right) = L_2^s \left(\dfrac{\partial \pi}{\partial \omega} + L_0^s \right) = 0$ in a W-equilibrium.

(i)   every trajectory of (B.13) in the δ-neighborhood of (p^*, w^*)
      for some $t = t_1$ is defined for $t_1 \leqslant t < \infty$, and
(ii) if a trajectory satisfies (i) it remains in the ϵ-neighborhood of
      (p^*, w^*) for $t > t_1$.
If, in addition, every trajectory $C: p = p(t)$, $w = w(t)$ satisfying (i)
and (ii) also satisfies:
(iii) $\lim\limits_{t \to \infty} p(t) = p^*$ and $\lim\limits_{t \to \infty} w(t) = w^*$,

then (p^*, w^*) is said to be (locally) asymptotically stable. Finally,
(iv) An equilibrium that is not stable according to (i) and (ii) is said
      to be unstable.

It is well known that the linearized system (B.14) will be locally
asymptotically stable if the roots λ of the characteristic equation:
$A - \lambda I = 0$ have negative real parts,[19] where A is the coefficient
matrix of the state variables in (B.14). This is the case if and only if
the trace (i.e., the sum of the elements in the main diagonal) of A is
negative and the determinant of the system is positive.

It is easy to verify that this stability condition holds for (B.14),
as both diagonal elements are negative[20] and the determinant is
positive:

$$|A| = D_3 L_1 \frac{\partial m}{\partial p} \frac{\partial \omega}{\partial w} - L_1^s D_3 \frac{\partial m}{\partial p} \frac{\partial \omega}{\partial w} + L_3^s D_1 \frac{\partial \omega}{\partial w} \frac{\partial m}{\partial p}$$

$$- Y_1 L_3^s \frac{\partial \omega}{\partial w} \frac{\partial m}{\partial p} > 0. \qquad (B.15)$$

All terms in this expression are positive. Hence, *a price mechanism
based on the traditional excess demand hypothesis is locally asymptotically stable.* To sum up, we have the following proposition.

Proposition 1
*In the Barro–Grossman model with assumption 1 holding, the price
adjustment process based on the* notional *excess demand functions
is locally asymptotically stable.*

Price adjustment based on effective excess demands
We now turn to an analysis of the *effective* excess demand hypothesis. When exchange occurs within the Barro–Grossman model and

---

[19] This follows from a theorem due to Liapunov.
[20] This is the reason why speeds of adjustment do not matter.

the fixed price vector is false (i.e., non-market-clearing), three "disequilibrium" situations are possible:

(1) general excess supply, i.e., effective excess supply in both the commodity and the labor markets (the K-region of Keynesian unemployment),

(2) general excess demand, i.e., effective excess demand in both the commodity and the labor markets (the R-region of repressed inflation), and

(3) an effective excess demand in the commodity market and an effective excess supply in the labor market (the C-region of classical unemployment).

A fourth situation where there is an effective excess supply in the commodity market and an effective excess demand in the labor market never arises in the present context where the production function specifies a one-to-one relationship between the sole variable input (labor) and output. With a single variable factor, a nonstorable output and no capital investment, the firm cannot be constrained simultaneously in both the labor and the goods markets.[21]

This oversimplification ignores possible discrepancies between output and sales, which may be important in practice. The firm may wish to produce for stockpiling, depending on the relationship between current prices and wages and their expected future values.

The *effective demand* (supply) or *Clower–Benassy demand* is defined as the net demand (supply) the agent expresses in one market, given all the restrictions he perceives in all other markets. In the K-region, therefore, the price adjustment process based on the effective excess demand hypothesis[22] would be:

$$\dot{p}_K = f_K(\hat{D} - Y), \qquad f_K(0) = 0, \qquad f_K' > 0,$$
$$(p, w) \in \text{interior } K, \tag{B.16a}$$
$$\dot{w}_K = g_K(\tilde{L} - L^s), \qquad g_K(0) = 0, \qquad g_K' > 0.$$

For the R-region we have:

$$\dot{p}_R = f_R(D - \hat{Y}), \qquad f_R(0) = 0, \qquad f_R' > 0,$$
$$(p, w) \in \text{interior } R, \tag{B.16b}$$
$$\dot{w}_R = g_R(\tilde{L} - L^s), \qquad g_R(0) = 0, \qquad g_R' > 0.$$

---

[21] Cf., e.g., Barro and Grossman (1976, pp. 91–2) or Malinvaud (1977, pp. 30–1).

[22] It should be emphasized that all authors do not regard the Clower effective excess demand as the indisputably best measure of the market imbalance. For a critical view, see Svensson (1980).

And in the C-region:

$$\dot{p}_C = f_C(\hat{D} - Y), \qquad f_C(0) = 0, \qquad f' > 0,$$
$$(p, w) \in \text{interior } C, \qquad\qquad (\text{B.16c})$$
$$\dot{w}_C = g_C(L - \tilde{L}^s), \qquad g_C(0) = 0, \qquad g'_C > 0.$$

In order to prove that the effective excess demand hypothesis is stable, it is necessary to show that: (1) each subsystem is stable, and (2) the misspecification of the switchpoints between the subsystems implied by the linearization of the model does not upset the local stability of the spillover process at the border between disequilibrium regimes. As Malinvaud (1977) has indicated, the complete model seems to converge toward a downward sloping border between the R-region and K-region ($\dot{p}_R = 0 = \dot{w}_K$). But, once a point on this curve has been reached, no clear trajectory for the economy can be established. This is because the effective excess demand for labor jumps from a positive to a negative value when this border separating regimes is crossed. The assumptions of the adjustment theory are not sufficient to determine what happens when this border is reached. Consider the phase diagram in figure B.1.

The borders between these regimes are, in general, surfaces where discontinuities occur. Take, e.g., the border between the regions of

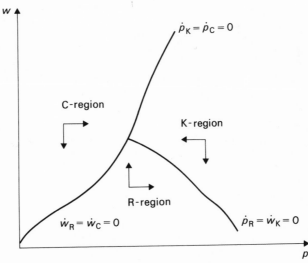

FIGURE B.1   A phase diagram of the Barro–Grossman model under the effective demand hypothesis

Keynesian and classical unemployment. It is easy to show that $\dot{p} = 0$ under each system on this border, but this does not necessarily mean that the process is "continuous" with respect to p and w, since the value of $\dot{w}$ implied by the C and K adjustment systems may differ. The vectors, however, do agree in direction if not in magnitude, so a trajectory that comes to this border will always leave the C-region.

Similar problems arise for a trajectory hitting the border between the R and C regions. The trajectory is not necessarily continuous on the border (although $\dot{w}_C = \dot{w}_R = 0$) due to the fact that $\dot{p}_R$ is, in general, different from $\dot{p}_C$. Again the vectors agree in direction, implying that a trajectory that hits this border will always enter the region of repressed inflation (R).

Given that the border between the K- and R-regions is downward sloping, it can be determined that a trajectory not reaching the Walrasian equilibrium will sooner or later end up on this border. Yet once this border is reached, the assumptions of the theory are not sufficient to determine what happens. (Note that the class of trajectories that end up on this border is not empty, as it contains at least all trajectories which start in the region in which price is higher and wage is lower than the general equilibrium ones. We will return to some of the possibilities in section 3.3 below.) We begin by checking to see whether assumption 1 (substitutes and normality) is sufficient to guarantee a downward sloping K–R border. Also the price dynamics in the R-region are made more explicit.

A potential destabilizing property of the present model is that within the R-region the household *decreases* its supply of labor if the supply of commodities decreases, because leisure and goods are net substitutes. If the price of commodities increases, it causes the effective demand for commodities to decrease. But it also causes a fall in the real wage rate. This in turn decreases the effective supply of labor and, hence, also indirectly the supply of commodities. If the latter change exceeds the former (in absolute value) effective excess demand will increase, i.e., the gap between demand and supply becomes *larger* when the price of the commodity is increased. Instability may result.

Given this possible instability in the R-regon, the impatient investigator starts his stability analysis with that regime. An explicit presentation of the price mechanism for the R-region is:

$$\dot{p}_R = f_R [D(\omega, \pi, m) - \hat{Y}(\tilde{L}^s)],$$

$$\dot{w}_R = g_R [L(\omega) - \tilde{L}^s(\omega, \pi, m, \bar{Y})].$$

$$(B.17)$$

Whenever $\dot{p}_R = 0$ it must be true that $\tilde{L}^s = L^s(\omega, \pi, m)$, because the household perceives no constraints in the commodity market when $D = \hat{Y}$. Moreover, whenever $\dot{w}_R = 0$ it must be true that $\bar{Y} = Y(\omega) = F(L(\omega))$, because the firm does not perceive any constraint in the labor market when $L = \tilde{L}^s$. A linearization of (B.17) at the W-equilibrium $(\dot{w}_R = \dot{p}_R = 0)$ taking into account equations (B.6) and (B.8b) yields:

$$
\dot{p}_R = \left(D_1 \frac{\partial\omega}{\partial p} + D_3 \frac{\partial m}{\partial p} - F_L L_1^s \frac{\partial\omega}{\partial p} - F_L L_3^s \frac{\partial m}{\partial p} \right)(p-p^*)
$$
$$
+ \left(D_1 \frac{\partial\omega}{\partial w} - F_L L_1^s \frac{\partial\omega}{\partial w} \right)(w-w^*),
$$

$$
\dot{w}_R = \left(L_1 \frac{\partial\omega}{\partial p} - \tilde{L}_1^s \frac{\partial\omega}{\partial p} + \tilde{L}_2^s F_L L_1 \frac{\partial\omega}{\partial p} - \tilde{L}_3^s \frac{\partial m}{\partial p} \right)(p-p^*)
$$
$$
+ \left(L_1 \frac{\partial\omega}{\partial w} - \tilde{L}_1^s \frac{\partial\omega}{\partial w} + \tilde{L}_2^s F_L L_1 \frac{\partial\omega}{\partial w} \right)(w-w^*).
$$

(B.18)

By making use of the fact that $F_L = \omega$ in a W-equilibrium, that $1 + \omega \tilde{L}_2^s = \tilde{m}_2^d$, and that $D_1 - \omega L_1^s = -m_1^d < 0$, the coefficient matrix can be written:

$$
\tilde{A} = \begin{bmatrix} -m_1^d \dfrac{\partial\omega}{\partial p} + (D_3 - \omega L_3^s) \dfrac{\partial m}{\partial p} & -m_1^d \dfrac{\partial\omega}{\partial w} \\[2ex] (L_1 \tilde{m}_2^d - \tilde{L}_1^s) \dfrac{\partial\omega}{\partial p} - \tilde{L}_3^s \dfrac{\partial m}{\partial p} & (L_1^d \tilde{m}_2^d - \tilde{L}_1^s) \dfrac{\partial\omega}{\partial w} \end{bmatrix}. \text{ (B.19)}
$$

In order to establish the possibility of instability, it is sufficient to show that the trace of the matrix is positive. The trace can be made positive whenever either one of its elements is positive by raising the speed-of-adjustment coefficient for the market with the positive diagonal element until the trace becomes positive. (All speed-of-adjustment coefficients are arbitrarily set equal to unity – in absolute value – in (B.19).)

The term $a_{22} = (L_1 \tilde{m}_2^d - \tilde{L}_1^s) \partial\omega/\partial w$ is unambiguously negative as $L_1 < 0$, $\tilde{m}_2^d > 0$, $\tilde{L}_1^s > 0$, and $\partial\omega/\partial w > 0$. On the other hand, it is not possible to show that $a_{11} = -m_1^d(\partial\omega/\partial p) + (D_3 - \omega L_3^s)(\partial m/\partial p)$ is negative. On the contrary, given that:

$$
-m_1^d \frac{\partial\omega}{\partial p} > 0,
$$

and

$$(D_3 - \omega L_3^s) \frac{\partial m}{\partial p} < 0,$$

whenever it is true that:

$$-m_1^d \frac{\partial \omega}{\partial p} > \left| (D_3 - \omega L_3^s) \frac{\partial m}{\partial p} \right|, \tag{B.20}$$

the relative speeds of adjustment in the two markets can be chosen so as to make the R-subsystem unstable.[23] Note that the fulfillment of condition (B.20) and assumption 1 imply that the border between the K- and R-regions is upward sloping.

In Löfgren (1979) it is shown by making use of a numerical example that the R-subsystem (B.17) may be unstable in the sense of Liapunov, i.e., there exists an ϵ-neighborhood of the Walrasian equilibrium which any solution always leaves independently of the proximity of the starting point to the Walrasian equilibrium. *In addition, it is shown that a solution will leave an ϵ-neighborhood in the interior of the R-region. When this is the case the R-region can be said to be unstable in the sense of Liapunov, and the whole model is unstable independently of the forces of work in the other regions of the (p, w) plane.*

We can sum up the foregoing discussion with the following proposition.

Proposition 2
The Barro–Grossman model (fulfilling assumption 1), which is locally asymptotically stable under the excess demand process, may be unstable when a price adjustment process governed by the effective excess demand process is specified.

Propositions 1 and 2 taken together are a refutation of Veendorp's conjecture mentioned in the introductory section of this appendix. They also shed some light on an interchange between Leijonhufvud and Grossman on effective demand failures.[24] Leijonhufvud argues that in a neighborhood of the equilibrium-generating price vector – within the "corridor" – the economy is characterized by good stability properties, but that with large deviations from the full-employment equilibrium, the economy can enter a state of lasting unemployment

---

[23] This is elementary as both roots are shown to be real, distinct, and positive.
[24] Compare Leijonhufvud (1973) and Grossman (1974).

equilibrium. Grossman does not share Leijonhufvud's views. He argues that even large (or perhaps especially large) deviations should influence the price vector in such a way that the economy converges toward the full-employment equilibrium.

Leijonhufvud's argument is based on liquidity considerations and on the effective demand functions. The point seems to be that large unanticipated deviations drain the system of liquid buffer stocks, causing households to revise their subjective estimates of permanent income downward. These downward revisions of permanent income tend to be self-fulfilling, because future income will be lower than the income along "the ideal self-regulation path," due to large downward multiplier effects of the downward revisions of permanent income.

Grossman's reasoning is based mainly on the formal properties of the effective excess demand functions as compared to the properties of the notional excess demand functions and on Veendorp's results, which were known to him.[25]

Our results show that in a sense, both are wrong.[26] The effective excess demand hypothesis can destabilize an economy, which is stable under the notional excess demand hypothesis, and instability can occur even if only small deviations are considered.

Note, however, if the border between the K- and R-regions is upward sloping (as described above), a Liapunov unstable trajectory that crosses this border will never return to the border again, and there is a distinct possibility that the Walrasian equilibrium will eventually be reached – see figure B.2.

This possibility, which was suggested in Löfgren,[27] has recently been studied by Raymon (1981). He proves a theorem which gives formal conditions for the existence of this somewhat degenerate corridor.[28]

We will end this section by briefly discussing the relationship between the stability properties of the short-run dynamics and the long-run dynamics. According to the analysis of the stability of the short-run quantity adjustments in the region of repressed inflation, a sufficient condition for global stabilities is that the marginal propensity to save $(\tilde{m}_2^d)$ is larger than zero but less than one. As should be obvious from the analysis of the effective excess demand hypothesis in the R-region, this condition is neither sufficient nor

[25] Grossman (1974) refers to a mimeographed version of Veendorp's paper.
[26] This is perhaps somewhat unfair to Leijonhufvud as the model in this section does not contain any liquid buffer stocks other than real balances.
[27] Löfgren (1979, pp. 36 and 46).
[28] Leijonhufvud's corridor is also discussed in papers by Howitt (1978) and Siven (1981).

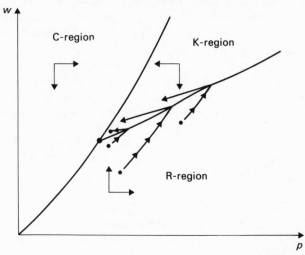

FIGURE B.2   Liapunov unstable but asymptotically stable model

necessary for the stability of the price adjustment process. A more comprehensive analysis reveals that this also holds true for the relationship between the short- and long-run dynamics of the remaining regimes. In other words the following claim holds true.

Proposition 3
The sufficient conditions for stability and uniqueness of quantity adjustment process toward fix-price equilibria, $0 < \tilde{m}_2^d < 1$ and $0 < \hat{D}_2 < 1$ derived in section 2 above, are neither necessary nor sufficient for the stability of long-run price dynamics governed by the effective excess demand process.

It should, however, be remembered that the stability conditions that have been derived regarding the short-run dynamics are only sufficient conditions. Further analysis aimed at finding necessary conditions may reveal some now hidden relationships between short- and long-run stability conditions.

Whatever the relationship between short-run and long-run analysis, both should be usable together, in a slightly extended version of Samuelson's correspondence principle.[29] By requiring that the model is stable with respect to both quantity and price adjustment, one

[29] Samuelson (1947, chapter 9).

may obtain conditions that are useful in signing various effects in comparative static analysis.

3.3 Overall Stability and How to Deal with Discontinuities

The previous section points out that the price adjustment mechanism is discontinuous on the borders between the regimes. A particularly difficult problem arises on the border between the region of Keynesian unemployment and the region of repressed inflation due to the fact that the values of $\dot{p}$ and $\dot{w}$ jump from positive values in the region of repressed inflation to negative values in the region of Keynesian unemployment. This has led some authors, including Malinvaud (1977) and Benassy (1978), to suggest that the border could be regarded as a set of stationary points. If this is the case and this border is downward sloping, as in figure B.1, the dynamic process will converge to this curve.

As pointed out above, this is a rather *ad hoc* manner of dealing with the convergence problem. The purpose of this section is to briefly introduce a superior approach originally suggested by Ito (1979). The discussion will be heuristic, but hopefully it will convey the general idea to the reader.

Discontinuities in the adjustment vectors appear on the borders between regions. If one ignores the vector directions on the borders and deals with a point on the border by taking some kind of "average vector direction" generated by shrinking the neighborhood ball of points on the border to zero, one can generate unique solutions to the price and wage dynamics of the Barro and Grossman model studied in sections 3.1–3.2 above. A continuous solution based on this kind of technique for dealing with differential equations with discontinuous right-hand sides is called a *Filippov solution*.[30] The property of a unique solution is that, in a situation where the vector fields point in different directions on either side of the border, *the solution will slide along the border toward or away from the Walrasian equilibrium*. Otherwise it will move smoothly across the border. (This is, e.g., true for movements across the border between classical and Keynesian unemployment, and the border between classical unemployment and repressed inflation.)

The *direction* the sliding trajectory takes depends on the relative strength of the vector fields on either side of the border. The analysis below, as well as figure B.3, is borrowed from Honkapohja and Ito (1983).

[30] See Filippov (1960) and Honkapohja and Ito (1983).

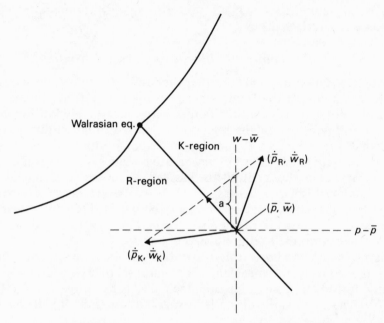

FIGURE B.3   The stable sliding Filippov solution

Figure B.3 depicts the downward-sloping border between the region of repressed inflation and the region of Keynesian unemployment. If a trajectory emanating from the R-region hits the border at $(\bar{w}, \bar{p})$ with limiting forces $\dot{w}_R$, and $\dot{p}_R$, the resultant will be $(\dot{w}_R, \dot{p}_R)$. Analogously a trajectory from the K-region hitting at $(\bar{w}, \bar{p})$ generates the resultant $(\dot{w}_K, \dot{p}_K)$.

The solution will slide along the border in the direction of the cone spanned by vectors $(\dot{p}_R, \dot{w}_R)$ and $(\dot{p}_K, \dot{w}_K)$. If we choose $(\bar{w}, \bar{p})$ as the origin, the Filippov solution (by definition) determines the direction in which the trajectory slides by drawing a straight line through points $(\dot{w}_R, \dot{p}_R)$ and $(\dot{w}_K, \dot{p}_K)$ and determines its ordinate at the origin. The trajectory will slide toward the Walrasian equilibrium if and only if the ordinate at the origin, a, is positive. It will stop at $(\bar{p}, \bar{w})$ if $a = 0$ and it will slide away from the Walrasian equilibrium if $a < 0$.

The equation of the straight line is:

$$w - \bar{w} = b(p - \bar{p}) + a,$$

with:

$$b = \frac{\dot{w}_R - \dot{w}_K}{\dot{p}_R - \dot{p}_K}, \qquad \text{and} \qquad a = \frac{\dot{w}_R(\dot{p}_R - \dot{p}_K) - \dot{p}_R(\dot{w}_R - \dot{w}_K)}{\dot{p}_R - \dot{p}_K}.$$

Moreover, as was mentioned above, a trajectory starting from an arbitrary point will eventually approach the border if it is not converging to the Walrasian equilibrium or diverging with $p \to +\infty$ inside the R-region. The latter problem can be handled by assuming that the subsystem R is stable (as this issue was already discussed above). We are now ready to sum up our discussion.

Proposition 4
(Honkapohja and Ito). *The price adjustment process (B.16) is globally asymptotically stable if: (1) the discontinuities on the borders are handled by a Filippov solution, (2) each regime is stable, and (3) for all $(\bar{p}, \bar{\omega})$ on the border between the region of repressed inflation and the region of Keynesian unemployment*

$$\text{sign}\, a = \text{sign}\, (-\dot{w}_R \dot{p}_K + \dot{p}_R \dot{w}_K) > 0.$$

We note that the speeds of adjustment in each market *do* matter here. In particular, downward rigid nominal wage under Keynesian unemployment $\dot{w}_K \approx 0$ is favorable for stability, as is a high value of $\dot{w}_R > 0$ under repressed inflation. Hence, *the conventional wisdom regarding the asymmetric response of nominal wages tends to promote stability when the method of the Filippov solution is employed.*

Note also that the border will be a set of stationary points in the Benassy and Malinvaud sense if $a = 0$ at *all* $(\bar{p}, \bar{w})$ on the border.[31] This is rather unlikely. It is a bit more likely that $a = 0$ for some $(\bar{p}, \bar{w})$ on the border, and if this stationary point is isolated it will be unstable.

It is also worth mentioning that the fact that the long-run price adjustment process is stable means that the model has the natural rate property, i.e., "left to themselves" quantities and prices will slowly adjust toward the Walrasian full-employment equilibrium.

---

[31] The so-called Malinvaud model has also been studied with respect to the discontinuity problems (in particular those at the border between the R- and K-regions) by Blad and Zeeman (1982).

Bibliography

Alchian, A. A. (1970) "Information Costs, Pricing and Resource Unemployment," in Phelps, E. S. (ed.), *Microeconomic Foundations of Employment and Inflation Theory* (London: Macmillan), pp. 27-53.

Alexander, S. S. (1952) "Effects of a Devaluation on a Trade Balance," *IMF Staff Papers* **2**, 263-278.

Arrow, K. J. (1951) *Social Choice and Individual Values* (New York: John Wiley & Sons).

Arrow, K. J. (1959) "Towards a Theory of Price Adjustments," in Abramowitz, M. (ed.), *The Allocation of Economic Resources* (Stanford: Stanford University Press).

Arrow, K. J. (1971) *Essays in the Theory of Risk Bearing* (Chicago: North-Holland).

Azariadis, C. (1975) "Implicit Contracts and Underemployment Equilibria," *Journal of Political Economy* **83**, 1183-202.

Azariadis, C. (1976) "On the Incidence of Unemployment," *Review of Economic Studies* **43**, 115-25.

Baily, M. N. (1974) "Wages and Employment under Uncertain Demand," *Review of Economic Studies* **41**, 27-50.

Balassa, B. (1982) "Disequilibrium Analysis in Developing Economics: An Overview," *World Development* **10** (December), 12.

Barro, R. J. and Grossman, H. I. (1971) "A General Disequilibrium Model of Income and Employment," *American Economic Review* **61**, 82-93.

Barro, R. J. and Grossman, H. I. (1976) *Money, Employment and Inflation* (Cambridge: Cambridge University Press).

Bell, C. and Devarajan, S. (1983) "Shadow Prices for Project Evaluation under Alternative Macroeconomic Specifications," *Quarterly Journal of Economics* **98**, 457-77.

Benassy, J. P. (1973) *Disequilibrium Theory*, unpublished Ph.D. Dissertation, University of California, Berkeley, CA.

Benassy, J. P. (1975) "Neo-Keynesian Disequilibrium Theory in a Monetary Economy," *Review of Economic Studies* **42**, 503-24.

Benassy, J. P. (1976a) "Regulation of the Wage–Profits Conflict and the Unemployment–Inflation Dilemma in a Dynamic Disequilibrium Model," *Economie Appliquée* **29**, 409-44.

Benassy, J. P. (1976b) "The Disequilibrium Approach to Monopolistic Price Setting and General Monopolistic Equilibrium," *Review of Economic Studies* **43**, 69–81.

Benassy, J. P. (1977) "On Quantity Signals and the Foundations of Effective Demand Theory," *Scandinavian Journal of Economics* **79**, 147–68.

Benassy, J. P. (1978) "A Neo-Keynesian Model of Price and Quantity Determination in Disequilibrium," in Schwödiauer, G. (ed.), *Equilibrium and Disequilibrium in Economic Theory*, Proceedings of a Conference held in Vienna (Boston: D. Reidel).

Benassy, J. P. (1982) *The Economics of Market Disequilibrium* (New York: Academic Press).

Bhagwati, J. N., Krueger, A. O., *et al.* (1978) *Foreign Trade Regimes and Economic Development* (Cambridge, MA: National Bureau of Economic Research, Ballinger).

Bhagwati, J. N. and Srinivasan, T. N. (1983) *Lectures in International Trade* (Cambridge, MA: MIT Press).

Blad, M. C. and Zeeman, E. C. (1982) "Oscillations between Repressed Inflation and Keynesian Equilibria due to Inertia in Decision Making," *Journal of Economic Theory* **28**, 165–82.

Blanchard, O. J. and Sachs, J. (1982) *Anticipations, Recessions and Policy: An Intertemporal Disequilibrium Model*, Working Paper No. 971, NBER, Cambridge, MA.

Blinder, A. (1982) "Inventories and Sticky Prices," *American Economic Review* **72**, 334–48.

Blitzer, C., Dasgupta, P. and Stiglitz, J. (1981) "Project Appraisal and Foreign Exchange Constraints," *Economic Journal* **91**, 58–74.

Boadway, R. W. (1974) "The Welfare Foundations of Cost–Benefit Analysis," *Economic Journal* **35**, 926–39.

Boadway, R. W. (1975) "Cost–Benefit Rules in General Equilibrium," *Review of Economic Studies* **42**, 361–373.

Boadway, R. W. (1978) "A Note on the Treatment of Foreign Reserves in Project Evaluation," *Economica* **45**, 391–99.

Bodkin, R. G. (1969) "Real Wages and Cyclical Variations in Employment," *Canadian Journal of Economics* **2**, 353–74.

Bohm, P. (1974) *Social Efficiency: A Concise Introduction* (London: Macmillan).

Boiteux, M. (1956) "Sur la Gestion des Monopoles Publics Astreints à L'Equilibre Budgétaire," *Econometrica* **24**, 22–40.

Borch, K. (1962) "Equilibrium in a Reinsurance Market," *Econometrica* **30**, 424–44.

Bruno, M. (1982) "Macroeconomic Adjustment under Wage–Price Rigidity," in Bhagwati, J. N. and Srinivasan, T. N. (eds), *Import Competition and Adjustment: Theory and Policy* (Chicago: Chicago University Press).

Casson, M. (1981) *Unemployment: A Disequilibrium Approach* (New York: Halstead Press).

Chan, K. S. (1978) "The Employment Effects of Tariffs under a Free Exchange Rate Regime: A Monetary Approach," *Journal of International Economics* **8**, 415–23.

Chan, K. S. (1979) "A Dynamic Disequilibrium Comparison of Fixed and Flexible Exchange Rate Regimes," *American Economic Review* **69**, 843–54.

Clower, R. W. (1965) "The Keynesian Counterrevolution: A Theoretical Appraisal," in Brechling, F. P. R. and Hahn, F. H. (eds), *The Theory of Interest Rates* (London: Macmillan).

Clower, R. W. (1967) "A Reconsideration of the Microfoundations of Monetary Theory," *Western Economic Journal* **6**, 1–9.

Cuddington, J. T. (1980) "Fiscal and Exchange Rate Policies in a Fix-Price Trade Model with Export Rationing," *Journal of International Economics* **10**, 319–40.

Cuddington, J. T. (1981) "Import Substitution Policies: A Two-Sector, Fix-Price Model," *Review of Economic Studies* **48**, 327–42.

Cuddington, J. T. (1983) *A Fix-Price Trade Model with Perfect Capital Mobility: Fixed versus Flexible Exchange Rates*, Seminar Paper No. 239, Institute for International Economic Studies, Stockholm.

Dasgupta, P., Sen, A. and Marglin, S. A. (1972) *Guidelines for Project Evaluation* (Vienna: United Nations Industrial Organization).

Dixit, A. K. (1978) "The Balance of Trade in a Model of Temporary Equilibrium with Rationing," *Review of Economic Studies* **45**, 393–404.

Dixit, A. K. and Norman, V. (1980) *The Theory of International Trade. A Dual General Equilibrium Approach* (London: Cambridge University Press).

Dornbusch, R. (1975) "Exchange Rates and Fiscal Policy in a Popular Model of International Trade," *American Economic Review* **65**, 859–71.

Dornbusch, R. (1976a) "Expectations and Exchange Rate Dynamics," *Journal of Political Economy* **84**, 1161–176.

Dornbusch, R. (1976b) "Exchange Rate Expectations and Monetary Policy," *Journal of International Economics* **6**, 231–44.

Dornbusch, R. (1980) *Open Economy Macroeconomics* (New York: Basic Books).

Drazen, A. (1980) "Recent Developments in Macroeconomic Disequilibrium Theory," *Econometrica* **48**, 283–306.

Drèze, J. H. (1975) "Existence of an Exchange Equilibrium Under Price Rigidities," *International Economic Review* **16**, 301–20.

Drèze, J. H. (1982) *Second Best Analysis with Markets in Disequilibrium: Public Sector Pricing in a Keynesian Regime*, Discussion Paper No. 8216, CORE, Louvain La Neuve.

Drèze, J. P. (1982) *On the Choice of Shadow Prices for Project Evaluation*, Discussion Paper No. 16, Indian Statistical Institute, New Delhi.

Dunlop, J. T. (1938) "The Movement of Real and Money Wage Rates," *Economic Journal* **48**, 413–34.

Eckalbar, J. C. (1980) "The Stability of Non-Walrasian Processes. Two Examples," *Econometrica* **48**, 371–86.

Eckalbar, J. C. (1981) "Stable Quantities in Fixed Price Disequilibrium," *Journal of Economic Theory* **25**, 302–13.

Eichengreen, B. J. (1981) "A Dynamic Model of Tariffs, Output and Employment under Flexible Exchange Rates," *Journal of International Economics* **11**, 341–59.

Filippov, A. F. (1960) "Differential Equations with Discontinuous Right-Hand Side," *Matematicheskii Sbornik* **51**, 99–128 (English translation, 1964, American Mathematical Society Translations, Ser. 2, Vol. 42, pp. 199–231).

Frenkel, J. A. and Johnson, H. G. (1976) *The Monetary Approach to the Balance of Payments* (Toronto: University of Toronto Press).

Friedman, M. (1968) "The Role of Monetary Policy," *American Economic Review* **58**, 1–17.

Frisch, R. (1965) *Theory of Production* (Dordrecht: D. Reidel).

Futia, C. A. (1977) *A Theory of Effective Demand*, Mimeo, Bell Laboratories, New Jersey.

Gale, D. (1979) "Large Economies with Trading Uncertainty," *Review of Economic Studies* **46**, 319–38.

Gordon, R. J. (1974) "A Neo-Classical Theory of Keynesian Unemployment," *Economic Inquiry* **12**, 431–59.

Gordon, R. J. (1981) "Output Fluctuations and Gradual Price Adjustment," *Journal of Economic Literature* **19**, 493–530.

Grandmont, J. M. (1977a) "Temporary General Equilibrium Theory," *Econometrica* **45**, 535–72.

Grandmont, J. M. (1977b) "The Logic of the Fix-Price Method," *Scandinavian Journal of Economics* **79**, 169–86.

Grossman, H. I. (1971) "Money, Interest and Prices in Market Disequilibrium," *Journal of Political Economy* **79**, 943–61.

Grossman, H. I. (1972) "A Choice-Theoretical Model of an Income–Investment Accelerator," *American Economic Review* **62**, 630–41.

Grossman, H. I. (1974) "Effective Demand Failures: Comment," *Swedish Journal of Economics* **76**, 358–65.

Grossman, H. I., Hanson, J. A. and Lucas, R. F. (1982) "The Effects of Demand Disturbances under Alternative Exchange-Rate Regimes," *Oxford Economic Papers* **34**, 78–97.

Hahn, F. H. (1977a) "Exercises in Conjectural Equilibria," *Scandinavian Journal of Economics* **79**, 210–26.

Hahn, F. H. (1977b) "Keynesian Economics and General Equilibrium Theory: Reflections on Some Current Debate," in Harcourt, G. C. (ed.), *The Microeconomic Foundations of Macroeconomics* (London: Macmillan).

Hahn, F. H. (1978) "On Non-Walrasian Equilibria," *Review of Economic Studies* **45**, 1–17.

Hall, R. E. and Lillien, D. M. (1979) "Efficient Wage Bargains under Uncertain Supply and Demand," *American Economic Review* **69**, 868–79.

Hanoch, G. and Fraenkel, M. (1979) "Income and Substitution Effects in the Two-Sector Open Economy," *American Economic Review* **69**, 455–8.

Hansen, B. (1951) *A Study in the Theory of Inflation* (London: Allen and Unwin).

Harberger, A. C. (1971) "Three Basic Postulates for Applied Welfare Economics: An Interpretative Essay," *Journal of Economic Literature* **9**, 785–97.

Helpman, E. (1977) "Nontraded Goods and Macroeconomic Policy under a Fixed Exchange Rate," *Quarterly Journal of Economics* **91**, 469–80.

Helpman, E. (1981) "An Exploration in the Theory of Exchange Rate Regimes," *Journal of Political Economy* **89**, 865–90.

Helpman, E. and Razin, A. (1979) "Towards a Consistent Comparison of Alternative Exchange Rate Systems," *Canadian Journal of Economics* **12**, 394–409.

Helpman, E. and Razin, A. (1981) *The Role of Saving and Investment in Exchange Rate Determination Under Alternative Monetary Mechanism*, Seminar Paper No. 181, Institute for International Economic Studies, University of Stockholm.

Hey, J. D. (1981) *Economics in Disequilibrium* (Oxford: Martin Robertson).

Hicks, J. R. (1965) *Capital and Growth* (Oxford: Oxford University Press).

Hoel, M. (1981) "Employment Effects of an Increased Oil Price in an Economy with Short-Run Labor Immobility," *Scandinavian Journal of Economics* **83**, 269–76.

Honkapohja, S. and Ito, T. (1983) "Stability with Regime Switching," *Journal of Economic Theory* **29**, 22–48.

Hool, B. (1980) "Monetary and Fiscal Policies in Short Run Equilibria with Rationing," *International Economic Review* **21**, 301–16.

Howitt, P. (1978) "The Limits to Stability of a Full Employment Equilibrium," *Scandinavian Journal of Economics* **80**, 265–82.

Howitt, P. and Patinkin, D. (1980) "Utility Function Transformation and Money Illusion: Comment," *American Economic Review* **70**, 819–22.

Isard, P. (1977) "How Far Can We Push the Law of One Price?," *American Economic Review* **67**, 942–8.

Ito, T. (1979) "A Filippov Solution of a System of Differential Equations with Discontinuous Right-Hand Sides," *Economic Letters* **4**, 349–54.

Ito, T. (1980) "Methods of Estimation for Multi-Market Disequilibrium Models," *Econometrica* **48**, 97–125.

Johansson, P. O. (1981) "On Regional Effects of Government Policies in a Small Open Economy," *Scandinavian Journal of Economics* **83**, 541–52.

Johansson, P. O. (1982a) "Cost–Benefit Rules in General Disequilibrium," *Journal of Public Economics* **18**, 121–37.

Johansson, P. O. (1982b) *On Cost–Benefit Rules when Markets do not Clear*, Umeå Economic Studies No. 105, Umeå.

Johansson, P. O. and Löfgren, K. G. (1980) "The Effects of Tariffs and Real Wages on Employment in a Barro–Grossman Model of an Open Economy," *Scandinavian Journal of Economics* **82**, 167–83.

Johansson, P. O. and Löfgren, K. G. (1981) "A Note on Employment Effects of Tariffs in a Small Open Economy," *Weltwirtschaftliches Archiv* **117**, 578–83.

Kantor, B. (1979) "Rational Expectations and Economic Thought," *Journal of Economic Literature* **17**, 1422–41.

Kemp, M. C. (1969) *The Pure Theory of International Trade and Investment* (New Jersey: Prentice-Hall).

Keynes, J. M. (1936) *The General Theory of Employment, Interest and Money* (London: Macmillan).

Keynes, J. M. (1939) "Relative Movements of Real Wages and Output," *Economic Journal* **49**, 34–51.

Kravis, I. B. and Lipsey, R. E. (1978) "Price Behaviour in the Light of Balance of Payments Theories," *Journal of International Economics* **8**, 193–246.

Kähkönen, J. (1982) *Credit Rationing, Unemployment and Economic Policies: Disequilibrium Models of Industrialized Economies with Underdeveloped Financial Markets*, Doctoral Dissertation Series A.38, Helsinki School of Economics, Helsinki.

Laffont, J. J. (1984) "Fix-Price Models: A Survey of Recent Empirical Work," in Arrow, K. J. and Honkapohja, S. (eds), *Frontiers of Economics* (Oxford: Basil Blackwell) (forthcoming).

Laroque, G. (1981) "A Comment on 'Stable Spillovers among Substitutes'," *Review of Economic Studies* **48**, 355–61.

Latham, R. W. (1980) "Quantity Constrained Demand Functions," *Econometrica* **48**, 307–13.

Leijonhufvud, A. (1968) *On Keynesian Economics and the Economics of Keynes* (London: Oxford University Press).

Leijonhufvud, A. (1973) "Effective Demand Failures," *Swedish Journal of Economics* **75**, 27–48.

Lesourne, J. (1975) *Cost–Benefit Analysis and Economic Theory* (Amsterdam: North-Holland).

Lindbeck, A. (1963) *A Study in Monetary Analysis* (Stockholm: Almqvist and Wiksell).

Lindbeck, A. (1982) "Tax Effects versus Budget Effects on Labor Supply," *Economic Inquiry* **20**, 473–89.

Lipsey, R. and Lancaster, K. (1956) "The General Theory of the Second Best," *Review of Economic Studies* **24**, 11–32.

Little, I. M. D. and Mirrlees, J. A. (1968) *Manual of Industrial Project Analysis in Developing Countries*, vol. 1 (Paris: Organization for Economic Cooperation and Development).

Liviatan, N. (1979) "A Disequilibrium Analysis of the Monetary Trade Model," *Journal of International Economics* **9**, 355–77.

Löfgren, K. G. (1977) *En studie i neokeynesiansk arbetslöshets- och inflationsteori*, Umeå Economic Studies No. 34, Umeå.

Löfgren, K. G. (1979) "The Corridor and Local Stability of the Effective Excess Demand Hypothesis: A Result," *Scandinavian Journal of Economics* **81**, 30–47.

Löfgren, K. G. (1982) "Contract Theory and the Phillips Curve," *Zeitschrift für Nationalökonomie* **42**, 31–59.

Lori, H. R. and Sheen, J. R. (1982) "Supply Shocks in a Two Country World with Wage and Price Rigidities," *Economic Journal* **92**, 849–67.

Lucas, R. F. (1980) "Tariffs, Nontraded Goods, and the Optimal Stabilization Policy," *American Economic Review* **70**, 611–25.

Malinvaud, E. (1977) *The Theory of Unemployment Reconsidered* (Oxford: Basil Blackwell).

Malinvaud, E. (1980) *Profitability and Unemployment* (London: Cambridge University Press).

Marchand, M., Mintz, J. and Pestieau, P. (1983) "Public Production and Shadow Pricing in a Model of Disequilibrium in Labour and Capital Markets." Discussion Paper No. 8315, Louvain La Neuve, CORE.

McDonald, I. M. and Solow, R. M. (1981) "Wage Bargaining and Employment," *American Economic Review* **71**, 896–908.

Miller, S. M. (1982) "Credit Rationing in a Disequilibrium Macroeconomic Model," *Journal of Macroeconomics* **4**, 129–54.

Muellbauer, J. and Portes, R. (1978) "Macroeconomic Models with Quantity Rationing," *Economic Journal* **88**, 788–821.

Neary, J. P. (1980) "Non-traded Goods and the Balance of Trade in a Neo-Keynesian Temporary Equilibrium," *Quarterly Journal of Economics* **95**, 403–29.

Neary, J. P. and Roberts, K. W. S. (1980) "The Theory of Household Behaviour under Rationing," *European Economic Review* **13**, 25–42.

Neary, J. P. and Stiglitz, J. E. (1983) "Towards a Reconstruction of Keynesian Economics: Expectations and Constrained Equilibria," *Quarterly Journal of Economics* (forthcoming).

Negishi, T. (1979) *Microeconomic Foundations of Keynesian Macroeconomics* (Amsterdam: North-Holland).

Noman, K. and Jones, R. W. (1979) "A Model of Trade and Unemployment," in Green, J. R. and Scheinkman, J. A. (eds), *General Equilibrium, Growth and Trade: Essays in Honor of Lionel McKenzie* (New York: Academic Press), pp. 297–322.

Okun, A. (1975) "Inflation: Its Mechanics and Welfare Cost," *Brookings Papers on Economic Activity* **2**, 351–401.

Okun, A. (1981) *Prices and Quantities* (Oxford: Basil Blackwell).

Owen, R. F. (1981) *A Two-Country Disequilibrium Model of International Trade and Finance*, unpublished Ph.D. Dissertation, Princeton University, Princeton, NJ.

Patinkin, D. (1956) *Money, Interest and Prices* (New York: Harper and Row).

Peisa, P. (1977) "Wages and the Demand for Labour in Unemployment Equilibria," *Scandinavian Journal of Economics* **79**, 227-38.

Persson, T. (1982a) "Global Effects of National Stabilization Policies under Fixed and Floating Exchange Rates," *Scandinavian Journal of Economics* **84**, 165-92.

Persson, T. (1982b) *Studies of Alternative Exchange Rate Systems: An Intertemporal General Equilibrium Approach*, Monograph Series No. 13, Institute for International Economic Studies, University of Stockholm.

Persson, T. and Svensson, L. E. O. (1983) "Is Optimism Good in a Keynesian Economy?," *Economica* (forthcoming).

Prachowny, M. F. J. (1975) *Small Open Economics: Their Structure and Policy Environment* (Toronto: Lexington Books).

Raymon, N. (1981) "Stability in the Barro–Grossman Model," *Scandinavian Journal of Economics* **83**, 563-9.

Roberts, K. W. S. (1982) "Desirable Fiscal Policies under Keynesian Unemployment," *Oxford Economic Papers* **34**, 1-22.

Rothbarth, E. (1940-1) "The Measurement of Changes in Real Income under Conditions of Rationing," *Review of Economic Studies* **8**, 100-7.

Samuelsson, P. A. (1947) *Foundations of Economic Analysis* (Cambridge, MA: Harvard University Press).

Sandmo, A. (1976) "Optimal Taxation, An Introduction to the Literature," *Journal of Public Economics* **6**, 37-54.

Silvestre, J. (1982) "Fix-price Analysis in Exchange Economies," *Journal of Economic Theory* **26**, 28-58.

Siven, C. H. (1981) "The General Supply–Demand Multiplier," *Scandinavian Journal of Economics* **83**, 22-37.

Smith, B. and Stephen, H. (1975) "Cost-Benefit Analysis and Compensation Criteria: A Note," *Economic Journal* **85**, 902-5.

Solow, R. M. (1979) "Alternative Approaches to Macroeconomic Theory: A Partial View," *Canadian Journal of Economics* **12**, 339-54.

Solow, R. M. (1980) "On Theories of Unemployment," *American Economic Review* **70**, 1-11.

Somers, G. G. and Wood, W. D. (1969) *Cost-Benefit Analysis of Manpower Policies*, Proceedings of a North American Conference, May 14-15, 1969 (Kingston, Ontario: Industrial Relations Centre, Queen's University).

Srinivasan, T. N. and Bhagwati, J. N. (1978) "Shadow Prices for Project Selection in the Presence of Distortions: Effective Rates of Protection and Domestic Resource Costs," *Journal of Political Economy* **86**, 97-116.

Starrett, D. (1979) "Second Best Welfare Economics in the Mixed Economy," *Journal of Public Economics* **12**, 329-49.

Steigum, E. (1980) "Keynesian and Classical Unemployment in an Open Economy," *Scandinavian Journal of Economics* **82**, 147-66.

Steigum, E. (1983) "Capital Shortage and Classical Unemployment," *International Economic Review* (forthcoming).

Svensson, L. E. O. (1980) "Effective Demand and Stochastic Rationing," *Review of Economic Studies* **47**, 339-55.

Svensson, L. E. O. (1981) "Effective Demand in a Sequence of Markets," *Scandinavian Journal of Economics* **83**, 1–21.

Svensson, L. E. O. and Razin, A. (1983) "The Terms of Trade, Spending and the Current Account: The Harberger–Laursen–Metzler Effect," *Journal of Political Economy* **91**, 97–125.

Tarshis, L. (1939) "Changes in Real and Money Wages," *Economic Journal* **49**, 150–4.

Tobin, J. and Houthakker, H. S. (1950–1) "The Effects of Rationing on Demand Elasticities," *Review of Economic Studies* **18**, 140–53.

Uzawa, H. (1961) "The Stability of Dynamic Processes," *Econometrica* **29**, 617–31.

Varian, H. R. (1975) "On Persistent Disequilibrium," *Journal of Economic Theory* **10**, 210–28.

Varian, H. R. (1977) "Non-Walrasian Equilibria," *Econometrica* **45**, 573–90.

Varian, H. R. (1978) *Microeconomic Analysis* (New York: Norton).

Veendorp, E. C. H. (1975) "Stable Spillovers among Substitutes," *Review of Economic Studies* **131**, 445–56.

Walras, L. (1874) *Eléments d'économie politique pure en théorie de la richesse sociale* (Paris).

Wijnbergen, S. (1984) "Inflation, Employment and The Dutch Disease in Oil Exporting Countries: A Short-Run Disequilibrium Analysis," *Quarterly Journal of Economics* (forthcoming).

Zabel, E. (1972) "Multiperiod Monopoly under Uncertainty," *Journal of Economic Theory* **5**, 524–36.

Index